Student Interactive

# myView®
## L I T E R A C Y

**SAVVAS**
LEARNING COMPANY

ISBN-13: 978-0-134-90883-0
ISBN-10:    0-134-90883-X

10   22

Julie Coiro, Ph.D.

Jim Cummins, Ph.D.

Pat Cunningham, Ph.D.

Elfrieda Hiebert, Ph.D.

Pamela Mason, Ed.D.

Ernest Morrell, Ph.D.

P. David Pearson, Ph.D.

Frank Serafini, Ph.D.

Alfred Tatum, Ph.D.

Sharon Vaughn, Ph.D.

Judy Wallis, Ed.D.

Lee Wright, Ed.D.

# Heroes

# Events

# Solutions

# Heroes

## Essential Question

## What makes a hero?

▶ **Watch**

"Being a Hero"

**TURN and TALK**

How would you describe a hero?

**SAVVAS**
**realize**™

Go ONLINE for
all lessons.

▶ VIDEO

◀ AUDIO

👆 INTERACTIVITY

🎮 GAME

✏ ANNOTATE

📖 BOOK

🔍 RESEARCH

# Spotlight on Historical Fiction

## READING-WRITING BRIDGE

- Academic Vocabulary • Word Study
- **Read Like a Writer • Write for a Reader**
- Spelling • Language and Conventions

## WRITING WORKSHOP

- Introduce and Immerse • Develop Elements       **Historical Fiction**
- Develop Structure • Writer's Craft
- Publish, Celebrate, and Assess

## PROJECT-BASED INQUIRY

- Inquire • Research • Collaborate

# Independent Reading

A genre is a category of text. The genres you will read in this unit include historical fiction, biography, and poetry. Before choosing an independent reading text, think about the genres that interest you most. Choosing texts in genres you like will help you read for a sustained period of time, or read continually without stopping.

Before you begin reading, set a purpose, such as to learn more about a time in history. Then use the thinking strategy called Reading Detective. Watch for elements of the genre as you read. Remember to record your sustained reading in the "Minutes Read" column of the chart.

| FICTION | NONFICTION and BIOGRAPHY |
|---|---|
| Notice WHO and WHAT the text is about. | Notice the MAIN TOPIC and boldface headings. |
| Notice how the SETTING influences the plot. | Notice the DETAILS that support the headings. |
| Notice how the PLOT develops: What is the problem or conflict? | Notice what the AUTHOR'S PURPOSE is. Ask what the author wants you to learn. |
| Notice personal connections you make to the text. | Notice parts that relate to your experience. |

# Independent Reading Log

| Date | Book | Genre | Pages Read | Minutes Read | My Ratings |
|------|------|-------|------------|--------------|------------|
|      |      |       |            |              | ☆☆☆☆☆ |
|      |      |       |            |              |            |
|      |      |       |            |              |            |
|      |      |       |            |              |            |
|      |      |       |            |              |            |
|      |      |       |            |              |            |
|      |      |       |            |              |            |
|      |      |       |            |              |            |
|      |      |       |            |              |            |

# Unit Goals

Shade in the circle to rate how well you meet each goal now.

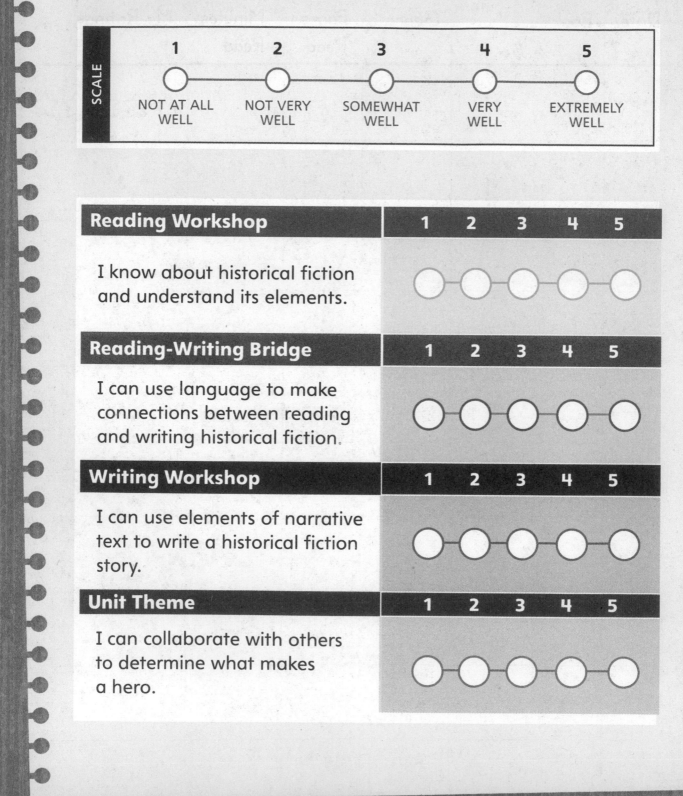

**SCALE**

| 1 | 2 | 3 | 4 | 5 |
|---|---|---|---|---|
| NOT AT ALL WELL | NOT VERY WELL | SOMEWHAT WELL | VERY WELL | EXTREMELY WELL |

**Reading Workshop**   1   2   3   4   5

I know about historical fiction and understand its elements.

**Reading-Writing Bridge**   1   2   3   4   5

I can use language to make connections between reading and writing historical fiction.

**Writing Workshop**   1   2   3   4   5

I can use elements of narrative text to write a historical fiction story.

**Unit Theme**   1   2   3   4   5

I can collaborate with others to determine what makes a hero.

# Academic Vocabulary

Use these vocabulary words to talk and write about this unit's theme, *Heroes: encourage, defeat, distinguish, achieve, command.*

**TURN and TALK** Read the vocabulary words and definitions. Then use each vocabulary word in a question and answer. Share your questions and answers with a partner.

[v] **encourage**—give someone hope to keep on trying

[n] **defeat**—a loss or setback of some kind

[v] **distinguish**—tell the difference between two things

[v] **achieve**—succeed at something or reach a goal

[v] **command**—direct or give an order

 INTERACTIVITY

# STEPS
## on the Moon

In 1969, astronaut Edwin E. "Buzz" Aldrin Jr. made history when he walked on the moon. He and astronaut Neil A. Armstrong flew the lunar module *Eagle* from the command ship to the moon's surface. A third astronaut, Michael Collins, stayed in the command module, *Columbia*.

The *Apollo 11* space vehicle launched from Kennedy Space Center on July 16, 1969. It was NASA's first lunar landing mission.

Lunar module pilot Aldrin steps out of the *Eagle* to begin his walk on the moon.

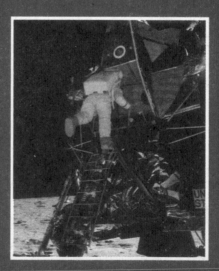

Aldrin poses for a photo with the United States flag on July 20, 1969.

Houston's command center cheered with relief when the astronauts radioed that the *Eagle* had safely landed. Here is part of the air-to-ground communication.

**Aldrin:** 413 is in.

**Command center:** We copy you down, *Eagle*.

**Armstrong** *(from the moon)*: Houston, Tranquility Base here. THE EAGLE HAS LANDED.

**Command center:** Roger, Tranquility. We copy you on the ground. You got a bunch of guys about to turn blue. We're breathing again. Thanks a lot.

## Weekly Question

**What qualities do we see in heroes?**

**Turn and Talk** Look at the photos of *Apollo 11*'s landing. Tell a partner how you would describe the astronauts and others involved in the mission. How were they heroic? Take notes about your shared ideas.

Aldrin photographed his footprint as part of an experiment to study the effects of pressure on lunar dust.

## Spotlight on Genre

# Historical Fiction

**Historical fiction** is a made-up story that could have happened in the past. It usually includes

- **Setting**, or the real place and time in which the story occurs; setting may influence the plot
- **Characters**, or the people the story is about; fictional characters may interact with real people from history
- **Plot**, or the series of things that happen; made-up events may occur at real places
- **Theme**, or message

Historical fiction tells a story set in the past.

**TURN and TALK** Think about historical fiction you have read. Discuss it with a partner. Then use the Historical Fiction Anchor Chart to help you determine if a text is historical fiction. Take notes on your discussion.

**My NOTES** _____

_____

_____

_____

_____

# Historical Fiction Anchor Chart

Historical fiction is one type of realistic fiction. Think of historical fiction as one "piece" of the realistic fiction "pie."

Realistic fiction

## Historical fiction

☀ **Characters** behave like real people.

☀ The **plot** may include both real and fictional events.

☀ The **resolution** of the story is realistic for the time period.

**Tony Bradman** is a British author who has written several books for children. Many readers enjoy his humorous stories and the popular series of books about Dilly the dinosaur. Before he wrote books, Bradman was a pop music journalist!

# Below Deck: A Titanic Story

## Preview Vocabulary

As you read *Below Deck: A Titanic Story*, notice these words and how they provide clues to the plot.

| | |
|---|---|
| **enormous** | **interfered** |
| **stationary** | **abandon** | **appeared** |

## Read

Readers preview images to make predictions about a story. Follow these strategies the first time you read this historical fiction text.

| **Notice** | **Generate Questions** |
|---|---|
| text and images that make you wonder about the text and help you predict. | before reading to better understand this historical event. |

**First Read**

| **Connect** | **Respond** |
|---|---|
| the text to what you already know about this event in history. | by discussing with classmates how the text answers the weekly question. |

# BELOW DECK

## A Titanic Story

by TONY BRADMAN

illustrated by
KEVIN HOPGOOD

 AUDIO

 ANNOTATE

Correct or Confirm Predictions

Highlight details that you could use to correct or confirm a prediction about what the *Titanic* is.

## Chapter One

1   The *Titanic* was the biggest thing Grace had ever seen in her life. She stood by the harbor with her Auntie Nora, the two of them looking up at it.

2   "Well, this is where we'll have to say goodbye," said Auntie Nora.

3   They were near the bottom of some stairs that had been placed against the side of the ship. Many people were climbing the stairs to an open door halfway up.

4   Grace could see tears in Auntie Nora's eyes. This was hard for them. Auntie Nora was Grace's mother's big sister, and she had taken Grace in at the age of five, after Grace's parents had died. She had been a mother to Grace, and they were very close.

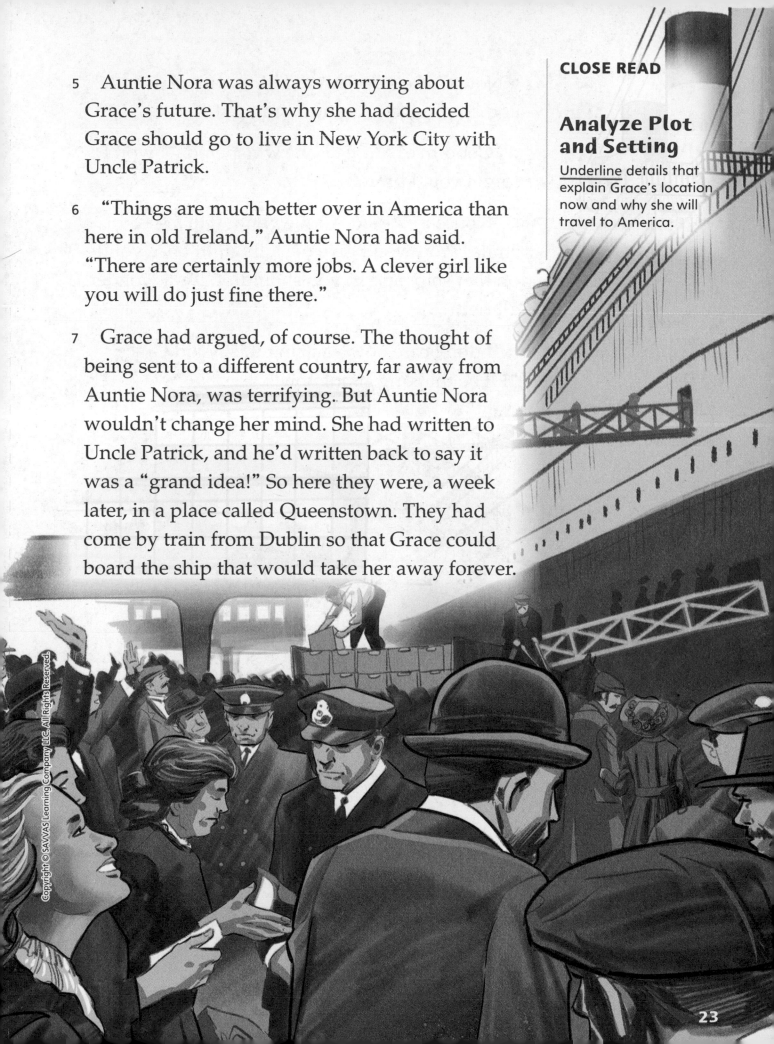

5   Auntie Nora was always worrying about Grace's future. That's why she had decided Grace should go to live in New York City with Uncle Patrick.

6   "Things are much better over in America than here in old Ireland," Auntie Nora had said. "There are certainly more jobs. A clever girl like you will do just fine there."

7   Grace had argued, of course. The thought of being sent to a different country, far away from Auntie Nora, was terrifying. But Auntie Nora wouldn't change her mind. She had written to Uncle Patrick, and he'd written back to say it was a "grand idea!" So here they were, a week later, in a place called Queenstown. They had come by train from Dublin so that Grace could board the ship that would take her away forever.

**Analyze Plot and Setting**

Underline details that explain Grace's location now and why she will travel to America.

## Vocabulary in Context

Context clues are words and sentences around an unfamiliar word that help readers understand the word. The context may appear beyond the sentence, in another paragraph on the page.

Use context beyond the sentence to determine the meaning of *forget* in paragraph 9.

Underline the context clue that supports your definition.

8    Now Grace's eyes were filling with tears too, and she hugged Auntie Nora tight.

9    "Good-bye, Auntie," she whispered. "I won't forget you, I promise."

10   "Nonsense," said Auntie Nora with a sad smile. "You won't give me a thought once you're on that ship, and so you shouldn't. It's a wonder, all right."

11   "I don't care how amazing it is," said Grace. "I'll be thinking about you."

12 But Grace had to admit she was a little excited about going on the ship. The *Titanic* had been built in Belfast, in the north of Ireland, and this was its first voyage. The whole world seemed to be talking about its size and speed and how it would never sink, whatever happened.

13 "Ah, Grace, you're a sweet girl," said Auntie Nora, kissing her. "You're too nice for your own good sometimes. Just take care of yourself."

14 They parted at last, and Grace went up the stairs with everybody else. She turned at the top and waved to Auntie Nora in the crowd far below.

15 Then she boarded the enormous ship.

**CLOSE READ**

## Correct or Confirm Predictions

Highlight historical facts that help you correct or confirm a prediction you made about what the *Titanic* is.

**enormous** huge or very large

# Chapter Two

## Correct or Confirm Predictions

Highlight details that help you correct or confirm a prediction you made about the setting inside the *Titanic*.

16    A man in uniform checked Grace's ticket and told her how to get to her cabin. There were long hallways that all looked the same, a lot of staircases, and people everywhere. The ship had started its voyage in Southampton, England, and then picked up more passengers in France before coming to Queenstown, the final stop before New York.

17    Auntie Nora had only been able to afford a third-class ticket for Grace. So her cabin—room F57—was at the bottom of the ship, where everything was cramped and there wasn't any fresh air. It took a long time to find it, but Grace opened the door to her cabin at last.

18   The cabin had six bunks, five already occupied by a family. They seemed kind, but they spoke a different language, so Grace couldn't communicate with them. There was space under Grace's bunk for her suitcase. There wasn't much in it—some clothes, a piece of paper with Uncle Patrick's address on it, and a photograph of Auntie Nora.

19   Once she had settled in, Grace realized she was hungry and set off to find the third-class dining hall. The ship was even more amazing than she had imagined. There was just so much to see; so many decks and cabins and other rooms, and she soon got lost in the enormous maze of hallways and staircases.

**CLOSE READ**

## Analyze Plot and Setting

Underline details about the setting that help you explain why Grace got lost on the ship. Briefly explain the influence this setting could have on the plot.

## Correct or Confirm Predictions

Highlight details that help you correct or confirm a prediction about how a third-class ticket will affect how Grace is treated on the *Titanic*.

20    The second-class decks certainly seemed better than the third-class ones. Grace spotted a cabin with an open door and peered through as she went past.

21    It was bigger than her own, and there were only two beds in it. They looked much more comfortable than the narrow metal bunk she would be sleeping in. Grace continued up the decks, curious to see more, but as she was about to go through a door a man in uniform stopped her. He asked to see her ticket, and said she wasn't allowed in the first-class areas.

22    Grace was disappointed. Everyone back home had been talking about how grand the first-class decks were—it had been in all the newspapers—and now she wouldn't be able to see them. But as she turned down the hallway, she noticed a window that would give her a glimpse into the first-class dining hall.

23   What a sight it was! The people inside were dressed in fine clothes and sitting at tables covered in spotless white linen. The silver knives and forks and the fine glasses gleamed like something from a fairy tale.

24   Two boys stood next to Grace and looked longingly through the window too. She recognized them from the third-class decks. Eventually one of them snuck in through the door, grabbed as much cake as he could from a cart, and then ran out again. Somebody at a table yelled, "Stop! Thief!" and several stewards came bustling after the boys. But they were long gone.

**CLOSE READ**

## Vocabulary in Context

Use a context clue beyond the sentence to determine the meaning of *thief* in paragraph 24.

Underline the context clues that support your definition.

## Chapter Three

Highlight details that help you correct or confirm a prediction about what plot event is being shown in the illustration.

25   "We'll never catch them," said one of the stewards. "I didn't even see their faces."

26   Some passengers had come out of the dining room—a girl of Grace's age followed by a man and a woman.

27   The girl pointed an accusing finger at Grace. "She knows those thieves!" she said in an American accent. "They were together!"

28   Grace stood rooted to the spot, her cheeks burning.

29   A steward grabbed Grace's arm. She tried to pull free, but his grip was too strong.

30   "You'd better tell us where we can find your friends," he said, scowling at her.

31   "I don't have a clue where they are," said Grace. "And they're not my friends."

32   "You're lying," said the girl. "You were standing right there with them."

33    Grace turned to her, suddenly feeling uncomfortable in her patched dress and scuffed old shoes. The girl's clothing looked brand new and probably cost a fortune.

34    "That will do, Catherine," the man said quietly. Grace realized he and the woman must be the girl's parents. He was tall and dark and wore a tailored suit and bow tie. His wife was fair, and her sparkling dress seemed to be something a queen might wear.

35    "Your father's right," said the girl's mother. "This is none of our business."

36    "I was only trying to help," said the girl. "I mean, stealing is wrong . . ."

37    "Maybe they were hungry," said Grace pointedly.

**CLOSE READ**

## Analyze Plot and Setting

Underline details that help you infer why the girl accused Grace of knowing the thieves.

## Analyze Plot and Setting

Underline details that help you analyze how the family's return to the dining room affects Grace.

**interfered** got involved in the matters of others

38 Stealing was wrong, of course, but Grace hated the way this girl, Catherine, had interfered. She expected Catherine to snap something rude back at her now, but she didn't. She looked down instead, and Grace could see she was blushing.

39 "Come along, Catherine," the girl's father said firmly, and they returned to their table in the dining room. The steward finally let go of Grace's arm.

40 "Go away," he hissed at her. "And don't let me see you here again!"

41 He needn't worry, thought Grace. She had already made up her mind to steer clear of the first-class areas from now on.

42    By the time Grace went to bed that night, the great ship was well on its way across the Atlantic Ocean. Over the next three days, they were lucky with the weather. The sea was so calm it was like a mirror reflecting the bright April sky, and only a few people were seasick.

43    Grace missed Auntie Nora terribly, but life on board was interesting, and she was excited about the future. There were people from almost every country in Europe in third class, and they all seemed to get along.

44    On the fourth evening some third-class passengers had a party. Grace went along and danced and sang with everyone else. It was late, and she felt tired, but she was having fun.

45    Suddenly, there was a sharp bump that threw Grace off balance, followed by a strange scraping noise.

46    Everyone stopped dancing and looked at each other.

## Correct or Confirm Predictions

Highlight details that help you confirm or correct a prediction you made about the experience of hitting an iceberg.

## Chapter Four

### Correct or Confirm Predictions

Highlight details that help you correct or confirm a prediction about how the setting would influence the plot of this story about the *Titanic*.

**stationary** not moving

47   It was just before midnight. The party-goers headed up through the hallways toward the main deck, and Grace followed them. A lot of other people from the first- and second-class decks were doing the same.

48   On the main deck, a large crowd was quickly gathering by the rail. The night air was freezing, and the stars glittered in the dark sky above them. The sea was strangely calm, and everybody was looking up at something white and glittering and enormous drifting past the stationary ship. Grace had never seen anything like it.

49   "It's an iceberg!" one man yelled. "We've hit an iceberg and we're going to sink!"

50   People in the crowd looked around, worried, and started to mutter to each other. Surely this man was talking nonsense?

51   Suddenly the bow of the ship lurched downward with a terrible grinding noise.

52   Moments later, one of the crew cried out that the captain had given the order to lower the lifeboats. They were going to abandon ship!

53   Grace felt very scared and alone. She thought of Auntie Nora, and tears filled her eyes. She couldn't believe the *Titanic* was sinking— the newspapers had said that the ship was unsinkable! But now lifeboats were splashing down into the sea. As Grace stood motionless in the chaos around her, word spread that there weren't enough lifeboats for everyone on board, and people started to panic.

54   Soon there was a lot of yelling and screaming and pushing and shoving. But Grace couldn't leave the ship without Uncle Patrick's address, or Auntie Nora's photograph. She had to go back to the cabin for her suitcase before trying to find a place on a lifeboat.

**CLOSE READ**

## Analyze Plot and Setting

Underline words and phrases that help you explain and analyze the sequence of events in this scene of Chapter Four.

**abandon** take leave of or desert

## Analyze Plot and Setting

Underline details that help you analyze the problem that Grace must overcome.

55  When Grace reached the staircases leading down to the third-class decks, she found they had been closed off. She had to go a different way, but soon she was lost inside the ship's maze of hallways. "Come on, think!" she whispered to herself. "Now where do I go?"

56  Just then, the floor shook beneath Grace's feet, and the ship groaned and creaked around her.

57  The lights flickered above her. Tears streamed down Grace's cheeks as she realized she would have to leave her belongings behind and return to the main deck. She was running out of time and she had never felt so alone. But she pulled herself together, wiped her eyes on her sleeve, and strode quickly toward the stairs.

58  Getting back to the main deck wasn't easy though. All the hallways were at steep angles now, and in some places Grace had to pull herself along the wall, as if she were climbing a mountain. The lights were flickering even more, and everywhere seemed eerily empty. At last, she spotted someone ahead of her—a girl.

59  As Grace got closer to her, she realized it was Catherine, the girl who had gotten her into trouble. Their eyes met, and Grace knew Catherine recognized her too.

60    Catherine ran up to Grace and grabbed her arm, sobbing uncontrollably.

61    "Please, you have to help me!" said Catherine, her voice cracking. "I got separated from my parents and I'm lost. I don't know what to do . . ."

62    "Let go of me," Grace snapped. She pulled her arm free. "Why should I help you after what you did? You must be joking!" Grace turned away from her.

63    "I'm sorry!" Catherine was screaming. "Don't leave me!"

**CLOSE READ**

## Vocabulary in Context

Use context clues within and beyond the sentence to determine the meaning of *snapped*.

Underline the context clues that support your definition.

64    Grace stopped with her back to Catherine and closed her eyes. She remembered what Auntie Nora had said. *You're too nice for your own good sometimes.*

65    That was true, but Grace also knew it would be wrong to leave Catherine here alone. She sighed, and turned back.

66    All of a sudden the lights went out, plunging them into darkness.

## Chapter Five

### Correct or Confirm Predictions

Highlight evidence that helps you correct or confirm a prediction you made about how the details of the setting inside the *Titanic* would be important to the plot of the story.

67  Catherine screamed. Grace knew she would have to take charge, even though she felt terrified herself. The two girls stumbled in the dark as she dragged Catherine along the hallway. After a while they came to an area where the lights were still flickering. But now the floor started to shake, and the hallway seemed to tip even more sharply . . .

68  Grace felt like she was in a nightmare as they turned down hallway after hallway, but at last they came to a staircase that Grace recognized. It would take them to the main deck. They climbed upward—only to discover that things had gotten much worse. The *Titanic* was creaking and groaning like a giant beast in agony, and its front part was now completely under water.

69　Most of the lifeboats had been launched, but there still seemed to be as many passengers on board the *Titanic* as ever. Grace saw quite a few people struggling into life preservers and jumping into the icy sea far below.

70　"Come on, this way!" Grace said, and she pulled Catherine toward a lifeboat that hadn't been launched yet. Suddenly a voice called out.

71　"Catherine! Oh, thank goodness we've found you." It was Catherine's mother, pushing through the crowd. She grabbed her daughter and held her tight.

72　Catherine's father appeared from the crowd. "We must hurry," he said. "They won't be able to launch the lifeboat if they have to wait any longer."

**CLOSE READ**

## Analyze Plot and Setting

Underline details about the lifeboats and passengers that help you explain how the setting influences the actions of the characters in this scene of Chapter Five.

**appeared** became visible or able to be seen

## Correct or Confirm Predictions

Highlight details that help you correct or confirm a prediction you made about who would be allowed into lifeboats.

73    The three of them started moving toward the ship's rail, Catherine's father roughly pushing people out of their way. Grace followed, and found herself at last looking down into a lifeboat. It was almost full, but there were still a few free places. A couple of the crew helped Catherine and her parents into the boat through a gate in the rail.

74    Just as Grace was about to climb down into the boat herself, one of the crewmen put his arm out to stop her. "Hold it," he said, looking Grace up and down. "Only first-class passengers are allowed in this lifeboat!"

75     "Shame on you!" a man yelled behind Grace. Others angrily called out too.

76     Grace stood shivering in the cold night air, jostled by the crowd, her eyes filling with tears once more. "But she saved me . . ." Catherine said quietly to her father.

77     Catherine's father stood up, "Let her on," he said to the crewman. "She's with us."

78     The man nodded and helped Grace down into the lifeboat.

**CLOSE READ**

## Analyze Plot and Setting

<u>Underline</u> details that help you describe the climax of the story.

**Correct or Confirm Predictions**

Highlight details that help you correct or confirm a prediction about how helping Catherine would affect Grace's safety.

79 She sat on a bench next to Catherine, who squeezed her hand. "I couldn't let them leave you behind," said Catherine. "I'd still be lost if it hadn't been for you."

80 Grace looked up at Catherine's parents, who were watching them.

81 "Thank you," Catherine's mother whispered to her through an exhausted smile.

82   Just then, the lifeboat was lowered and they splashed down into the sea. The crewmen at the oars rowed them away from the sinking ship. Grace turned around and saw that the *Titanic* was sliding beneath the water in a huge cloud of steam.

83   Catherine's father leaned over. "Don't worry Grace," he said, with a kind expression on his face. "We'll take care of you."

84   As the lifeboat bobbed gently on the waves, Grace wondered what would happen next. She was only halfway to America, but at least she felt safe for now, sitting between Catherine and her parents.

**CLOSE READ**

## Analyze Plot and Setting

A resolution is a story's outcome. Underline details and descriptions that help you analyze the resolution of the story.

# Develop Vocabulary

In fiction, authors use vivid language to tell about events in the story. These words help readers picture and better understand the plot.

**My TURN** Choose two vocabulary words from the word bank and tell how the words are related. Then use each in a sentence about the story.

## Word Bank

| abandon | appeared | enormous | interfered | stationary |
|---|---|---|---|---|

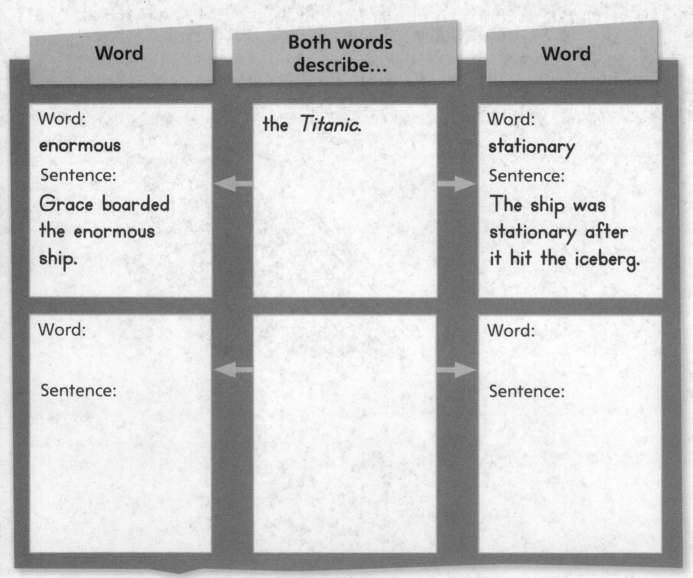

**Word**

**Both words describe...**

**Word**

Word:
**enormous**

Sentence:
Grace boarded the enormous ship.

the *Titanic.*

Word:
**stationary**

Sentence:
The ship was stationary after it hit the iceberg.

Word:

Sentence:

Word:

Sentence:

# Check for Understanding

**My TURN** Look back at the text to answer the questions.

**1.** How do you know the text is historical fiction?

**2.** Why do you think the author includes dialogue in the story?

**3.** What effect do Catherine's comments in paragraphs 27 and 32 have on events?

**4.** Which evidence would be most convincing in an argument that the ship and its crew were unprepared for an emergency?

# Analyze Plot and Setting

The **plot** of a story includes the sequence of events, the conflict, and the resolution. The **setting** includes where and when the story takes place. The setting often influences the plot.

1. **My TURN** Go to the Close Read notes in *Below Deck: A Titanic Story*, and underline parts that help you analyze plot and setting.

2. **Text Evidence** Use some of the parts you underlined to complete the chart.

| Setting | Text Evidence about Plot | Connection Between Setting and Plot |
|---|---|---|
| Queenstown, Ireland | "That's why she had decided Grace should go to live in New York City." | Grace gets on a ship to America at Queenstown because her aunt wants her to have a better life. |
|  |  |  |
|  |  |  |

Use the connections between plot and setting to analyze how each chapter builds on the one before it.

# Correct or Confirm Predictions

Before reading, readers make **predictions**, or tell what they think will happen next, using clues from the text and characteristics of the genre. During and after reading, they use text details to **correct or confirm** their predictions.

1. **My TURN** Go back to the Close Read notes and highlight evidence that helps you correct or confirm your predictions.

2. **Text Evidence** Use some of your highlighted text to correct or confirm predictions about the plot and setting.

| My Prediction | Related Text Evidence | Correct or Confirm Prediction |
|---|---|---|
| The *Titanic* was a big and famous ship. | "The whole world seemed to be talking about its size and speed and how it would never sink." | I was right. The *Titanic* was a famous ship. I did not know people thought it was unsinkable. |
|  |  |  |

# Reflect and Share

**Talk About It** Grace helped Catherine even though Grace was also afraid and lost. Think about the other characters you have read about this week. Which characters acted like heroes? What motivated them to help others? Use examples from the texts to support your opinion.

**Make Thoughtful Comments** When discussing your opinion, make sure your comments relate to the topic. Include specific details in the text that support your ideas.

- Identify key details that support your opinion.
- Use quotations to support your opinion. Be specific about where your quotations came from.
- Connect a character's traits to his or her actions.

Use these sentence starters when discussing specific ideas:

Key details that support my opinion include . . .

This quotation from Chapter ___ of *Below Deck* supports my opinion because . . .

## Weekly Question

**What qualities do we see in heroes?**

# Academic Vocabulary

**Related Words** can be words that share roots or word parts. These words can have different meanings based on how the word is used, such as *mind*, *minded*, and *mindful*.

**Learning Goal**

I can develop knowledge about language to make connections between reading fiction and writing historical fiction.

**My TURN** For each sentence below,

1. **Use** print or digital resources, such as a dictionary or thesaurus, to find related words and their meanings.

2. **Add** an additional related word in the box.

3. **Choose** the correct form of the word to complete the sentence.

| Word | Related Words | Use the Correct Form of the Word |
|---|---|---|
| encourage | encouraged<br>encourages<br>_____ | Mom _____ me to do well on the test last week. |
| defeat | defeats<br>undefeated<br>_____ | The basketball team was _____ until they lost their first game. |
| distinguish | distinguished<br>distinguishable<br>_____ | The twins are _____ because Hazel has a freckle on her nose. |
| achieve | achievement<br>achievable<br>_____ | There was an assembly to recognize the students' _____. |
| command | commanded<br>commands<br>_____ | Yesterday Julio _____ that we follow the rules of the game. |

# Prefixes

**Prefixes** *pre-*, *dis-*, *in-*, *im-*, and **non-** are added to the beginning of base words. In the prefix *pre-*, the e usually spells a long e sound. In the prefixes *dis-*, *in-*, *im-*, and *non-*, the vowels are all short. Knowing the meaning of a prefix can help you figure out the meaning of a word.

**My TURN** Read each base word in the left column. Then add the prefix *pre-*, *dis-*, *in-*, *im-*, or *non-* to create a new word, and then define it. Then read each new word.

| Base Word | Prefix (meaning) | New Word | Definition |
|---|---|---|---|
| heat | pre- (before) | | |
| like | dis- (not) | | |
| effective | in- (not) | | |
| polite | im- (not) | | |
| living | non- (not) | | |

# High-Frequency Words

**High-frequency words** appear often in texts. Practice reading them during independent reading. Read these high-frequency words: *surface*, *produce*.

# Read Like a Writer

Authors use graphic features, such as illustrations, to achieve a specific purpose. Illustrations often emphasize ideas.

**Model !** Read the sentence from *Below Deck: A Titanic Story.*

> The whole world seemed to be talking about its size and speed and how it would never sink, whatever happened.

*illustrated idea*

1. **Identify** The illustration near paragraph 12 shows a crowd of people around the *Titanic*.

2. **Question** What idea does this illustration emphasize?

3. **Conclude** It helps me understand the interest in its size.

Read the sentence.

> So her cabin—room F57—was at the bottom of the ship, where everything was cramped and there wasn't any fresh air.

**My TURN** Follow the steps to analyze the text. Describe how the author uses illustrations to emphasize ideas.

1. **Identify** The illustration near paragraph 17 shows _____

_____ .

2. **Question** What idea does this illustration emphasize?

3. **Conclude** It helps me understand _____

_____ .

# Write for a Reader

Writers use illustrations to give visual information. Illustrations help readers better understand important story elements, such as setting.

Graphic features help me write about big ideas!

**My TURN** Think about how the illustrations in *Below Deck: A Titanic Story* help you understand the setting. Then decide how you might use illustrations to achieve the specific purpose of helping readers understand the setting of your own historical fiction story.

1. Choose and describe a historical setting from the past.

   My chosen historical setting:

   _____

   _____

   My description of that historical setting:

   _____

   _____

   _____

2. Choose a detail from your description that could be illustrated. Explain how you could use that illustration to achieve a specific purpose in a story.

   _____

   _____

   _____

   _____

# Spell Prefixes

**Prefixes *pre-*, *dis-*, *in-*, *im-*,** and ***non-*** are added to the beginning of base words. Knowing how to spell prefixes can help you spell new words.

**My TURN** Read the words. Sort the words by their prefix.

**SPELLING WORDS**

| | | |
|---|---|---|
| prepay | preapprove | impolite |
| nonstop | indirect | insecure |
| disagree | imperfect | incorrect |
| nonfiction | | |

| Prefix | Words |
|---|---|
| pre- | |
| non- | |
| dis- | |
| im- | |
| in- | |

# High-Frequency Words

Learn to spell high-frequency words. Write each high-frequency word on the line.

surface _____

produce _____

# Subject-Verb Agreement

**Subject-verb agreement** occurs when a singular or plural verb agrees with the singular or plural noun or pronoun in the subject.

The subject of a simple sentence is usually a noun or a pronoun that may be singular or plural. The subject and the verb in a sentence must work together, or agree. To make most present tense verbs agree with singular subjects, add -s. If the subject is a plural noun or pronoun, the present tense verb usually does not end with -s.

| Noun | Pronoun | Singular or Plural |
|---|---|---|
| **Billy** plays guitar. | **He** plays guitar. | singular |
| The **girl** runs. | **She** runs. | singular |
| The **dogs** chase the ball. | **They** chase the ball. | plural |
| The **boys** laugh. | **They** laugh. | plural |

**My TURN** Edit this draft by correcting any errors in subject-verb agreement in each simple sentence.

Jamal walk his dogs, Cricket and Snowflake, to the park. They likes to chase tennis balls. Jamal throw the ball for Cricket. Cricket run after the ball. He bring it back to Jamal. Jamal throw the ball for Snowflake. He runs after it too. Then they all walks back home.

# Historical Fiction

**Historical fiction** takes place in the past. The story is made up, but the setting, events, and characters may be based on facts. Other elements, such as dialogue and characters' thoughts, are fictional.

Writers compose historical fiction to help readers imagine events from an earlier time and place.

**My TURN** Choose historical fiction that you have read and fill in the chart.

| SETTING: *Where* does the story happen? | SETTING: *When* does the story happen? |
|---|---|
| | |
| **CHARACTERS:** *Who* is in the story? | **PROBLEM:** *What* problem needs to be solved? |
| | |

# Identify Characters and Setting

**Characters** are people (and sometimes animals) in a story. They move the plot forward through their thoughts, actions, and feelings. The characters in historical fiction are realistic, which means they are like real people.

**Setting** is the place and time in which the story events happen. Historical fiction always takes place during a specific place and time in the past.

**My TURN**  Use a historical fiction story you have read. Write details about the characters and setting.

| Name of Character | Short Description of Character |
|---|---|
|  |  |
|  |  |
|  |  |

## Setting

1. *Where* does the story take place? _____

   How do you know? _____

2. *When* does the story take place? _____

   How do you know? _____

# Develop Plot

The **plot** is the series of events in a story. A plot includes a problem to be solved. Events often happen in sequence and lead up to an ending, or solution. Writers develop an engaging plot so that readers stay interested from beginning to end.

**My TURN** With a partner, choose a historical fiction story from your classroom library. Discuss the plot and outline it in the chart.

| Beginning (Introduce the Problem) |
| --- |
| |

| First Event |
| --- |
| |

| Second Event |
| --- |
| |

| Third Event |
| --- |
| |

| Ending (Solution) |
| --- |
| |

# Brainstorm Ideas

**Brainstorming** means thinking about and writing ideas as quickly as possible. Before you brainstorm, determine your purpose for writing and consider topics that will be interesting to your audience.

**My TURN** Brainstorm ideas for a historical fiction story.

| Settings | Characters | Problems |
|----------|------------|----------|
|          |            |          |

Put a checkmark next to your favorite ideas in each column.

Use this checklist to brainstorm ideas for your historical fiction story.

**BRAINSTORM IDEAS**

- ☐ I will think about events that happened in the past.
- ☐ I will list all of the possible characters, settings, and plots.
- ☐ I will write down all ideas, even if they do not seem as good as other ideas.
- ☐ I will know my purpose and write about topics that will be interesting to my audience.

# Plan Your Historical Fiction Story

Writers may plan a story by **mapping**. Mapping can help you see the direction a story might go. Mapping can help you develop the plot and other elements, such as dialogue. Telling a story aloud can also help you map details and events.

**My TURN** Use the chart to map a first draft of your historical fiction story. Then tell your story to your Writing Club. Include relevant details and historical facts. Speak at a natural pace.

**Beginning**

How will you introduce the characters, the setting, and the problem within the plot? How will you show that the story takes place in the past?

**Middle**

What events will help solve the problem?

**End**

How will you tell about a character's role in solving the problem?

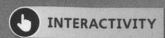
INTERACTIVITY

# You Are
# MY HERO

A hero does not shy away

When action must be taken!

He rustles up his courage

And she faces fear unshaken.

Selfless and quite humble,

Caring and always kind,

Heroes come in many sizes,

But their actions always shine.

Heroes could go unnoticed,

While quietly doing good,

With helping hands and loving words,

They take action when they should.

Can a person be a hero

With no one else to save?

Can a hero be a hero,

Alone, though feeling brave?


Consider those around you,

And what they truly need,

Take someone's hand in yours,

And help them with your deeds.

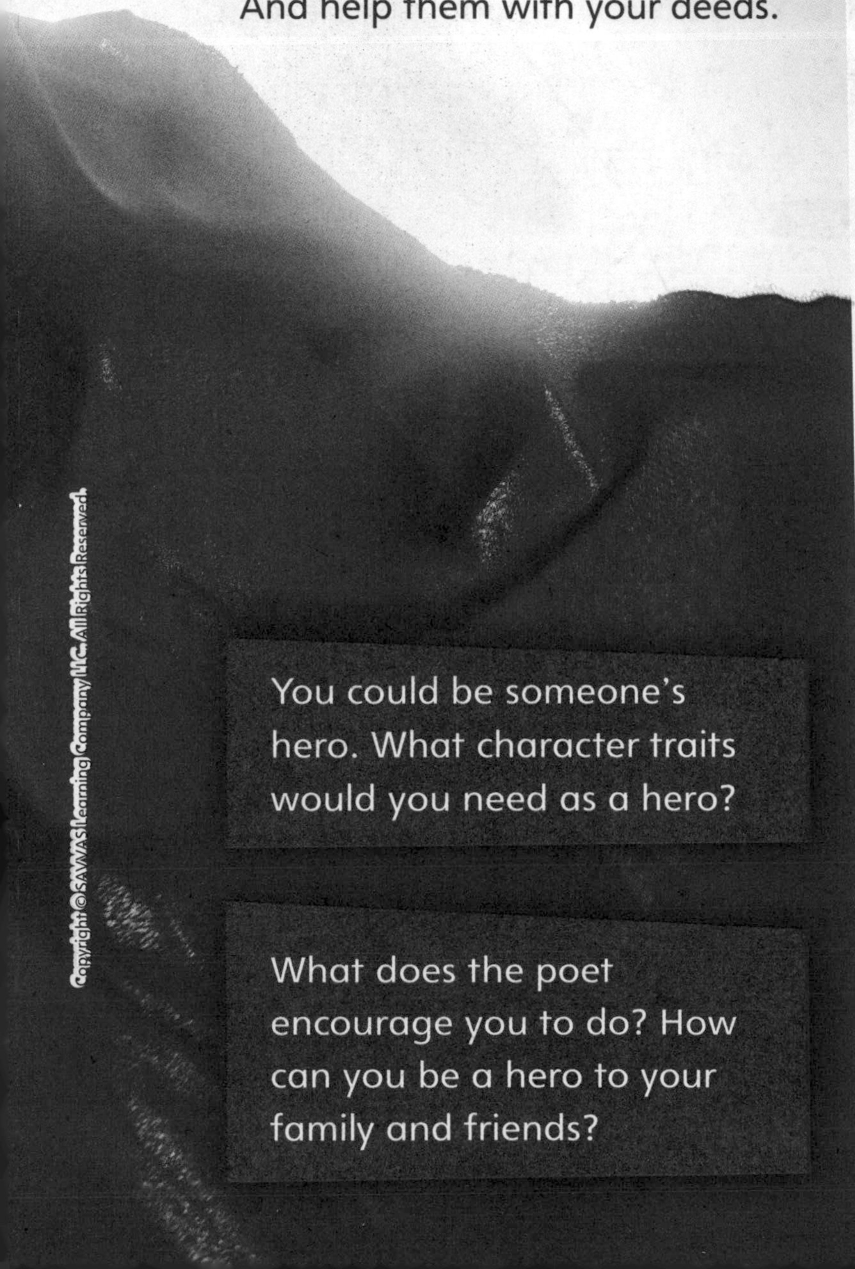

You could be someone's hero. What character traits would you need as a hero?

What does the poet encourage you to do? How can you be a hero to your family and friends?

## Weekly Question

### How can a hero's actions affect other people?

**Illustrate** *To illustrate* means "to provide visual information in a drawing or another graphic feature." Think of ways you could be a hero to someone. Illustrate what your actions would look like.

**Spotlight on Genre**

# Historical Fiction

In **historical fiction**, characters

- Live in a setting that is a real place
- Can be real people or fictional characters
- Face real problems that people experienced in the time and place in which the story is set

**Establish a Purpose** The **purpose**, or reason, for reading historical fiction may be for enjoyment or to learn about people and events from the past.

Notice what characters think, say, and do.

---

My **PURPOSE**

_____

_____

_____

_____

_____

**TURN and TALK** With a partner, discuss different purposes for reading *Granddaddy's Turn: A Journey to the Ballot Box*. For instance, you may want to find out what the title means. Establish your purpose for reading this text.

# Historical Fiction Anchor Chart

## Purpose

★ To entertain using events from the past

★ To give information about history

★ To show how the past and present are similar and different

## Characters

★ May be real people from the past or made-up characters

★ Are understood through their thoughts, actions, feelings, and dialogue

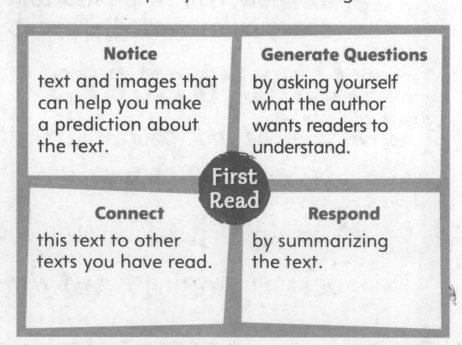

**Michael S. Bandy** and **Eric Stein** have written books for children, as well as scripts for television and movies. Their book *White Water* tells the story of a young African American boy in the 1960s. This story is set during the same time period.

# Granddaddy's Turn

## Preview Vocabulary

As you read *Granddaddy's Turn: A Journey to the Ballot Box*, notice what these vocabulary words tell about the characters.

| | figured | complain |
|---|---|---|
| patience | temper | remembered |

## Read

Before you begin, skim the text and establish a purpose for reading. Follow these strategies when you read this **historical fiction** text the first time, in order to deepen your understanding.

**Notice** text and images that can help you make a prediction about the text.

**Generate Questions** by asking yourself what the author wants readers to understand.

**First Read**

**Connect** this text to other texts you have read.

**Respond** by summarizing the text.

# GRANDDADDY'S TURN

## A JOURNEY TO THE BALLOT BOX

*by* Michael S. Bandy and Eric Stein   *illustrated by* James E. Ransome

🔊 AUDIO

✏️ ANNOTATE

65

## Make Connections

Highlight details that help you connect Granddaddy to adult characters in other texts you have read.

**figured** believed or thought

1 Where we lived, I didn't need an alarm clock.

2 I woke up to the *cock-a-doodle-doo* of my pet rooster and the *chucka, chucka, chucka* of my granddaddy's tractor.

3 "Hurry up, boy" he would shout.

4 "I'm coming, Granddaddy," I'd say.

5 "We got work to do," my granddaddy would say. "Hard work will keep you out of trouble."

6 I guess he figured I was going to get in a whole passel of trouble, because he sure gave me lots of chores.

7    We fed the animals. We milked the cows. And we worked in the fields.

8    My granddaddy was a big, strong man—who always said he "didn't take nothing off nobody." He could do anything—plow fields, chop wood, and dig fence posts, all without breaking a sweat.

9    Not like me! Sometimes when I did my chores, I made so much sweat, it was like I was raining.

## Make Connections

Highlight details that help you connect Granddaddy to a hard-working character in another text you have read.

## Vocabulary in Context

Use context clues within the sentence to determine the meaning of the phrase *right away* in paragraph 11.

<u>Underline</u> the context clues that support your definition.

**complain** express a feeling of unhappiness about something

**patience** the ability to wait without getting upset

10   We worked together a lot. But we played a lot, too. We really loved to go fishing.

11   Sometimes I would complain when I didn't get a bite right away, but my granddaddy always said, "Patience, son, patience."

12  One morning while we were eating breakfast, my grandmother brought out a surprise for my granddaddy. She had cleaned and ironed his suit. I didn't understand that, since he only wore his suit to church—and it wasn't a church day.

13  "It's our time, and you got to look your best!" my grandma said.

14  My granddaddy was so excited, he leaped up from the table and gave her a big hug.

15  "What's going on, Granddaddy?" I asked.

16  "You'll see," he said with a big, beaming smile.

17  I didn't like neckties too much, but since my granddaddy was wearing one, I guess I was, too.

18  "Y'all be careful, now," my grandma said. "And don't forget to take pictures," she said as she handed my granddaddy the camera.

CLOSE READ

## Analyze Characters

Underline details that help you explain the relationship between the narrator's grandmother and Granddaddy.

## Make Connections

Highlight details that help you connect the narrator to a character in another text you have read who feels excited about going to an event.

19  We walked and walked—it seemed like a hundred miles. I asked my granddaddy where we were going again.

20  "Patience, son, patience," he reminded me with a smile.

21  *Oh, boy*! I thought. *We must be going to the county fair.* I walked faster. I couldn't wait to get there. I could almost hear the music and smell the barbecue.

22  "Where are all the rides and animals?" I asked my granddaddy.

23   He laughed and said, "What are you talking about, son?"

24   "I thought we were going to the county fair," I said.

25   "Take a look around," my granddaddy said. "This is better than any old fair."

26   Then I saw the VOTE HERE sign and shouted to my granddaddy, "Are you voting today?"

27   "Yes, I am," my granddaddy proudly replied.

**Analyze Characters**

Underline details that help you explain why Granddaddy and the narrator stay calm as others cut in line in front of them.

28  Nobody in my family had ever voted before. Where we lived, some people were allowed to vote and some people were not. I never knew anyone who had voted before.

29  But I heard my teacher say that some new laws had changed all that.

30  I hoped that was true, because I didn't want us to get in trouble.

31  It felt like we were standing in line forever, and every time we seemed to get a little closer, someone would cut in line in front of us. That's just how things worked where we lived.

32  It didn't seem to bother my granddaddy, though. He said, "Patience, son. Takes patience to get what you've got coming to you!"

72

33   When we finally got to the front of the line, my granddaddy proudly signed a paper and was handed a ballot.

34   He clutched the ballot to his chest and said, "Son, this is the happiest day of my life."

35   I took the camera from him and said, "Smile, Granddaddy."

36   "Now, come on—let's go vote," he said.

37   But before we could even walk to the voting booth, a deputy stopped us and asked my granddaddy, "What are you doing, Uncle?"

38   Where we lived, if the white folks didn't know your name, they usually called you either Uncle or George—or Auntie if you were a lady.

39   "I'm voting today, sir," my granddaddy replied.

**CLOSE READ**

## Make Connections

Highlight details that help you connect the deputy to a character in another text who does not treat all people equally.

73

## Analyze Characters

Underline details that help you explain the deputy's feelings about Granddaddy's plan to vote.

40   The deputy got out a big, thick book and slammed it on the table. He opened it to a page with words that looked longer than crawfish.

41   "Can you read this, Uncle?" the deputy asked.

42   My granddaddy just stared at the pages and shook his head. "No, sir, I can't," he replied.

43   The deputy slammed the book shut, saying, "Well, Uncle, if you can't read this, then you can't vote." He tore up my granddaddy's ballot and threw it on the ground.

44   I was pretty sure that man wasn't playing by the rules, but he was in charge. I could see my granddaddy was mad.

45     As we headed back down the road toward home, my granddaddy didn't say a word. But I saw something I'd never seen before—my big, strong granddaddy had tears in his eyes.

46     "Don't worry, Granddaddy. I'll vote for you one day," I said to him.

47     Granddaddy passed away before he ever got a chance to vote.

48     I never forgot that day he tried to vote. My granddaddy was so mad, he might've lost his temper. But he knew better than me how important that day was. Even though it wasn't his time to vote that day, he looked to the future.

**CLOSE READ**

## Make Connections

Highlight details that help you connect Granddaddy's feelings to the feelings of a character in another text you have read who was treated unfairly.

**temper** a person's state of mind or feelings of anger

## Make Connections

Highlight details that help you connect the narrator with characters in other texts you have read who value something special.

**remembered** thought of something that occurred in the past

49   When I went to vote for the first time, I remembered what my granddaddy always said: "Patience, son, patience." He was right. The day finally came. And I knew that—just like my granddaddy—I would never take it for granted.

50    With his picture in my hand, I put my ballot in the box, smiled, and said to myself, *Now it's Granddaddy's turn.*

## Analyze Characters

<u>Underline</u> evidence that helps you infer and explain the narrator's feelings about Granddaddy when the narrator first voted.

# Develop Vocabulary

In *Granddaddy's Turn*, the author chooses specific words to tell the reader what the grandfather thought and said and how he acted when he was not allowed to vote.

**My TURN** Complete the chart using words from the word bank. Write a synonym for each word. Then write a sentence that uses the word to describe something that happened in the story.

## Word Bank

| figured | complain | patience | temper | remembered |
|---------|----------|----------|--------|------------|

| Word | Synonym | | Sentence |
|------|---------|---|----------|
| figured | believed | → | Granddaddy figured that hard work was good for the boy. |
| | | → | |
| | | → | |
| | | → | |
| | | → | |

# Check for Understanding

**My TURN** Look back at the text to answer the questions.

**1.** How can the reader tell that *Granddaddy's Turn* is historical fiction?

**2.** What is the most likely reason that the authors chose to tell the story from the grandson's point of view?

**3.** Which text details would you select to support the key idea that Granddaddy was a patient man?

**4.** What is the author's message? Connect this message to problems in society today.

# Analyze Characters

When you **analyze characters**, you think about what the characters' words and actions reveal about their traits, or qualities and experiences. You also notice details that explain the relationships among the major and minor characters.

1. **My TURN** Go to the Close Read notes in *Granddaddy's Turn*. Underline parts that help you analyze characters.

2. **Text Evidence** Use some of the parts you underlined to complete the graphic organizer.

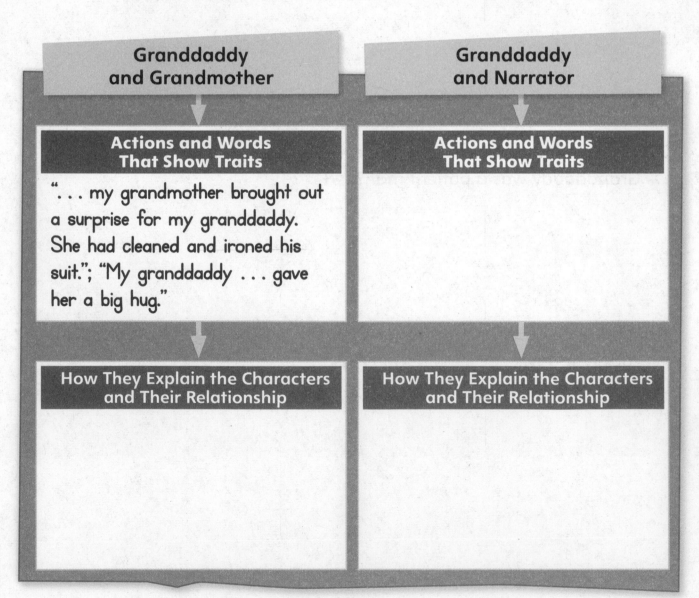

| Granddaddy and Grandmother | Granddaddy and Narrator |
|---|---|
| **Actions and Words That Show Traits** | **Actions and Words That Show Traits** |
| ". . . my grandmother brought out a surprise for my granddaddy. She had cleaned and ironed his suit."; "My granddaddy . . . gave her a big hug." | |
| **How They Explain the Characters and Their Relationship** | **How They Explain the Characters and Their Relationship** |
| | |

# Make Connections

Readers **make connections** between the text they are reading and other texts. To make these connections, notice details in the text you are reading and describe how they remind you of ideas in other texts you have read.

1. **My TURN** Go back to the Close Read notes and highlight evidence that helps you make connections.

2. **Text Evidence** Use some of the highlighted text to make connections to characters and ideas in other texts.

| Details About a Character in *Granddaddy's Turn* | How the Details Connect to Other Texts I Have Read |
|---|---|
| "'Hurry up, boy'"; "'We got work to do.'" | |
| | |
| | |

# Reflect and Share

**Write to Sources** You have read two historical fiction texts. How did reading historical fiction help you understand more about people and events from the past? Use evidence from these texts and your independent reading to describe personal connections to texts. For example, perhaps an event you read about in a text also happened to someone you know.

**Describe Personal Connections to Texts** Before you write your response, consider how you feel about the characters and events in the texts and what you already know about the topics.

Then, freewrite about the texts in this unit and your independent reading. Ask yourself questions such as:

What did I learn about these people and events from the past?

How do I feel about these historical events?

Finally, use what you wrote during freewriting to describe a personal connection you can make to the texts. Write your response on a separate sheet of paper.

## Weekly Question

How can a hero's actions affect other people?

# Academic Vocabulary

**Learning Goal**

I can develop knowledge about language to make connections between reading and writing historical fiction.

**Synonyms and Antonyms** A synonym is a word that has the same or nearly the same meaning as another word. An antonym is a word that means the opposite of another word.

**MyTURN** For each sample thesaurus entry below,

**1.** **Define** each entry word.

**2.** **Identify** two synonyms and antonyms for each word.

**3.** **Confirm** and **explain** your definitions, synonyms, and antonyms using your glossary or a print or online dictionary or thesaurus.

encourage, *v.* _____

Synonyms: _____

Antonyms: _____

defeat, *n.* _____

Synonyms: _____

Antonyms: _____

distinguish, *v.* _____

Synonyms: _____

Antonyms: _____

achieve, *v.* _____

Synonyms: _____

Antonyms: _____

command, *v.* _____

Synonyms: _____

Antonyms: _____

# Abbreviations

**Abbreviations** are shortened forms of longer words and phrases. If you see an abbreviation in something that you are reading, you would read the word for which it stands. For example, if you see the abbreviation *St.*, you would read it as the word *Street*.

He lives on Highland Ave.       Ave. = Avenue

Mr. Hall is my neighbor.         Mr. = Mister

**My TURN** Read each abbreviation. Then draw a line from the abbreviation to the word or phrase it stands for.

| | |
|---|---|
| Dept. | Doctor |
| St. | Junior |
| Jr. | Missus |
| Mt. | Street |
| Mrs. | Mountain |
| Dr. | Department |

# High-Frequency Words

High-frequency words often do not follow regular word-study patterns. Read these high-frequency words: *building, ocean.* Try to memorize them so you can identify them in your reading.

# Read Like a Writer

An author's message is the idea he or she is expressing to the reader. Analyze key details to determine the author's message.

**Model !** Read the passage from *Granddaddy's Turn*.

> He said, "Patience, son. Takes patience to get what you've got coming to you!"

*Repetition emphasizes a message.*

1. **Identify** Michael S. Bandy and Eric Stein emphasize their message by repeating the word *patience*.

2. **Question** What message are the authors expressing?

3. **Conclude** The authors' message is that it is better to be patient than angry, even when you are treated unfairly.

Read the passage.

> When I went to vote for the first time, I remembered what my granddaddy always said: "Patience, son, patience." He was right. The day finally came.

**My TURN** Follow the steps to explain the author's message.

1. **Identify** Michael S. Bandy and Eric Stein emphasize their message by

_____ .

2. **Question** What message are the authors expressing?

3. **Conclude** The authors' message is that _____

_____ .

# Write for a Reader

Think about what is important to repeat.

To make sure their message is understood, writers craft their language to make their message stand out.

**My TURN** Consider how the authors used repetition in *Granddaddy's Turn* to help you recognize the message. Think of a way to tell readers about the value of hard work. Plan how to emphasize this message in your writing.

1. What message could you tell readers about the value of hard work? What details or techniques could you use to make this message clear in your writing?

_____

_____

_____

2. Write a passage about a character who works hard to reach a goal. Emphasize your message about hard work in your writing. Then briefly explain the message within the text.

_____

_____

_____

_____

_____

_____

_____

# Spell Abbreviations

**Abbreviations** are shortened versions of words and phrases. Some abbreviations use capital letters and periods. Memorize how to spell abbreviations.

**My TURN**   Sort the list of abbreviations by the use of capital letters. If you don't know what an abbreviation stands for, look it up in a dictionary.

| SPELLING WORDS | | |
|---|---|---|
| A.M. | no. | Rd. |
| ASAP | P.M. | vs. |
| Blvd. | P.S. | wt. |
| etc. | | |

**All Capital Letters**    **First Letter Capitalized**    **No Capital Letters**

_____    _____    _____

_____    _____    _____

_____    _____    _____

# High-Frequency Words

High-frequency words are words that appear in many texts you read. Write the following high-frequency words on the lines.

building _____

ocean _____

# Edit for Subject-Verb Agreement

A simple sentence's subject and verb must work together, or agree, as singular or plural, even for the verb *to be* (*am, is, are, was, were*). With the subject *you*, use the verbs *are* and *were*, whether you mean one or more than one person.

My **mom** (singular) **bakes** (singular) cakes. **Dogs** (plural) **are** (plural) cuddly.

**You** (singular or plural) **are** (plural) the winner.

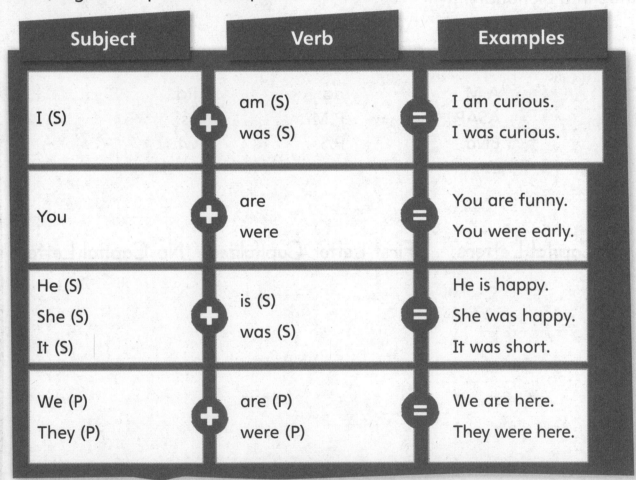

| Subject | Verb | Examples |
|---------|------|----------|
| I (S) | am (S)<br>was (S) | I am curious.<br>I was curious. |
| You | are<br>were | You are funny.<br>You were early. |
| He (S)<br>She (S)<br>It (S) | is (S)<br>was (S) | He is happy.<br>She was happy.<br>It was short. |
| We (P)<br>They (P) | are (P)<br>were (P) | We are here.<br>They were here. |

**My TURN** Edit this paragraph for subject-verb agreement.

My teacher assigned us a class project. She were very excited about it. We was not as excited as she were. She said, "You is not excited now, but you'll see that it are fun."

# Compose Characters

**Learning Goal**

I can use elements of narrative text to write a historical fiction story.

**Characters** in historical fiction can be real or imaginary, but they must be realistic. Their actions should make sense for the time period.

The **major**, or main, **character** is the most important character. **Minor characters** have less important roles. Writers explain relationships among characters as the story unfolds.

**My TURN** Read a historical fiction text from the classroom library. Complete the graphic organizer with details about the main character.

| Who is the main character? | What does he or she wear? | What are his or her chores or jobs? |
| --- | --- | --- |
| | | |

| What are the beliefs and attitudes of the character? |
| --- |
| |

| Name a minor character. How would you describe the minor character's relationship to the main character? |
| --- |
| |

**My TURN** As you compose your historical fiction story in your writing notebook, include realistic details that will develop the main character.

# Compose a Setting

The **setting** of historical fiction influences the plot. The setting determines if story events are realistic for the time period.

- The time is a particular historical time period.
- The place is real or seems as though it could be real.

**My TURN** Review a historical fiction text you have read. Then complete the chart.

| When and where does the story take place? | |
|---|---|
| **What does the place look like?** | **Text Evidence** |
| **What is life like in the place?** | **Text Evidence** |
| **How does the setting influence the plot?** | |

**My TURN** On a separate sheet of paper, compose a setting for your historical fiction story.

# Plot: Establish a Problem

In historical fiction, writers use events to establish a problem. The problem must be actual or believable for the time in history. The events help shape the challenge that the main character faces.

**My TURN** Read the passage. Complete the chart.

In 1775, most of the men of Bedford left to join other Americans in the Revolutionary War. However, Samuel was too young to be a soldier. He needed to stay home. His job was to watch over his mother and younger sisters. To earn money, he cleaned out Mrs. Walsh's barn. Sometimes she sent him home with fresh eggs. Samuel knew how to hunt and fish, but going into the woods alone was not safe.

**Historical Event and Year**

What actual problem did the event create for men at that time?

What problem did the event create for the fictional main character?

**My TURN** As you compose your historical fiction story, establish a problem that makes sense for the time period you are writing about.

# Plot: Plan a Resolution

The **resolution** provides a satisfactory ending to the story. It reveals an outcome or solution. In historical fiction, writers think about historical events before writing an ending. The character's actions must be believable too. A resolution may reveal the character's thoughts and feelings. It may also tell what happens to the character as a result of the ending.

**My TURN** Use the chart to plan, or map, what leads to the resolution of your historical fiction story. Use the completed chart as you compose a draft of your story.

---

**What is the problem?**




**What happens to lead to an outcome or solution?**

1.

2.

3.

**What is the resolution?**




---

# Select a Genre

To write historical fiction, authors must have knowledge of a particular time in the past. They may use that knowledge to write in another genre, or category of writing. To select another genre, authors consider a topic, a purpose for writing, and an audience to write for.

**My TURN** Use a strategy such as brainstorming, freewriting, or mapping to think about writing your story in another genre. Then answer the questions in the chart. For the last question, choose a genre that is different from your story's genre. Share your answers with your Writing Club.

| | Question | Answer |
|---|---|---|
| **Topic** | What do I want to share about this topic? | |
| **Purpose** | Why do I want to share this knowledge? | |
| **Audience** | Who do I want to share it with? | |
| **Genre** | In what genre can I best share it? | |

When you write in another genre, you can use what you already know and new things you learn!

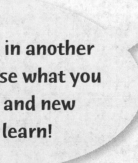

# American HEROES

For a United States president performing duties as the nation's top leader requires courage. Presidents face unexpected problems that call for difficult decisions. Many Americans consider some presidents to be heroes.

## GEORGE WASHINGTON

Before he was elected president, George Washington led the military as Americans fought for independence from England. As the first president of the United States, Washington planned how the highest office would work. The judicial branch of government was formed during his presidency. This branch includes the courts and judges who interpret the laws.

## ABRAHAM LINCOLN

Abraham Lincoln, our sixteenth president, led the United States during the Civil War. The outcome of the Civil War determined that the Northern and Southern states would remain united as one country. He is remembered for issuing the Emancipation Proclamation, which led to the end of slavery.

**How do challenges turn ordinary people into heroes?**

**Turn and Talk** Take turns reading aloud each section with your partner. Discuss the main idea and key details of each section. What challenges did these three presidents face? How did they show courage when facing these challenges? What can you infer about heroic traits these men had?

## FRANKLIN ROOSEVELT

President Franklin D. Roosevelt, the thirty-second president, helped the United States recover from the Great Depression, when people did not have jobs or enough money. He was known for Fireside Chats, radio messages that comforted and encouraged Americans.

## Spotlight on Genre

# Historical Fiction

In **historical fiction**, authors use imagination and historical facts to tell a realistic story.

Historical fiction takes place in the past. Authors include realistic and factual details about the setting, plot, and characters. The **theme**, or central message, is made clear through events that happen during a particular time period.

**Establish Purpose** In this lesson, you will read two historical fiction texts. Before you start, establish a purpose, or reason, for reading these texts. For example, you may want to learn about a time period in history by comparing and contrasting the settings.

Historical fiction texts can help you learn about the past!

MY **PURPOSE**

_____

_____

_____

_____

**TURN and TALK** With a partner, discuss different purposes for reading the excerpts from _Little House on the Prairie_ and _By the Shores of Silver Lake_. Then set your purpose for reading.

# HISTORICAL FICTION
## ANCHOR CHART

### SETTING
realistic historical setting with factual or made-up details

### PLOT
fictional plot that weaves together historical and fictional events

### CHARACTERS
may be fictional or real people involved in the events of the time period

**Laura Ingalls Wilder** is one of the country's most influential children's book authors. The first book in her *Little House* series was published in 1932, and the books continue to be widely read today. Her *Little House* stories have even been made into a television series and a musical play!

*from*

# Little House on the Prairie

## Preview Vocabulary

As you read the excerpt from *Little House on the Prairie*, notice how these vocabulary words provide clues about the text.

| horribly | furious |
|---|---|

## Read

Establish a purpose for reading by asking yourself, "How can I find clues about the theme in this text?" Follow these strategies when you read this **historical fiction** text the first time.

**Notice** when and where the action takes place.

**Generate Questions** about what the author wants you to understand.

First Read

**Connect** this text to what you know about the past.

**Respond** by marking parts you find most interesting or surprising.

Genre **Historical Fiction**

# *from*
# LITTLE HOUSE
# *on the* PRAIRIE

## *by* Laura Ingalls Wilder

AUDIO

ANNOTATE

### BACKGROUND

*Little House on the Prairie* is the third novel in a series
of books written by Laura Ingalls Wilder. The books
are based upon the experiences of her family in the
1800s. In this excerpt, Laura and her family face an
unexpected danger and struggle to save their home
and animals, including their dog, Jack, and their horses,
Pet, Patty, and Bunny.

**Compare and Contrast Texts**

Highlight details that help you analyze how the conflict, or problem, the characters face in this story is different from the problem they face in the second story.

1   One day they were helping Ma get dinner. Baby Carrie was playing on the floor in the sunshine, and suddenly the sunshine was gone.

2   "I do believe it is going to storm," Ma said, looking out of the window. Laura looked, too, and great black clouds were billowing up in the south, across the sun.

3   Pet and Patty were coming running from the field, Pa holding to the heavy plow and bounding in long leaps behind it.

4   "Prairie fire!" he shouted. "Get the tub full of water! Put sacks in it! Hurry!"

5    Ma ran to the well, Laura ran to tug the tub to it. Pa tied Pet to the house. He brought the cow and calf from the picket-line and shut them in the stable. He caught Bunny and tied her fast to the north corner of the house. Ma was pulling up buckets of water as fast as she could. Laura ran to get the sacks that Pa had flung out of the stable.

6    Pa was plowing, shouting at Pet and Patty to make them hurry. The sky was black now, the air was as dark as if the sun had set. Pa plowed a long furrow west of the house and south of the house, and back again east of the house. Rabbits came bounding past him as if he wasn't there.

**CLOSE READ**

**Infer Theme**

<u>Underline</u> details that describe how the family members work together when facing a dangerous situation.

## Infer Theme

Underline evidence that describes Pa's and Ma's actions and the great dangers they face. Use this evidence to infer the theme of the selection. Be sure to distinguish the theme from the topic, or what the story is about.

7    Pet and Patty came galloping, the plow and Pa bounding behind them. Pa tied them to the other north corner of the house. The tub was full of water. Laura helped Ma push the sacks under the water to soak them.

8    "I couldn't plow but one furrow; there isn't time," Pa said. "Hurry, Caroline. That fire's coming faster than a horse can run."

9    A big rabbit bounded right over the tub while Pa and Ma were lifting it. Ma told Laura to stay at the house. Pa and Ma ran staggering to the furrow with the tub.

10    Laura stayed close to the house. She could see the red fire coming under the billows of smoke. More rabbits went leaping by. They paid no attention to Jack and he didn't think about them; he stared at the red under sides of the rolling smoke and shivered and whined while he crowded close to Laura.

11    The wind was rising and wildly screaming. Thousands of birds flew before the fire, thousands of rabbits were running.

12    Pa was going along the furrow, setting fire to the grass on the other side of it. Ma followed with a wet sack, beating at the flames that tried to cross the furrow. The whole prairie was hopping with rabbits. Snakes rippled across the yard. Prairie hens ran silently, their necks outstretched and their wings spread. Birds screamed in the screaming wind.

13    Pa's little fire was all around the house now, and he helped Ma fight it with the wet sacks. The fire blew wildly, snatching at the dry grass inside the furrow. Pa and Ma thrashed at it with the sacks, when it got across the furrow they stamped it with their feet. They ran back and forth in the smoke, fighting that fire. The prairie fire was roaring now, roaring louder and louder in the screaming wind. Great flames came roaring, flaring and twisting high. Twists of flame broke loose and came down on the wind to blaze up in the grasses far ahead of the roaring wall of fire. A red light came from the rolling black clouds of smoke overhead.

**CLOSE READ**

## Compare and Contrast Texts

Highlight details about the prairie fire that can help you explain how the setting's influence on the plot is similar and different in the two stories.

## Compare and Contrast Texts

Highlight details that help you analyze how Laura's response to the family's problem in this story is different from her response to the problem in the second story.

**horribly** in a very bad way

14   Mary and Laura stood against the house and held hands and trembled. Baby Carrie was in the house. Laura wanted to do something, but inside her head was a roaring and whirling like the fire. Her middle shook, and tears poured out of her stinging eyes. Her eyes and her nose and her throat stung with smoke.

15   Jack howled. Bunny and Pet and Patty were jerking at the ropes and squealing horribly. The orange, yellow, terrible flames were coming faster than horses can run, and their quivering light danced over everything.

16    Pa's little fire had made a burned black strip. The little fire went backing slowly away against the wind, it went slowly crawling to meet the racing furious big fire. And suddenly the big fire swallowed the little one.

17    The wind rose to a high, crackling, rushing shriek, flames climbed into the crackling air. Fire was all around the house.

18    Then it was over. The fire went roaring past and away.

19    Pa and Ma were beating out little fires here and there in the yard. When they were all out, Ma came to the house to wash her hands and face. She was all streaked with smoke and sweat, and she was trembling.

20    She said there was nothing to worry about. "The back-fire saved us," she said, "and all's well that ends well."

**CLOSE READ**

### Infer Theme
<u>Underline</u> details in the conclusion that help you infer the theme of this story.

**furious** intense, raging, or violent

**Laura Ingalls Wilder's** family moved from place to place when she was a young girl. Her younger sister Grace, an important character in *By the Shores of Silver Lake*, was born in 1877 in Burr Oak, Iowa. However, the family soon returned to Wisconsin that same year after an unsuccessful try at running a hotel.

*from*

# By the Shores of Silver Lake

## Preview Vocabulary

As you read the excerpt from *By the Shores of Silver Lake*, pay attention to these vocabulary words. Notice what they suggest about story events.

> **insisted   terribly   disturbed**

## Read and Compare

Establish a purpose for reading by asking yourself, "How will the theme of this text be similar to and different from the theme of the previous text?" Follow these strategies when you read this **historical fiction** text the first time.

**Notice**
events that take place in the story.

**Generate Questions**
about what seems different from what you already know.

**First Read**

**Connect**
this text to other texts you have read.

**Respond**
by discussing your thoughts about the text as you read.

**Genre** Historical Fiction

*from*
# BY *the* SHORES *of* SILVER LAKE

## *by* Laura Ingalls Wilder

🔊 AUDIO

✏️ ANNOTATE

### BACKGROUND

The story of the Ingalls family continues in the fifth book of the series, *By the Shores of Silver Lake*. Years after the prairie fire, the family has moved to the Dakota Territory. Shortly after settling into their new home, the family discovers that Laura's youngest sister, Grace, is missing.

**Infer Theme**

Underline details that describe how the family works together to solve its problem.

**insisted** stated firmly

1  "She can't be lost," Pa said.

2  "I left her outdoors. I thought she was with you," said Ma.

3  "She can't be lost," Pa insisted. "She wasn't out of my sight a minute." He shouted, "Grace! Grace!"

4  Laura ran panting up the hill. She could not see Grace anywhere. Along the edge of the Big Slough toward Silver Lake she looked, and over the flowery prairie. Quickly, quickly she looked, again and again, seeing nothing but wild flowers and grasses. "Grace! Grace!" she screamed. "Grace!"

5  Pa met her on the slope as she ran down and Ma came up gasping for breath. "She must be in sight, Laura," Pa said. "You must have missed seeing her. She can't be—" Terribly he exclaimed, "The Big Slough!" He turned and ran.

**terribly** in an awful or very bad way

6  Ma ran after him, calling back, "Carrie, you stay with Mary! Laura, look for her, go look!"

7  Mary stood in the doorway of the shanty calling, "Grace! Grace!" More faintly from Big Slough came Pa's shouts and Ma's, "Grace! Where are you? Grace!"

8    If Grace was lost in the Big Slough, how could anyone find her? The old, dead grass stood higher than Laura's head, over acres and acres, for miles and miles. The deep mud sucked at bare feet, and there were water holes. Laura could hear, where she stood, the sound of the coarse slough grass in the wind, a muffling sound that almost smothered even Ma's shrill call, "Grace!"

9    Laura felt cold and sick.

10    "Why don't you look for her?" Carrie cried. "Don't stand there! Do something! I'm going myself!"

11    "Ma told you to stay with Mary," said Laura. "So you'd better stay."

12    "She told you to look!" Carrie screamed. "Go look! Go look! Grace! Grace!"

13    "Shut up! Let me think!" Laura screeched, and she started running across the sunny prairie.

**CLOSE READ**

**Compare and Contrast Texts**
Highlight details that help you explain how the dangers of this setting are similar to and different from those in the first story. Explain how the setting influences the plot in this story.

## Infer Theme

<u>Underline</u> evidence on this page that shows that Laura does not give up hope even though finding a small child in the Big Slough seems impossible.

14   Laura was running straight toward the south. Grass whipped soft against her bare feet. Butterflies fluttered over the flowers. There wasn't a bush nor a weed that Grace could be hidden behind. There was nothing, nothing but grass and flowers swaying in the sunshine.

15   If she were little and playing all by herself, Laura thought, she wouldn't go into the dark Big Slough, she wouldn't go into the mud and the tall grass. "Oh, Grace, why didn't I watch you?" she thought. Sweet pretty little helpless sister—"Grace! Grace!" she screamed. Her breath caught and hurt in her side.

16    She ran on and on. "Grace must have gone this way. Maybe she chased a butterfly. She didn't go into Big Slough! She didn't climb the hill, she wasn't there. Oh, baby sister, I couldn't see you anywhere east or south on this hateful prairie." "Grace!"

17    The horrible, sunny prairie was so large. No lost baby could ever be found on it. Ma's calling and Pa's shouts came from Big Slough. They were thin cries, lost in wind, lost on the enormous bigness of the prairie.

## CLOSE READ

## Vocabulary in Context

To determine the meaning of multiple-meaning words, readers use context, or other words within the sentence, to help them.

The word *thin* can mean "having little body fat" or "weak."

Use context clues within the sentence to determine the meaning of *thin* in paragraph 17.

Underline the context clue that supports your definition.

CLOSE READ

## Vocabulary in Context

Readers often come across multiple-meaning words in texts. As they read, they use context to determine the words' meanings. The context may be found in the same sentence or in other sentences nearby.

The word *bank* can mean "a place or object in which money is stored" or "the edge of a hillside."

Use context clues within and beyond the sentence to determine the meaning of the word *bank* in paragraph 18.

Underline the context clues that support your definition. Be sure to underline context within as well as beyond the sentence.

**disturbed** bothered or moved the position of

18    Laura's breathing hurt her sides under the ribs. Her chest was smothering and her eyes were dizzy. She ran up a low slope. Nothing, nothing, not a spot of shadow was anywhere on the level prairie all around her. She ran on, and suddenly the ground dropped before her. She almost fell down a steep bank.

19    There was Grace. There, in a great pool of blue, sat Grace. The sun shone on her golden hair blowing in the wind. She looked up at Laura with big eyes as blue as violets. Her hands were full of violets. She held them up to Laura and said, "Sweet! Sweet!"

20    Laura sank down and took Grace in her arms. She held Grace carefully and panted for breath. Grace leaned over her arm to reach more violets. They were surrounded by masses of violets blossoming above low-spreading leaves. Violets covered the flat bottom of a large, round hollow. All around this lake of violets, grassy banks rose almost straight up to the prairie-level. There in the round, low place the wind hardly disturbed the fragrance of the violets. The sun was warm there, the sky was overhead, the green walls of grass curved all around, and butterflies fluttered over the crowding violet-faces.

21   Laura stood up and lifted Grace to her feet. She took the violets that Grace gave her, and clasped her hand. "Come, Grace" she said. "We must go home."

22   She gave one look around the little hollow while she helped Grace climb the bank.

23   Grace walked so slowly that for a little while Laura carried her. Then she let her walk, for Grace was nearly three years old, and heavy. Then she lifted her again. So, carrying Grace and helping her walk, Laura brought her to the shanty and gave her to Mary.

24   Then she ran toward the Big Slough, calling as she ran. "Pa! Ma! She's here!" She kept on calling until Pa heard her and shouted to Ma, far in the tall grass. Slowly, together, they fought their way out of Big Slough and slowly came up to the shanty, draggled and muddy and very tired and thankful.

**CLOSE READ**

## Compare and Contrast Texts

Highlight details in paragraph 24 that help you infer the theme. Compare and contrast the themes of the two stories.

# Develop Vocabulary

In historical fiction, authors choose precise words that help a reader hear, see, and feel the action. These words connect to the reader's senses.

**My TURN** Complete the word equation with a suffix and a vocabulary word from the word bank. Then use the word in a sentence about the story.

**Word Bank**

**disturbed**    **horribly**    **insisted**    **terribly**

| Base Word | Suffix | Vocabulary Word |
|---|---|---|
| terrible | ➕ -ly | ＝ terribly<br>Sentence:<br>Pa became terribly worried about Grace. |
| horrible | ➕ ____ | ＝ _____<br>Sentence: |
| insist | ➕ ____ | ＝ _____<br>Sentence: |
| disturb | ➕ ____ | ＝ _____<br>Sentence: |

# Check for Understanding

**My TURN** Look back at the text to answer the questions.

**1.** What identifies these texts as historical fiction?

**2.** How does the author convey a feeling of panic in each story? Cite text evidence.

**3.** Based on the details in the second text, what can you conclude about the influence of the setting on the plot?

**4.** Synthesize, or combine, what you know from both texts to answer this question: Why do you think these two texts were paired together?

# Infer Theme

The **theme** of a story is its central message, or what the author wants the reader to understand about life. The theme is usually not directly stated. Instead, you need to **infer**, or figure out, the theme. To infer the theme, consider the problems the characters face, how they respond, and what they learn.

1. **My TURN** Go to the Close Read notes in the texts and underline parts that help you infer theme.

2. **Text Evidence** Use some of the parts you underlined to infer the theme of both stories and distinguish it from the topic, or what each text is about.

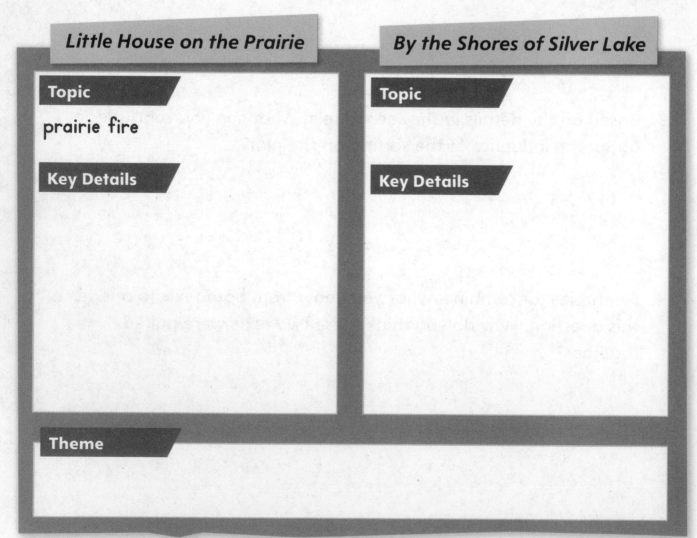

*Little House on the Prairie*

**Topic**

prairie fire

**Key Details**

*By the Shores of Silver Lake*

**Topic**

**Key Details**

**Theme**

# Compare and Contrast Texts

After reading two or more texts by the same author about the same or similar characters, you can **compare and contrast** plot elements, including the conflict. Comparing shows how text elements are alike. Contrasting shows how they are different. Analyzing story conflicts in this way helps you better understand the text.

1. **My TURN** Go back to the Close Read notes and highlight evidence that helps you compare and contrast the plot elements in both texts.

2. **Text Evidence** Use some of your highlighted text to compare and contrast the two texts.

| *Little House on the Prairie* | Both | *By the Shores of Silver Lake* |
| --- | --- | --- |
| Conflict | Setting | Conflict |
| "great black clouds were billowing up"; "'Prairie fire!'" | Plot | |
| Laura's Response to the Conflict | Theme | Laura's Response to the Conflict |

# Reflect and Share

**Write to Sources** Consider the excerpts from *Little House on the Prairie* and *By the Shores of Silver Lake*. Compare and contrast how the characters respond to challenges. In your opinion, what traits best help a person face challenges? Use examples from the texts to write and support your response.

**Use Text Evidence** When writing an opinion, use text evidence to support your ideas. Before writing, follow these steps:

- Write your opinion about the traits that best help a person face challenges.
- Identify two or three characters in the texts who demonstrate these traits.
- Locate evidence in both of the texts that best supports your opinion.

On a separate sheet of paper, write a short paragraph to state your opinion on traits that help people face challenges. Use text evidence to support your opinion.

**Weekly Question**

How do challenges turn ordinary people into heroes?

# Academic Vocabulary

**Learning Goal**

I can develop knowledge about language to make connections between reading and writing historical fiction.

**Context Clues** are words and phrases that help you determine the meanings of unfamiliar words. Context clues can be found within sentences and in surrounding sentences.

**My TURN** For each sentence below,

**1. Underline** the academic vocabulary word.

**2. Highlight** the context clue or clues.

**3. Write** a brief definition of the word based on the clues.

Salim worries about the math test. I encourage him by reminding him how well he does on his homework.

Definition: _____

As the general of the army, I command the soldiers by telling them not to retreat.

Definition: _____

The two puppies looked so much alike, I could distinguish them only by comparing the small differences on their tails.

Definition: _____

Even though our team suffered a defeat in the final game, we did not let the loss ruin our season.

Definition: _____

I will achieve my goal when I cross the finish line.

Definition: _____

# Suffixes

**Suffixes -*ful*, -*y*, -*ness*** can be added to the end of a base word to change a word's meaning. The word *joyful* has the base word *joy* and the suffix -*ful*. The suffix -*ful* means "full of," so *joyful* means "full of joy." The word *flowery* has the base word *flower* and the suffix -*y*. The suffix -*y* means "full of" or "having the character of," so *flowery* means "full of flowers." The word *brightness* has the base word *bright* and the suffix -*ness*. The suffix -*ness* means "the state or quality of," so *brightness* means "the state or quality of being bright."

Sometimes you need to change the spelling of the base word. To change the word *happy* to *happiness*, change the *y* to an *i* and add -*ness*. To change the word *chat* to *chatty*, double the final consonant before adding -*y*.

**My TURN** Read the sentences. Underline the word that has the suffix -*ful*, -*y*, or -*ness*. Read the words with suffixes, and then write the definition of the word on the line.

1. They fought their way out of Big Slough and came up to the shack, draggled and muddy.

   _____

2. They were very tired and thankful.

   _____

3. The smokiness in the air warned Pa of the fire.

   _____

# High-Frequency Words

**High-frequency words** appear frequently in texts. They often do not follow regular word study patterns. Read these high-frequency words: *nothing, scientists.* Try to identify them in your reading.

# Read Like a Writer

**Hyperbole,** or extreme exaggeration, overstates something in a serious or funny way. Hyperbole is a figure of speech and is not meant to be read as literal, or factual, information. "He is as tall as a giraffe" and "I have told you a million times" are examples of hyperbole.

**Model**   Read the passage from *Little House on the Prairie.*

> Thousands of birds flew before the fire, thousands of rabbits were running.

**Hyperbole exaggerates.**

**1. Identify** Laura Ingalls Wilder uses hyperbole to exaggerate the number of rabbits and birds escaping the fire.

**2. Question** How does hyperbole help me imagine the events?

**3. Conclude** Hyperbole helps me imagine the panic during the prairie fire.

Read the sentence.

> The whole prairie was hopping with rabbits.

**My TURN** Follow the steps to analyze the passage. Describe how the author uses hyperbole.

**1. Identify** Laura Ingalls Wilder uses hyperbole to exaggerate _____

**2. Question** How does hyperbole help me imagine the events?

**3. Conclude** Hyperbole helps me imagine _____

# Write for a Reader

Writers use hyperbole for a funny or serious effect.

With hyperbole, the more exaggeration, the better!

**My TURN** Think about how Laura Ingalls Wilder used hyperbole to describe events in *Little House on the Prairie*. Identify how you can use hyperbole to describe events in your historical fiction story.

1. If you wanted to write about someone who is about to achieve a goal, what hyperboles might you include? Briefly explain how the use of hyperbole would help readers understand the character.

_____

_____

_____

2. Write a passage that takes place in the past about a person who tried to achieve a challenging goal. Use hyperbole to describe and emphasize the events of your story.

_____

_____

_____

_____

_____

_____

# Spell Words with Suffixes

**Suffixes -ful, -y, -ness** are added to base words to create new words. Sometimes you need to change the spelling of the base word when a suffix is added. To change the word *happy* to *happiness*, change the *y* to *i* and add *-ness*. To change the word *chat* to *chatty*, double the final consonant before adding *-y*.

**My TURN** Read the words. Sort the listed words by their suffixes.

**SPELLING WORDS**

readiness     illness
cloudy     freshness
stormy     happiness
peaceful     graceful
eagerness     frightful

*-ful*     *-y*     *-ness*

# High-Frequency Words

High-frequency words often do not follow regular word study patterns. Write each high-frequency word on the line.

nothing

scientists

# Simple Verb Tenses

Verbs have **simple tenses: past, present,** and **future**. Different verb tenses have different forms.

| Simple Verb Tenses | Examples |
|---|---|
| Many **present tense** verbs end in -s. | Stephanie *sews* pillows for dogs. |
| Form the **past tense** of most verbs by adding -*ed*. Change the spelling before adding -*ed* in the following cases:<br>• When a verb ends with e, drop the e before adding -*ed*.<br>• When a one-syllable verb ends with a vowel and a consonant, double the final consonant before adding -*ed*.<br>• When a verb ends with a consonant followed by *y*, change the *y* to *i* before adding -*ed*. | • I *baked* a cake for Sammy.<br>• Miners *panned* for gold in California.<br>• Mr. Sharp *hurried* to get to his appointment. |
| The **future tense** tells what will happen in the future. Add the helping verb *will* to a present tense verb. | I *will run* for president.<br>She *will plant* a garden. |

**My TURN** Edit this draft by correcting any mistakes in verb tense.

Sam want to walk to school today. Yesterday his mom want him to take the bus. Sam tells her he find someone to walk with him. She say that, if he find someone, she allow him to walk to school.

# Develop an Introduction

An **introduction** in historical fiction

- ○ introduces the main characters of the story
- ○ provides details about the historical setting
- ○ highlights a challenge the characters face

Copyright © SAVVAS Learning Company LLC. All Rights Reserved.

**Learning Goal**

I can use elements of narrative text to write a historical fiction story.

**My TURN** Read the paragraph. Highlight details about the setting, underline the characters, and summarize the situation.

> Margaret was a happy-go-lucky teenager living in Chicago. Like most American teens, she enjoyed going to the movies and riding in her parents' new car. But in 1929, the Great Depression changed all that. Her father lost his job and, with it, the family's house. With no place to live, Margaret and her parents moved to the West to make a new home with her grandparents.

**Summarize the Situation**

**My TURN** On a separate sheet of paper, write an introduction for your own historical fiction story.

# Draft an Event Sequence

Historical fiction describes events that really happened or could have happened. Often the **event sequence** is chronological, or in time order, meaning one event leads to the next. Using a story map to identify plot elements can help you plan an event sequence.

**Beginning**: Introduces the historical time period, characters, and a problem using signal words and phrases, such as *first*, *once*, or *many years ago*, or a specific date

**Middle**: Describes events and how characters face problems

**Ending**: Tells the solution or lesson learned using signal words and phrases, such as *finally*, *at last*, or *in the end*

**My TURN** Use the story map to draft a focused, structured, and clear event sequence for your historical fiction story.

| Characters: | Setting: |
|---|---|
| | |

| Beginning: | |
|---|---|

↓

| Middle: | |
|---|---|

↓

| End: | |
|---|---|

# Create an Audio Recording of a Story

Writers have many ways of sharing their work with an audience. Some writers choose to publish their stories as printed books. Others choose to publish to blogs or other Web sites, where they might add images or other visuals to go with the story. Some writers choose to record their stories and publish them as audiobooks.

An audiobook

- allows a storyteller to emphasize specific ideas or words

- reveals information about characters, such as their tone of voice or accent

- appeals to audiences who are not able to read a book

**My TURN** Work with a partner. Take turns reading your stories aloud. Use the checklist to help you practice. Then ask an adult to help you record your story.

**READING A STORY ALOUD**

- [ ] I say each word, and I pronounce the words correctly.
- [ ] I read at an understandable pace and loud enough volume.
- [ ] I pause when needed, such as when showing shock or humor.
- [ ] I read with appropriate expression, changing my voice for each character as appropriate.

Think about who your characters are. Let their motivations and traits guide how you read their dialogue.

**127**

# Compose Dialogue

Writers use **dialogue** to show the conversation between characters. The dialogue is often made up. Dialogue must sound realistic and appropriate for the time period.

---

"Go along, child," Grandmother said. "The radio is broken. Nothing but bad news, anyhow. Bad news and false hope. There's no time for music here."

Margaret looked at her grandmother's gray eyes. "Will you sing me a song, Grandmother? Sing your favorite Kansas song."

---

**My TURN** Compose some dialogue for your historical fiction story.

_____

_____

_____

_____

**CHECKLIST FOR WRITING DIALOGUE**

☐ Indent to indicate a new speaker.

☐ Follow capitalization and punctuation rules for dialogue, including quotation marks.

☐ Use dialogue to show how characters think and feel, how they respond to events, and to move the story along.

# Describe Events with Details

**Details** help authors focus their writing and allow readers to visualize story events. In historical fiction, writers take readers back in time. Writers research to find accurate details about the setting and possible situations for the time period they are writing about.

The dust storm blackened the Kansas sky for a third day. Margaret rubbed her dusty eyes as she swept the front porch. The sand and grit drifted and blocked the front door. She covered her mouth with her kerchief. It was hard to breathe.

**My TURN** Complete the chart with details from the passage.

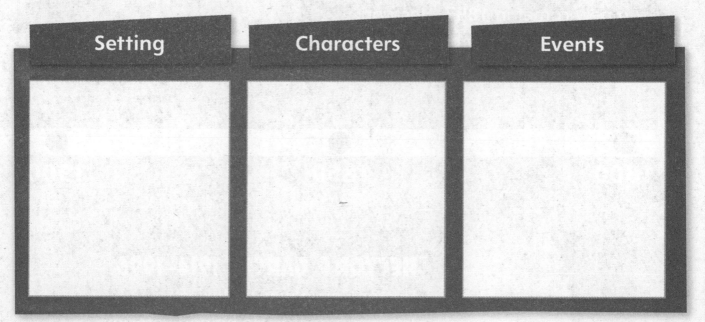

| Setting | Characters | Events |
| --- | --- | --- |
| | | |

**My TURN** Begin to focus your draft by identifying a topic, purpose, and audience. Then select any genre, and plan a draft by freewriting your ideas.

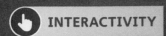INTERACTIVITY

# Needing Heroes

People have always needed heroes. We admire heroes because of their courage, determination, honesty, or other traits. Heroes inspire others because of their sacrifices or desire to make life better. This time line shows some important heroes over the years.

## MARIA MITCHELL, 1818-1889

Maria Mitchell was an astronomer and a professor. She discovered a new comet in **1847**. Her work inspired women to be scientists.

**1800**          **1850**          **1900**

## HECTOR P. GARCIA, 1914-1996

Hector Garcia was a Mexican-American doctor. He helped veterans and people in need to get medical care. He argued that everyone had the right to a good education.

## MAHATMA GANDHI, 1869-1948

Mohandas Gandhi was called Mahatma, or "Great Soul." He worked for years to make India a free nation. His belief in peaceful protest inspired other heroes, including Martin Luther King Jr.

## Weekly Question

### Why do people need heroes?

**Turn and Talk** Discuss with your partner which heroes featured on the time line are most inspiring and why. Remember to express ideas politely.

1950　　　2000　　　2050

## FIRST RESPONDERS, 2001

On September 11, 2001, terrorists attacked the World Trade Center in New York. Police officers and firefighters rushed toward danger to save others' lives.

# Biography

A **biography** tells about a real person's life. An author of a biography writes about the life events or experiences of someone else. Biographies usually

- Take place during a real **historical time**
- Tell about a person's life in **time order**
- Give **facts** and **details** about the person's life

**TURN and TALK** Think about a biography you have read. How was the biography like historical fiction? How was it different? Share your thoughts with a partner. Use the Biography Anchor Chart to guide your discussion.

Reading biographies helps me learn about many kinds of people.

**Be a Fluent Reader** Reading fluently requires that you read accurately at an appropriate pace, or rate. When you read a biography, adjust your reading rate by slowing down to better understand facts and details in the text.

Practice reading with fluency. Ask yourself:

- Do I understand what I just read?

- Should I read the text faster or slower for better understanding?

# BIOGRAPHY
## anchor chart

Purpose
: To inform or explain events from a real person's life

Elements
: *A biography is written in the third person.

  * Setting is a real time and a real place.

  * The subject of the text is real, and other real people may be included.

  * Text includes important events, challenges, and struggles in the person's life.

Text Structure
: Time order

Theme
: Inspiring message or lesson learned

**Donna Jo Napoli** is a grandmother who has written many books for children and young adults. She has traveled around the world several times to learn about people and animals in her stories. Her books have been translated into more than a dozen different languages.

# Mama Miti

## Preview Vocabulary

As you read *Mama Miti: Wangari Maathai and the Trees of Kenya*, notice how these vocabulary words help to develop themes about heroes.

| | |
|---|---|
| ceremonies | tradition |
| medicine | lamenting | offering |

## Read

Before you begin, scan the text to establish a purpose for reading. Follow these strategies when you read this **biography** the first time.

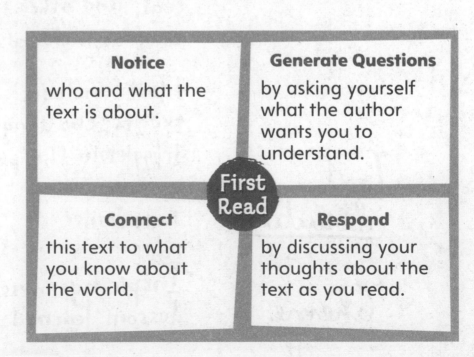

**Notice** who and what the text is about.

**Generate Questions** by asking yourself what the author wants you to understand.

**First Read**

**Connect** this text to what you know about the world.

**Respond** by discussing your thoughts about the text as you read.

# MAMA MITI

## WANGARI MAATHAI and the TREES of KENYA

 AUDIO

ANNOTATE

BY **Donna Jo Napoli**  ILLUSTRATIONS BY **Kadir Nelson**

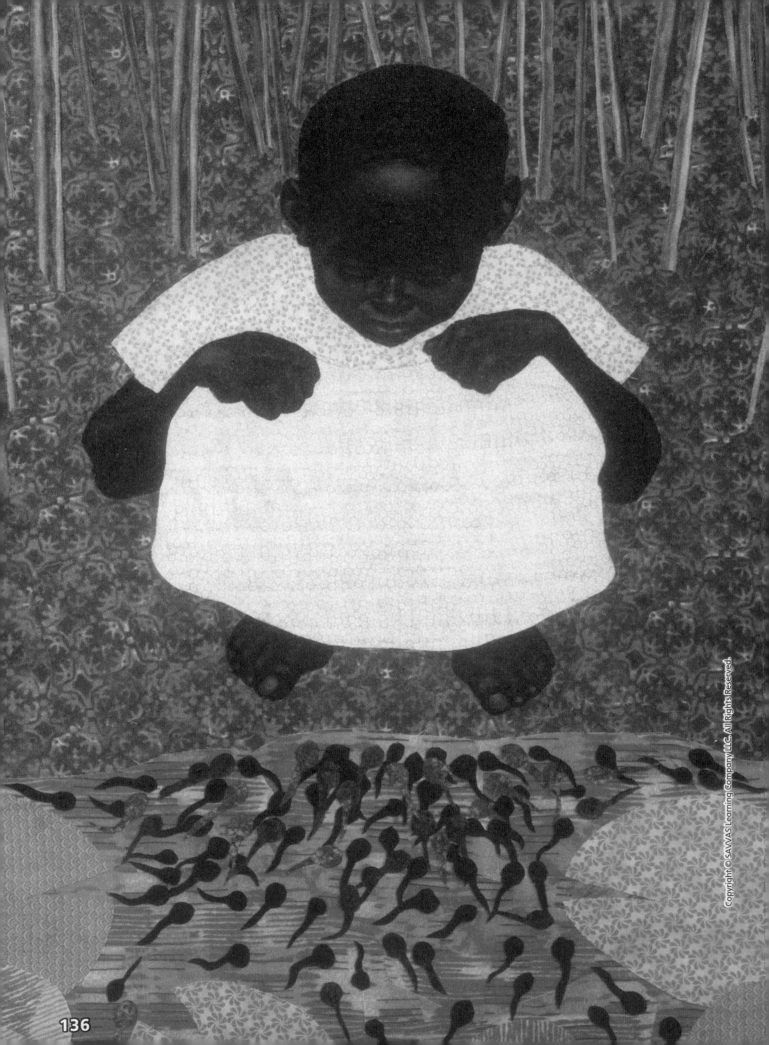

1 *On the highlands of Africa, near forests and plains and a huge salt lick, Wangari was born. The face of Mount Kenya smiled down on her. People told stories of how in the old days sometimes the sun shone too bright too long, and droughts came. Creatures suffered. Plants wilted. People fought.*

2 *So the men held ceremonies under the* mugumo—*the spreading sacred fig tree—and the skies blessed them with shimmering rains to slake their thirst and water their farms. Village elders placed staffs from the* thigi *tree between angry men, and enemies became friends.*

3 Wangari listened to these stories. That's how she came to love and respect trees. That's how she came to be wise in the tradition of her family and village, of her country and continent.

4 When Wangari grew up, she worked in the city, but she always remembered her roots. She planted trees in her backyard and sat under them to refresh her body and spirit.

Copyright © SAVVAS Learning Company LLC. All Rights Reserved.

## CLOSE READ

### Analyze Text Structure

<u>Underline</u> details about Mount Kenya, the sun, and skies that help you explain the author's purpose for beginning the biography with the italicized text in paragraphs 1 and 2.

**ceremonies** formal religious or public events

**tradition** customs or beliefs passed down among a group of people

**Vocabulary in Context**

Use a context clue within the sentence to determine the meaning of *squiggles* in paragraph 5.

Underline the context clue that supports your definition.

5    One day a poor woman came from the western valley to see the wise Wangari. Her children peeked out from behind her at the smiling woman in bright blue cloth with squiggles all through it, like tadpoles squirming in a pool. "I have too little food to feed my family," said the poor woman. "There is no longer a job for me in the timber mill. And I have no other skills. What can I do?"

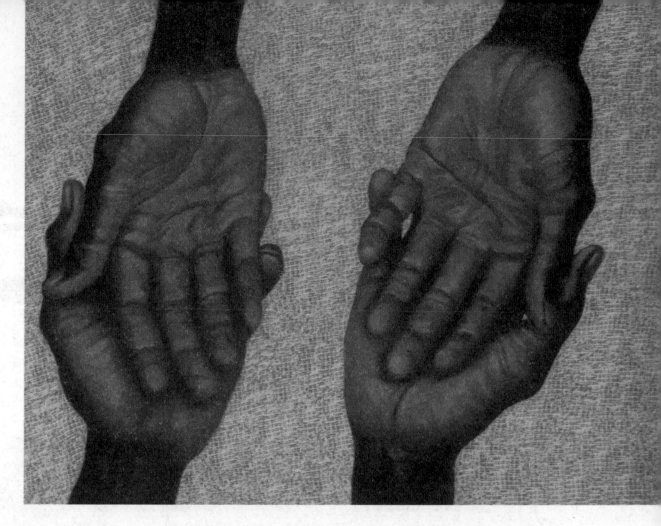

6    Wangari took the woman's hands and turned them over. She took the children's hands, one by one. "These are strong hands. Here are seedlings of the *mubiru muiru* tree. Plant them. Plant as many as you can. Eat the berries."

7    *Thayu nyumba*—

8    Peace, my people

9    The woman and her children returned home and planted trees with their strong hands, one by one. In the years to come, when flowering season was over, the family ate the shiny round fruits. They shared with their neighbors, who carried home the seeds, planted them, and grew their own *mubiru muiru* trees.

**CLOSE READ**

## Summarize Informational Text

Highlight key details that help you summarize the effect that Wangari's advice had on the family and its neighbors.

## Summarize Informational Text

Highlight key details that help you summarize how the event described in paragraphs 10–13 is similar to the event described in paragraphs 5–9.

10  Another woman came to the wise Wangari, as poor as the first. This one traveled from the mountain in the south. Her daughters stood beside her, thin as ropes. "My daughters and I walk hours every day to find firewood to cook with," said the poor woman. "It takes so long, we have no time for anything else. What can I do?"

11  Wangari took the woman by the arms. "These arms are strong," she said. "Plant a tree. Here are seedlings of the *mukinduri*. This tree makes good firewood. Plant as many as you can."

12  *Thayu nyumba*—

13  Peace, my people

14    The woman and her daughters planted those seedlings. In time the trees grew huge with many wide branches. The woman and her daughters cut branches for warmth. They shared new seedlings with their neighbors, who carried them home and grew their own *mukinduri* trees.

15    Word passed from woman to woman, until all over Kenya women knew about the wise Wangari. They came to her from every direction, one after another, as the years went by.

**CLOSE READ**

**Analyze Text Structure**

Underline words and phrases that help you understand the order of the events.

16 "Our goats are starving," said a woman from near the northern desert. "I have barely enough food to feed my family; how can my husband feed the animals, too?"

17 "Plant a tree. A *muheregendi*. The leaves are good animal fodder. Plant as many as you can."

18 *Thayu nyumba*—Peace, my people

19 "My cows are sick," said another, from the savanna. "I have no money to buy medicine for them."

20 "Plant a tree. A *muthakwa wa athi*. The leaves cure gall sickness in cattle."

21 *Thayu nyumba*—Peace, my people

22 "Wild animals come in the night and steal my chickens," said a woman from a fishing village. She shook her head in worry.

23 "Plant a tree. A *mukawa*. Its thorns will keep out predators."

24 *Thayu nyumba*—Peace, my people

25 "My home fell apart," came the cry of another woman, who had come all the way from the coast. "We have no shelter."

26 "Plant a tree. A *muluhakuha*. The timber makes good building poles."

27 *Thayu nyumba*—Peace, my people

**CLOSE READ**

## Analyze Text Structure

Underline details that help you recognize the people's problems and Wangari's solutions. Explain how the problem-and-solution text structure in paragraphs 16–26 contributes to the author's purpose of helping readers understand how Wangari assisted the people of Kenya.

**medicine** a substance used for treating an illness

## Analyze Text Structure

<u>Underline</u> examples of repetition in paragraphs 28–31. Explain how the author's use of repetition contributes to her purpose of accurately describing how Wangari helped the women.

28  Wangari told women to plant *murigono*, whose branches make good stakes for training yam vines.

29  She told them to plant *muhuti* as a living fence around their animal yards.

30  She told them to plant *muigoya*, whose leaves could be wrapped around bananas to ripen them.

31  She told them to plant *muringa* for the pure joy of their white flowers.

32　And when a woman from her own village came, lamenting that the water in her stream was too dirty to drink, Wangari told her to plant *mukuyu*, the giant sacred fig, the drinker of water, which acts as nature's filter to clean streams.

33　*Thayu nyumba—*

34　Peace, my people

35　Soon cool, clear waters teemed with black wriggling tadpoles, like the ones on Wangari's clothes—like the ones Wangari marveled at in the waters when she was small, when Kenya was covered with trees and animals, when people lived in peace with nature.

**CLOSE READ**

**Summarize Informational Text**

Highlight key details that help you recognize and summarize the cause and effect of planting *mukuyu* trees.

**lamenting** expressing feelings of sadness

**Summarize Informational Text**

Highlight key details that help you summarize the effect of Wangari's teachings on Kenya.

**Fluency** Read paragraphs 36–40 aloud with a partner to practice reading at an appropriate rate. Make sure you are not reading too quickly nor too slowly.

**offering** giving or presenting

36  All over the countryside the trees that had disappeared came back. Nairobi, the capital city, had been known as Kiinuini, "the place where there are many *miinu* trees." Now it was Kiinuini again.

37  Kenya was strong once more, strong and peaceful.

38  Wangari changed a country, tree by tree. She taught her people the ancient wisdom of peace with nature. And now she is teaching the rest of the world. She is known these days as Mama Miti—the mother of trees. A green belt of peace started with one good woman offering something we can all do: "Plant a tree."

39  *Thayu nyumba*—

40  Peace, my people

# Develop Vocabulary

In biographies and other nonfiction texts, authors carefully choose words to help the reader connect events in the text to personal experiences.

**My TURN** Add the vocabulary words from the word bank to complete the first column. Then, use each word in a sentence about the story.

**Word Bank**

ceremonies    tradition    medicine    offering

| Word | Sentence |
|---|---|
| medicine <br> a substance used for treating an illness | A woman cannot pay for medicine to treat her sick cows. |
| customs or beliefs passed down among a group of people | |
| formal religious or public events | |
| giving or presenting | |

# Check for Understanding

**My TURN** Look back at the text to answer the questions.

1. How can the reader identify *Mama Miti* as a biography?

2. What is the author's purpose for including the information in paragraphs 1 and 2?

3. Based on evidence in the biography, what conclusions can you draw about Wangari Maathai?

4. What evidence from the text supports the idea that Wangari Maathai wanted to provide long-lasting solutions to the women's problems?

# Analyze Text Structure

**Text structure** is how information is organized. Text structures include description, cause and effect, problem and solution, compare and contrast, and time order. Look for details in a text that suggest how it is structured. For example, specific dates and words and phrases such as *first*, *then*, and *after that* suggest a time-order text structure. Recognizing text structure and explaining how it contributes to the author's purpose can help you better understand a text.

1. **My TURN** Go to the Close Read notes in *Mama Miti* and underline parts that help you analyze the text structure.

2. **Text Evidence** Use some of the parts you underlined to complete the chart.

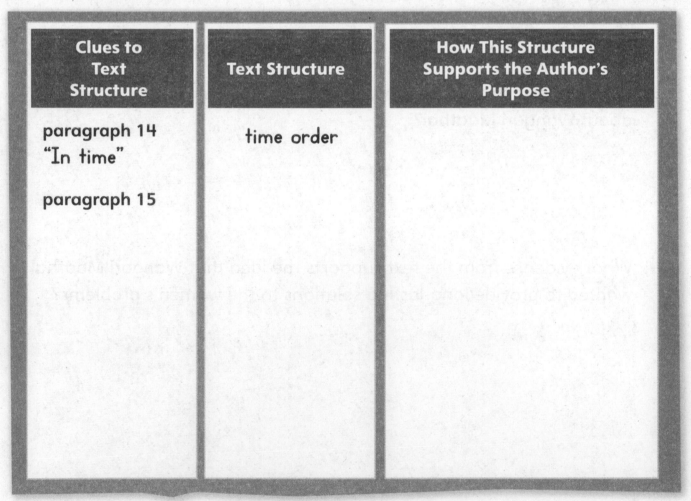

| Clues to Text Structure | Text Structure | How This Structure Supports the Author's Purpose |
|---|---|---|
| paragraph 14 "In time"  paragraph 15 | time order | |

# Summarize Informational Text

You can **summarize**, or recount, the key ideas of a text in your own words. Use text structure to help you identify and evaluate details and recount the most important ideas in a text.

1. **My TURN** Go back to the Close Read notes and highlight text evidence that helps you summarize the text.

2. **Text Evidence** Use some of your highlighted evidence to evaluate details and determine key ideas. Use these key ideas to write a brief summary of the text.

| Summary |
| --- |
|  |

# Reflect and Share

**Write to Sources** Consider all the heroes you have read about in this unit. Choose two heroes, each from a different text, and compare and contrast their heroic actions. Based on your comparison, what conclusions can you draw about the importance of heroes? Use examples from each text to write and support your response.

**Ask and Answer Questions** When writing a response to a text, ask and answer questions about the text to guide your writing.

- ◎ What heroes did we read about in this unit?
- ◎ How are the two heroes I chose alike and different?
- ◎ What can I conclude about the importance of heroes?

On a separate sheet of paper, write a paragraph that states your response. Use linking words, such as *also*, *and*, and *but*, to connect your ideas. Support your response with text evidence. End your paragraph with a sentence that restates your ideas.

## Weekly Question

**Why do people need heroes?**

# Academic Vocabulary

**Learning Goal**

I can develop knowledge about language to make connections between reading and writing.

**Figurative Language** gives words meanings beyond their dictionary definitions. One type of figurative language is simile, which compares two things using the word *like* or *as*.

**My TURN**  For each sentence below,

**1.** **Read** each sentence and underline the simile.

**2.** **Match** the word in the box with the simile that best relates to the definition of the word.

**3.** **Choose** two similes. Then use each simile and its related academic vocabulary word in a sentence.

| Word Bank | | | | |
|---|---|---|---|---|
| encourage | defeat | distinguish | achieve | command |

I can tell the twins apart because they are as different as night and day.

_____

Getting a good grade in math was like winning a prize. _____

My friend's words of support were as kind as a mother's praise.

_____

The dog barked forcefully, like he was giving orders. _____

Missing the party felt as upsetting as losing the big game.

_____

_____

**153**

# Vowel Teams

**Vowel Teams *oo, ew, ue, ui, eu*** are letter combinations that spell one sound. These vowel teams spell the vowel sound in *tool* or the vowel sound in *cue*. You can use print or digital dictionaries to check pronunciations.

| Vowel Sound in *Tool* | Vowel Sound in *Cue* |
|---|---|
| stool     fruit | few |
| stew     sleuth | hue |
| clue | |

**My TURN** Read the vowel team in each word in the box. Write each word in the correct column. Underline each vowel team.

> feud     neutral     argue
>
> juicy     nephew     mushroom

Vowel Sound in *Tool*

Vowel Sound in *Cue*

# High-Frequency Words

**High-frequency words** often do not follow regular word-study patterns. Read these high-frequency words: *island, machine.*

# Read Like a Writer

Authors choose words and use language in a style that shows their **voice**, or personality. The author's attitude toward a subject is called **tone**. Tone and other use of language contribute to the writer's voice.

**Model** Read the sentence from *Mama Miti*.

> So the men held ceremonies under the mugumo—the spreading sacred fig tree—and the skies blessed them with shimmering rains to slake their thirst and water their farms.

*establishes a tone*

**1. Identify** Donna Jo Napoli uses language that shows her attitude toward the ceremony.

**2. Question** What tone is revealed?

**3. Conclude** Donna Jo Napoli's use of language reveals a peaceful tone, almost like a fairy tale.

Read the passage.

> Wangari took the woman by the arms. "These arms are strong," she said. "Plant a tree. . . ."

**My TURN** Follow the steps to analyze the passage. Describe how the author uses tone.

**1. Identify** Donna Jo Napoli uses language that shows her attitude toward _____.

**2. Question** What tone is revealed?

**3. Conclude** Donna Jo Napoli's use of language reveals a _____ tone.

# Write for a Reader

Use language that reveals a tone.

Choose words carefully to express a certain tone in your writing. Use tone with other style elements to build your voice as a writer.

**My TURN** In *Mama Miti*, Donna Jo Napoli chooses language that reveals a tone and contributes to her writer's voice. Choose language that shows your tone, or attitude toward a subject, as one way to develop a strong writer's voice.

1. Think of a subject that makes you happy. Write the subject.

   **Subject:** _____

2. Write some positive words describing your subject.

   _____

   _____

3. Write a paragraph that has a positive tone about your subject. Use some of the positive words you listed.

   _____

   _____

   _____

   _____

4. Discuss how your tone contributes to your writer's voice.

   _____

   _____

   _____

# Spell Vowel Teams

**Vowel Teams *oo, ew, ue, ui, eu*** can spell the vowel sound in *tool* or the vowel sound in *cue*. Learning the spellings of these sounds can help you be a better speller and writer.

**My TURN** Read the words. Sort the words into groups by their vowel sounds.

**SPELLING WORDS**

| balloon | recruit | statue |
|---------|---------|--------|
| choose | rescue | suitable |
| feud | spooky | threw |
| newest | | |

| Vowel Sound in *Tool* | Vowel Sound in *Cue* |
|---|---|
| oo: | eu: |
| ew: | ue: |
| ui: | |

# High-Frequency Words

High-frequency words appear frequently in texts. Write the following high-frequency words on the lines.

island _____

machine _____

# Irregular Verbs

The suffix -ed is added to a regular verb to show action in the past, but some verbs do not follow this rule. They are called **irregular verbs.** Instead of using -ed forms to show past time, these verbs change to other words. Many irregular verbs have a special past form when used with *has, have,* or *had.* Here are some examples of irregular verbs.

| Irregular Verb | Past Tense | Past Forms with *has, have, had* |
|---|---|---|
| begin | began | (has, have, had) begun |
| do | did | (has, have, had) done |
| find | found | (has, have, had) found |
| go | went | (has, have, had) gone |
| take | took | (has, have, had) taken |

**My TURN** Edit this paragraph for the correct forms of irregular verbs.

We begin our homework, but Jasmine was still downstairs. That is when we figured out that Jasmine had did her homework already. She had went to the library after school. We were upset, but then we remembered that she had invited us to go too. We had took a different way home.

# Edit for Capitalization

Learning Goal

I can use elements of narrative text to write a historical fiction story.

**Capitalization** is the use of capital, or uppercase, letters. Writers use capitalization for specific reasons. Examples are shown in the chart.

| 1. Begin the names of holidays with a capital letter. | 2. Begin a title for a person with a capital letter. | 3. Begin specific geographical names and places with a capital letter. |
| --- | --- | --- |
| We are visiting our grandparents on **Thanksgiving**. | She listened to a speech by **President Kennedy**. | They sailed across the **Pacific Ocean**. |
| On **Groundhog Day**, we get a weather prediction. | I saw a picture of **Queen Elizabeth**. | Have you ever been to **Japan**? |

**My TURN** Edit the following paragraph for correct capitalization of titles of people, holidays, and geographical names and places.

Princess Katherine was ten years old when she left europe. On thanksgiving, her family came across the atlantic ocean on a large ship. They built a house near a Lake. In the distance, they could see the Appalachian mountains. At first, princess Katherine missed her old Country. By memorial day, her new country felt like home.

**My TURN** Edit your historical fiction story for capitalization.

# Add Ideas for Coherence and Clarity

Writers revise for coherence and clarity. **Coherence** means that ideas belong together. **Clarity** means that ideas are expressed clearly. Writers may ask themselves:

- What am I trying to say?
- Is what I am saying clear and interesting?
- Do all ideas relate to one another?
- What specific words or sentences should I add?

**My TURN** Read the passage. Then read the three sentences or phrases below the passage. Write the number of each sentence or phrase where it should be added to the passage.

Billy and Sharon stood next to their parents. Every other person from their small town stood with them.

Suddenly, Billy put a finger to his mouth. They heard a roar get louder and louder. In the distance, they saw puffs of smoke. It was the train! Neither of them had seen a train in person until now.

**1.** They were all facing the steel track that stretched across the prairie.

**2.** Sharon stopped talking and listened with him.

**3.** in the tall grass

**My TURN** On one of your own drafts, identify details you might add for better coherence and clarity.

# Delete Ideas for Coherence and Clarity

To make historical fiction stories clearer, writers delete ideas that

- do not relate directly to the main events.
- are unnecessary or unimportant to the story.
- are unclear or confusing.

**My TURN** Read the edited passage. Then answer the questions on the lines below the passage.

The year was 1775. Sheila was in the kitchen kneading dough for a loaf of bread. ~~The recipe for the bread came from her grandmother. It was for white bread.~~ Her father ran into the room and yelled, "We are going to fight for our freedom!"

Sheila knew what he meant. ~~Yesterday, he had said something she did not understand. But she understood this.~~ America was going to fight England. There would be a war.

1. Why is this information deleted?

2. Why is this information deleted?

1. _____

_____

2. _____

_____

**My TURN** On one of your drafts, identify ideas to delete for better coherence and clarity.

# Edit for Verbs

A **verb** tells what the subject is or does. Writers use verbs to express thoughts and feelings and to tell actions. Verb tense tells when actions happen—in the past, present, or future.

- **Present tense verbs** tell what is happening now.
- **Past tense verbs** tell what happened in the past. Verbs that end with -ed tell about the past.
- **Future tense verbs** tell about action in the future. The word will appears before the verb.

| Verb | Present Tense | Past Tense | Future Tense |
|------|---------------|------------|--------------|
| sail | The ship sails. | The ship sailed. | The ship will sail. |
| move | I move boxes. | I moved boxes. | I will move boxes. |

**My TURN** Edit the following paragraphs for the correct use of present, past, and future verb tense.

Last year, Frank hear about a trip around the world. He

say, "One day, I travel the world!"

His mom tell him to made a list of the places he visit.

Then, she say, "For now, though, you needs to finish school."

**My TURN** Edit one of your own drafts for the correct use of present, past, and future verb tenses.

# Edit for Subjective, Objective, and Possessive Pronouns

Pronouns take the place of nouns. Writers use pronouns to create variety. Since a pronoun replaces a noun, writers must make sure the meaning of each sentence is still clear.

| Subjective Pronouns | Objective Pronouns | Possessive Pronouns |
|---|---|---|
| Subject position | Object position | Show ownership |
| I, you, he, she, it, we, they | me, you, him, her, it, us, them | my/mine, your/yours, her/hers, our/ours, his, their/theirs, its |
| **I** went to the store with Casey. **She** wanted to see the puppies. | Sarah made **me** a saddle for the horse. I thanked **her**. | **Our** trip to **your** house was difficult. |

**My TURN** Edit the following paragraph for pronoun errors.

Jim and Helen go to a one-room country school. Them desks are in the coldest part of the room. Jim gives she his warm jacket. Helen gladly wears them.

**My TURN** Edit one of your own drafts for correct use of subjective, objective, and possessive pronouns. Share and discuss the reasons for your edits with your Writing Club.

 INTERACTIVITY

# ACTING
## Heroically

When we think of heroes, we may think about soldiers, firefighters, and others who show great courage. However, you do not have to save lives to be a hero. In fact, people can be heroes in many ways, big and small.

**PROTECTING OUR COUNTRY**
Men and women in the U.S. armed forces help prevent war. They may be sent anywhere in the world where there is a conflict. They sacrifice their safety to protect our country.

**BREAKING BARRIERS** African Americans were not allowed to play major league baseball until Jackie Robinson joined the Brooklyn Dodgers in 1947. Robinson's courage helped to change the game. People continue to work today to break racial and gender barriers.

33 USA

Jackie Robinson

**SHOWING HEROISM** Have you ever said a kind word to a classmate? Helped a neighbor with a chore? Similar actions can help others feel cared about. Being helpful and kind to others is a form of heroism!

## Weekly Question

**What kinds of actions can be heroic?**

**Take Notes** Write your ideas about each kind of heroic action described in the text. Use your own words to summarize different ways of acting heroically. Then write about ways you have been heroic.

**MAKING SACRIFICES** During World War II, a ship carrying American soldiers started to sink. There were not enough life vests. Four religious leaders gave their life vests to save soldiers. The Four Chaplains, as they are called, are remembered for acting selflessly.

**165**

# Poetry

**Poetry** is a form of writing in which words are arranged in lines. Poets use language creatively to express deep feelings or thoughts.

Poetry often includes **sound devices**, or language that creates an effect using the sounds of words. Sound devices may include

- **Rhyme:** two or more words with the same ending sound
- **Rhyme scheme:** the pattern of rhyme in a poem
- **Rhythm:** the pattern of sounds from stressed and unstressed syllables
- **Onomatopoeia:** words that sound like their meaning, such as *hum* and *squeak*

**TURN and TALK** With a partner, discuss how poetry is different from historical fiction. Use the chart to help you contrast the genres.

**Be a Fluent Reader** Fluent readers read poetry with accuracy, at an appropriate rate, and with expression.

When you read poetry aloud:

- ◎ Read at a comfortable pace.
- ◎ Try not to skip any words.
- ◎ Pay attention to rhyming words and words that create rhythm.

# Poetry Anchor Chart

## Purpose

To express deep feelings or thoughts

## Elements

* **Line breaks** that emphasize words or ideas
* **Stanzas,** or groups of lines
* **Sound devices,** such as rhyme and rhythm
* **Imagery,** or sensory language
* **Figurative language,** which gives words meaning beyond their dictionary definitions

## Some Types of Poetry

* **Narrative:** tells a story
* **Free verse:** no rhymes or stanza patterns
* **Concrete:** forms a shape that suggests the subject of the poem

**Jennifer Trujillo** is passionate about language and culture. She is an author, a teacher, and an expert in educating students who are learning English as a second language. Her love of languages can be seen in her writing, including her poem "The Race."

# Poems About Heroes

## Preview Vocabulary

As you read the poems, pay attention to these vocabulary words. Notice how they help you better understand the qualities of heroes.

| | | |
|---|---|---|
| triumphant | | company |
| challenge | twinkle | curious |

## Read

Before you begin, preview the poems to establish a purpose for reading. Follow these strategies when you read **poetry** the first time.

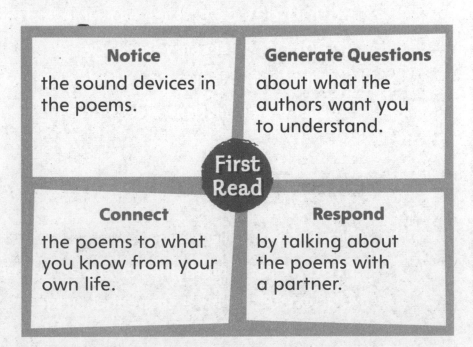

**Notice** the sound devices in the poems.

**Generate Questions** about what the authors want you to understand.

First Read

**Connect** the poems to what you know from your own life.

**Respond** by talking about the poems with a partner.

# FIREFIGHTER FACE
by Mary E. Cronin

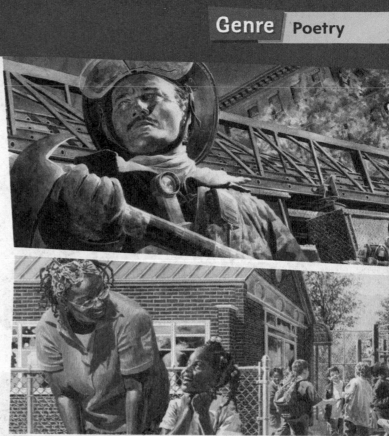

# MISS STONE
by Nikki Grimes

# THE RACE
by Jennifer Trujillo

## in daddy's arms
by Folami Abiade

🔊 AUDIO

✏️ ANNOTATE

# THE WRIGHT BROTHERS
by Charles R. Smith, Jr.

# FIREFIGHTER FACE

by Mary E. Cronin

**CLOSE READ**

**Explain Poetic Elements**

Underline words that help you explain the poem's rhyme scheme.

1  Trickles of sweat etch silvery trails

down wind-bitten cheeks coated with ash.

Curtains of vapor, with each breath he exhales,

wreathe his tired smile, his drooping mustache.

5  Framed by smoke-smudged wrinkles,

soot-black eyebrows cannot hide

a flash of blue eyes that twinkle

with strength and triumphant pride.

**twinkle** sparkle or shine with a flickering light

**triumphant** joy-filled or winning

# MISS STONE

by Nikki Grimes

1  My wishes gathered like ants.

I wished there was no recess.

I wished there was no first day.

I wished somebody, anybody

5  Would come over and ask me to play.

Then you said, "Excuse me.

Would you keep me company?

I'm feeling all alone."

Remember, Miss Stone?

10  I loved you that day.

You made my unhappy thoughts

Scamper away.

**CLOSE READ**

## Monitor Comprehension

Highlight details that you can reread to check your understanding of how the speaker's feelings change from the first stanza of this poem to the last stanza.

**company** being together with another person or other people

## Explain Poetic Elements

Poets often use sound devices to help their readers understand, enjoy, and visualize their poems. One example is *onomatopoeia*, or a word that sounds like its meaning.

Find onomatopoeia in this poem. Then, <u>underline</u> words that help you describe how the author uses this sound device to help you "hear" what is happening.

**challenge** a difficult situation or contest

# THE RACE

by Jennifer Trujillo

1   She rode a horse named Fina
     when women didn't ride.
     They galloped around the mountain,
     her legs on Fina's side.

5   She let her hair down from its bun
     and felt it whip and fly.
     She laughed and sang and whooped out loud.
     Up there she wasn't shy!

     One day great-grandma found her out
10  and planned to stop it all.
     But down in town they'd heard some news ...
     they told her of a call.

     A call for the caballeros
     from all the highs and lows
15  to race their fancy caballos
     to try and win the rose.

     Abuela looked at Fina,
     a twinkle in her eye.
     Abuela said, "Let's enter!
20  This race deserves a try."

     At dawn she was the only girl,
     but didn't even care.
     She came to meet the challenge, and
     her horse was waiting there.

25 They swept across the finish line
much faster than the rest.
She flung her hat without surprise;
she'd always done her best.

Fina shook her mane and stomped.
30 Abuela flashed a smile.
She sniffed the rose and trotted off
in caballera style!

**CLOSE READ**

## Monitor Comprehension

Highlight details that
are supported when
you check for visual
cues in the illustration.

# in daddy's arms

by Folami Abiade

**Monitor Comprehension**

Highlight stanzas that you can understand better if you use your background knowledge about the sun and moon when you read them.

1   in daddy's arms i am tall

    &close to the sun & warm

    in daddy's arms


    in daddy's arms

5   i can see over the fence out back

    i can touch the bottom leaves of the big
       magnolia tree

    in Cousin Sukie's yard

    in daddy's arms


    in my daddy's arms the moon is close

10  closer at night time when I can almost touch it

    when it grins back at me from the wide
       twinkling skies


    in daddy's arms i am tall

    taller than Benny & my friends Ade & George

    taller than Uncle Billy

15  & best of all

    i am eye-ball-even-steven with my big brother
       Jamal

in my daddy's arms

i am strong & dark like him & laughing

happier than the circus clowns

20  with red painted grins

when daddy spins me round & round

& the whole world is crazy upside down

i am big and strong & proud like him

in daddy's arms

25  my daddy

# THE WRIGHT BROTHERS

by Charles R. Smith, Jr.

**CLOSE READ**

### Explain Poetic Elements

<u>Underline</u> details about the plane that help you explain why the author structured the lines of the poem in this shape.

**Fluency** Reread "The Wright Brothers" at a comfortable pace so you can identify the poem's meaning. You can pause to sound out unfamiliar words if needed.

**curious** interested in knowing or seeing

day to remember.

creating a historic

one day in December,

and *Flyer* took off

10   to reach and explore,

a plane named *Flyer*

to soar,

with an engine

so they built a plane

5   looked to climb high,

Orville and Wilbur,

as the Wright Brothers,

past clouds in the sky,

1   Curious eyes gazed

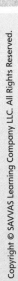

# Develop Vocabulary

Poets choose describing words to express their thoughts and feelings. These words help readers feel what the poet is trying to express.

**My TURN** Add the vocabulary word from the word bank that completes each group of synonyms. Then name who is described by the word in one of the poems you read. Write a sentence using the vocabulary word.

### Word Bank

**twinkle**    **triumphant**    **company**    **challenge**    **curious**

| Synonyms | Who Is Described? | Sentence |
|---|---|---|
| winning | | |
| _____ | | |
| victorious | | |
| interested | | |
| _____ | | |
| nosy | | |
| contest | | |
| _____ | | |
| difficulty | | |
| friendship | | |
| _____ | | |
| community | | |
| shine | | |
| _____ | | |
| sparkle | | |

# Check for Understanding

**My TURN** Look back at the texts to answer the questions.

1. How can the reader identify the texts as poems?

2. In lines 25–28 of "The Race," why does the poet use the words *swept* and *flung* to describe the girl and her horse as they cross the finish line?

3. Compare the themes of "in daddy's arms" and "Miss Stone." In what ways are the themes alike?

4. Synthesize details from two poems to answer this question: What are the different qualities that make a person a hero?

# Explain Poetic Characteristics

Poets choose and arrange words to express meaning. They may use a **rhyme scheme**, or a special pattern of rhyme. For example, the ending sound in every line may rhyme. Poets may use **sound devices**, or language that uses the sounds of words, to create interesting effects. They may choose a specific **structure**, or form, for the poem. For example, a **stanza** is a group of lines that work together as a unit.

1. **My TURN** Go to the Close Read notes in the poems and underline parts that help you explain poetic characteristics.

2. **Text Evidence** Use some of the parts you underlined to complete the chart.

| Rhyme Scheme of "Firefighter Face" |
|---|
| Explain the rhyme scheme. The first and third lines rhyme, and the second and fourth lines rhyme. The fifth and seventh lines almost rhyme, and the sixth and eighth lines rhyme. |

| Sound Devices in "The Race" |
|---|
| Explain the author's purpose for using a sound device. |

| Structural Elements of "The Wright Brothers" |
|---|
| Explain how the shape of the poem fits with its ideas. |

# Monitor Comprehension

As you read, monitor your comprehension and make any needed adjustments. Use the most helpful strategies, including rereading, using background knowledge, asking questions, and annotating to strengthen your understanding.

1. **My TURN** Go back to the Close Read notes and highlight details that help you monitor your comprehension.

2. **Text Evidence** Monitor your comprehension of the poems using some of your highlighted text. Use the strategies listed in the chart.

| Details from the Poem | How the Strategy Helps Me Understand the Text |
|---|---|
| "in daddy's arms i am tall / & close to the sun & warm / in daddy's arms"; "in my daddy's arms the moon is close / closer at night time when i can almost touch it / when it grins back at me"/ from the wide twinkling skies" | **Comprehension Strategy:** Use Background Knowledge<br><br>I know that a hug can feel warm, like sunshine, and that the moon sometimes looks like it has a face. |
|  | **Comprehension Strategies:** Ask Questions and Reread |

# Reflect and Share

**Talk About It** Which characters in the poems you read this week acted like heroes? Compare their actions with those of another character from a text you read this week. Use specific lines and stanzas to support your response.

**Ask and Answer Relevant Questions** When having a discussion, ask questions that are relevant, or related, to the topic. Answer questions from your partners.

- Ask questions to clarify something you do not understand.
- Ask questions to better understand someone else's thoughts or ideas.
- Answer questions about your own points to clarify or add detail to your response.
- Consider how your partners' comments may have changed your ideas.

Use these sentence starters to guide your questions to make sure they are relevant:

What did you mean when you said . . . ?

What words in the text make you think that . . . ?

**Weekly Question**

**What kinds of actions can be heroic?**

# Academic Vocabulary

**Parts of Speech** are categories of words.

- **nouns:** words that name people, places, things
- **verbs:** words that tell what something or someone is or does
- **adjectives:** words that describe nouns
- **adverbs:** words that tell how, when, or where something happens

Words can often be used as more than one part of speech.

**My TURN** For each sentence below,

1. **Underline** the academic vocabulary word in the sentence.

2. **Identify** the word's part of speech.

3. **Write** your own sentence using the same base word as a different part of speech. Write the new part of speech.

| Sentence | Part of Speech | My Sentence |
|---|---|---|
| Dentists encourage their patients to brush their teeth regularly. | | |
| The flavors were so similar, I could not distinguish one from the other. | | |
| I feel proud when I work hard and achieve my goals. | | |
| Miranda and her brother command their dog to come back. | | |

# Irregular Plural Nouns

**Irregular Plural Nouns** are plural nouns that do not follow the usual pattern of adding -s. There are some useful irregular plural nouns that you should become familiar with and learn to read. The plural of the word *life* is *lives*. The plural of the word *leaf* is *leaves*. The plural of the word *foot* is *feet*. The plural of the word *hero* is *heroes*. The plural of the word *man* is *men*.

### My TURN

1. Read these irregular plural nouns: *leaves, women, deer, teeth, sheep, loaves, heroes.*

2. Write a sentence using the correct plural form of each noun.

1. leaf _____

2. deer _____

3. foot _____

4. tomato _____

5. woman _____

# High-Frequency Words

**High-frequency words** are words that you will see many times as you read. Read these high-frequency words: *ago, stood*. Try to identify them as you read.

# Read Like a Writer

Authors use descriptive language to make their writing more interesting. Imagery is the use of words that engage readers' senses or their imaginations.

**Model** Read the lines from the poem "Firefighter Face."

> Trickles of sweat etch silvery trails
> down wind-bitten cheeks coated with ash.

*Imagery appeals to the senses.*

1. **Identify** Mary E. Cronin uses descriptive language to describe the firefighter's face.

2. **Question** How does the descriptive language help me use my senses to experience what is happening in the poem?

3. **Conclude** It helps me picture the way the firefighter's face looks after he battles a fire.

Read these lines from the poem "The Race."

> She let her hair down from its bun
> and felt it whip and fly.

**My TURN** Follow the steps to analyze the lines from the poem.

1. **Identify** Jennifer Trujillo uses descriptive language to describe

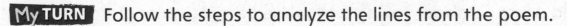

_____.

2. **Question** How does the descriptive language help me use my senses to experience what is happening in the poem?

3. **Conclude** It helps me _____

_____.

# Write for a Reader

When writing, try to use words for each of the five senses.

Writers use descriptive language, including imagery, to engage readers' senses and capture their imaginations. The words writers choose help readers see, smell, taste, feel, and hear what is happening in a text.

**My TURN** Think about how descriptive language in "Firefighter Face" and "The Race" affects you as a reader. Think about how you can use descriptive language to help your own readers use their senses.

1. If you were writing about going to the zoo, what would you describe? Write something you could describe for each sense below.

   sight _____

   hearing _____

   smell _____

   touch _____

   taste _____

2. Begin a passage about taking a trip. Use descriptive language to stimulate your readers' senses and imaginations. Describe how this use of imagery achieves the purpose of helping your readers imagine the scene.

   _____

   _____

   _____

   _____

# Spell Irregular Plural Nouns

**Irregular Plural Nouns** do not follow the usual spelling rules. Some have their own rules or no rule at all.

**My TURN** Read the words. Sort the words by their spelling rule. Then write both the singular and plural forms of each word.

### SPELLING WORDS

| | | | |
|---|---|---|---|
| wolves | sheep | geese | volcanoes |
| knives | heroes | calves | loaves |
| children | scarves | | |

| Rule | Plural |
|---|---|
| Drop the -f or -fe and add -ves. | |
| Change oo to ee. | |
| Singular and plural are the same. | |
| Add -es to words that end with o | |
| No rule | |

# High-Frequency Words

Memorizing high-frequency words will help you read more fluently. Read the following high-frequency words. Write them on the lines.

ago _____

stood _____

# Pronouns

**Pronouns** take the place of nouns. Writers use pronouns to make their writing less repetitive. Subjective pronouns are used as the subject of a sentence. Objective pronouns are used after action verbs. Possessive pronouns show who or what owns, or possesses, something.

| Pronoun | Examples |
|---|---|
| **Subjective:** *I, you, he, she, it, we, they* | Suki and *I* took a walk. *She* stopped to pick flowers. *They* were roses. |
| **Objective:** *me, you, him, her, it, us, them* | Mom made cookies for Jack and *me*. She told *us* to enjoy *them*. |
| **Possessive:** *my, mine, your, yours, her, hers, our, ours, his, their, theirs, its* | *My* garden is pretty. *Their* cat gets into *our* yard. |

**My TURN** Edit this draft. Replace the underlined nouns with pronouns.

Mr. Davis had organized a class trip to the museum. Jerome and Stacy liked the museum. <u>The museum</u> was <u>Jerome and Stacy's</u> favorite place. Mr. Davis told <u>Jerome and Stacy</u>, "I think <u>Stacy and Jerome</u> will be the first ones on the bus!"

On the day of the trip, <u>Mr. Davis</u> watched <u>Stacy and Jerome</u> board the bus before anyone else. Stacy said, "Mr. Davis, Jerome and I were first on the bus. You know <u>Jerome and Stacy</u> really well!"

# Edit for Punctuation Marks

Edit your drafts for punctuation marks. Knowing punctuation rules makes text easy to understand.

**Learning Goal**

I can use elements of narrative text to write a historical fiction story.

| Rule | Example |
|---|---|
| **Compound Sentence:** Use a comma before a conjunction (*and, but, or*) to combine two simple sentences. | I ordered ham, but Jen wanted chicken. |
| **Items in a Series:** With three or more items, put a comma after all but the last item. | I bought milk, sugar, and soup. |
| **Show Possession:** Use an apostrophe (')*s* to show singular ownership and *s* (') to show plural ownership. | The dog's bowl is empty. Five dogs' bowls are empty. |
| **Contractions:** Use an apostrophe to replace a missing letter or letters in a contraction. | I can't find my keys. |

**My TURN** Edit the paragraph for punctuation marks.

   Kiya waited at the rivers edge. The queen was sailing today. Kiya had heard the queen was beautiful strong, and wise. Kiya pushed aside the reeds and the boat passed by. Kiya could'nt believe her luck!

**My TURN** Edit one of your drafts for punctuation marks.

# Edit for Prepositions and Prepositional Phrases

Writers use prepositions to relate nouns or pronouns to other words in a sentence. A prepositional phrase begins with a preposition, and it ends with a noun or pronoun.

- He brought water <u>from the well.</u>
- She rode the horse <u>up the mountain.</u>

Some common prepositions are *above, across, around, at, before, behind, by, down, during, for, from, in, into, of, off, on, through, to, toward, with,* and *without.*

To identify prepositions and prepositional phrases when you edit, answer these questions:

1. Does the prepositional phrase begin with a preposition?
2. Does the prepositional phrase end with a noun or pronoun?
3. Is the prepositional phrase in the right place?

**My TURN** Edit the paragraph for prepositions and prepositional phrases.

> Margaret sat with the living room in her family. Their attention on the television was fixed and its black-and-white picture. The news reporter announced that for the first time, a man would walk to the moon!

**My TURN** Edit one of your own drafts for prepositions and prepositional phrases.

# Publish and Celebrate

Writers publish their work in order to share it with an audience. Some writers choose to produce audio recordings of their stories and create visuals to go with them.

**My TURN** After you have published your historical fiction story, reflect on your experience. Write complete words, thoughts, and answers legibly in cursive. Leave appropriate spaces between words.

The biggest challenge of writing a setting for a historical
fiction story is _____

_____

_____ .

I think readers of my historical fiction story will like _____

_____

_____

_____ .

When I revised my story, I improved _____

_____

_____

_____ .

The events I included are realistic because _____

_____

_____

_____ .

I would like to write another historical fiction story set during this time
and place: _____

_____

_____ .

# Prepare for Assessment

**My TURN** Follow this plan to help you write a historical fiction story in response to a prompt.

**1. Study the prompt.**

Read the prompt. Highlight the kind of writing you will do. <u>Underline</u> the key details you need to include in your response.

**Prompt:** Write a historical fiction story about an inventor who made something that continues to affect people's lives today.

**2. Brainstorm.**

Brainstorm ideas that are connected to the prompt. Highlight your favorite idea.

_____

_____

**3. Organize and plan your historical fiction story.**

Create your characters. Think of a problem and a resolution. Develop a sequence of events.

**4. Write your draft.**

Include dialogue as well as details about the events and setting.

**5. Revise and edit your historical fiction story.**

Use the skills you have learned to make changes and corrections as needed.

# Assessment

**My TURN** Before you write a historical fiction story for your assessment, rate how well you understand the skills you have learned in this unit. Go back and review any skills you mark "No."

|  |  | Yes | No |
|---|---|---|---|
| **Ideas and Organization** | ◐ I can brainstorm ideas. | ☐ | ☐ |
| | ◐ I can plan a historical fiction story. | ☐ | ☐ |
| | ◐ I can establish a problem and plan a resolution. | ☐ | ☐ |
| | ◐ I can add or delete ideas for coherence and clarity. | ☐ | ☐ |
| **Craft** | ◐ I can create characters and dialogue. | ☐ | ☐ |
| | ◐ I can develop a historical fiction setting. | ☐ | ☐ |
| | ◐ I can describe events with details. | ☐ | ☐ |
| | ◐ I can develop a plot and event sequence. | ☐ | ☐ |
| **Conventions** | ◐ I can correctly use capitalization. | ☐ | ☐ |
| | ◐ I can use verbs in the present, past, and future tenses. | ☐ | ☐ |
| | ◐ I can use subjective, objective, and possessive pronouns. | ☐ | ☐ |
| | ◐ I can edit for punctuation marks. | ☐ | ☐ |
| | ◐ I can edit for prepositions and prepositional phrases. | ☐ | ☐ |

## UNIT THEME
# Heroes

**TURN**and**TALK**

## QUESTION THE ANSWERS

Read the sentence attached to each text. Then, with a partner, go back into each text, evaluate details, synthesize information, and write a question that goes with each answer. Use evidence from the texts. Talk with your partner about how each answer relates to themes about heroes.

**WEEK 3**

### *from* Little House on the Prairie and By the Shores of Silver Lake

Against all odds, she found her missing sister.

_____

**BOOK CLUB**

**WEEK 2**

### Granddaddy's Turn: A Journey to the Ballot Box

This trait of Granddaddy's helped him stay strong when he was prevented from voting.

_____

**BOOK CLUB**

**WEEK 1**

### Below Deck: A Titanic Story

She saved a girl when the ship was sinking.

_____

**BOOK CLUB**

## Mama Miti: Wangari Maathai and the Trees of Kenya

Wangari Maathai gave this advice and changed Kenya.

**BOOK CLUB**

## Poems About Heroes

She was the only girl who dared to enter the horse race.

## Essential Question

**My TURN**

In your notebook, answer the Essential Question: **What makes a hero?**

**BOOK CLUB**

**BOOK CLUB**

### Project

Now it is time to apply what you learned about heroes in your **WEEK 6 PROJECT: Be a Hero!**

# Be A HERO!

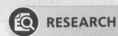 RESEARCH

## Activity

How can ordinary people become heroes? Everyone has opportunities to be heroic. Compose an opinion speech about why it is important to take advantage of opportunities to be heroic.

## Research Articles

With your partner, read "Heroes Aren't Just for Comic Books" to generate questions you have about the inquiry topic. Then, with help from an adult, make a research plan for writing your speech.

1. **Heroes Aren't Just for Comic Books**

2. **I'm a Volunteer!**

3. **A Helping Hand**

## Generate Questions

**COLLABORATE** After reading "Heroes Aren't Just for Comic Books," generate three questions you have about the article. Share these questions with your classmates.

1. _____

2. _____

3. _____

# Use Academic Words

**COLLABORATE** In this unit, you learned many words related to the theme of *Heroes*. Work with your partner to add more academic vocabulary words to each category. Be respectful when discussing, and do not interrupt. If appropriate, use this vocabulary in your opinion speech.

| Academic Vocabulary | Word Forms | Synonyms | Antonyms |
|---|---|---|---|
| encourage | encouragement<br>encourages<br>encouraging | inspire<br>cheer<br>urge | discourage<br>dishearten<br>deter |
| defeat | defeats<br>defeated<br>defeating | loss<br>failure<br>overthrow | win<br>success<br>victory |
| distinguish | distinguishes<br>distinguished<br>distinguishable | identify<br>specify<br>separate | overlook<br>confuse<br>miss |
| achieve | achieves<br>achieved<br>achievement | finish<br>reach<br>accomplish | lose<br>fail<br>begin |
| command | commander<br>commanded<br>commandment | order<br>demand<br>direct | submit<br>obey<br>follow |

# Speaking to Persuade

The goal of an opinion speech is to persuade the audience to agree with your opinion.

People write opinion speeches to persuade an audience to think or do something. When reading or listening to an opinion speech, notice

- who the audience is;
- the author's claim, or opinion, about the topic;
- reasons that support the claim and persuade the audience;
- linking words, such as *because* or *for example*, that connect the claim to the reasons; and
- how the speaker uses tone and emphasis to appeal to the audience.

 **RESEARCH**

**COLLABORATE** Read "I'm a Volunteer!" with your partner. Then, answer the questions. Discuss your answers with your partner.

**1.** What is the author's claim?

_____

_____

**2.** How does the author support the claim?

_____

_____

**3.** Did the speech persuade you to agree with the author's claim? Explain.

_____

_____

# Plan Your Research

**COLLABORATE** Before you begin researching opportunities for heroism, you and your partner will need to plan your research. With adult assistance, complete this activity to make a research plan.

| Definition | Example |
|---|---|
| A **claim** is a statement that tells the author's opinion about a topic.<br><br>**Example:** Families should recycle their paper and plastic waste. | In your opinion, why should people try to be heroic?<br><br>My claim:<br><br>_____<br>_____ |
| Authors use **reasons** to support their claims. Reasons can help persuade the audience to agree with the author's opinion.<br><br>**Example:** Families produce a lot of paper and plastic waste that can be made into new things. | Why should the audience agree with your claim?<br><br>Reason 1:<br>_____<br><br>Reason 2:<br>_____ |
| **Evidence** is information, such as facts, details, and examples, that authors use to support their claim and reasons.<br><br>Look for evidence in **sources**, such as books, newspapers, and Web sites. | Where can you find evidence to cite about your topic?<br><br>Source 1:<br>_____<br><br>Source 2:<br>_____ |

With your partner, discuss how you can improve your research plan.

# SEARCHING the WEB

A **search engine** is an online tool for finding information about a topic. It allows you to search a topic on the Internet and access a list of Web sites that contain information about the topic. The list will include a URL, or Web address, for each Web site. The URL can help you figure out if the Web site will have reliable information. Learning how to use a search engine is one way to recognize the characteristics and structures of digital texts.

**EXAMPLE** Juan wants to persuade his neighbors to join a neighborhood recycling program. He enters the keywords *reasons to recycle* into the search engine and gets a list of Web sites. How can Juan determine which Web sites will have relevant and reliable information?

reasons to recycle 🔍

Type keywords in the **search engine** to find information about a topic.

## Reduce, Reuse, Recycle | US EPA
https://www.epa.gov/recycle/html
Learn the benefits of **recycling**. Find out how you can save money, energy, and natural resources. **Recycle** all types of materials from aluminum to plastic and more. **Recycling** centers are located ...

Click on the blue text, or **hyperlink**, to visit the Web site.

Look at the **URL**, or Web address, to evaluate the source of the information:
- *.gov* (government Web site, reliable)
- *.edu* (educational Web site, reliable)
- *.org* (organization Web site, usually reliable)
- *.com* (commercial Web site, sometimes reliable)

The **Web site description** helps you decide if the Web site will have the information you need.

**COLLABORATE** With your partner, identify keywords that could help you find relevant information online. Use a search engine and evaluate the Web sites. Show that you understand the information you gather by taking notes on the Web sites that will support the claim of your opinion speech.

Keywords used in search engine:

URL:

Notes from Web site:

Keywords used in search engine:

URL:

Notes from Web site:

Discuss your search results. Did you find Web sites with relevant and reliable information? Do you need to change your keywords? Which Web sites are most reliable?

# A Call to ACTION!

People write **opinion speeches** to persuade an audience to think or act in a certain way. An opinion speech states a claim, includes reasons that support the claim, and persuades listeners to agree.

Before you begin writing, answer the following questions:

- What is your claim, or opinion?
- Who is the audience or reader you are trying to persuade?
- What reasons will you use to support your claim and persuade your audience?

**COLLABORATE** Read the Student Model. Work with your partner to recognize the characteristics of an opinion speech.

## Now You Try It!

Discuss the checklist with your partner. Work together to follow the steps as you write your opinion speech.

**Make sure your opinion speech includes**

☐ an introduction that states your claim, or opinion.

☐ reasons that support your claim.

☐ linking words, such as *because* or *for example*, that connect reasons to the claim.

☐ evidence, such as facts and examples, from research.

☐ a strong conclusion that restates your claim.

## Student Model

Have you ever noticed litter along your street but did not pick it up? Have you seen a neighbor trying to carry groceries but did not offer to help? Imagine how your neighborhood might be different if everyone took a little time to help one another. I believe families should take an hour each month to do something nice for a neighbor or their neighborhood.

**Underline** the claim.

In some communities, people do not know their neighbors. Lending a hand or surprising new neighbors with a treat is a great way to meet the people who live near you. Building relationships leads to a strong and happy community. It can make neighborhoods safer too. For example, studies show that crime rates can drop more than 10 percent in communities where people get to know their neighbors and look out for one another.

**Highlight** reasons that support the author's claim.

**Underline** a fact from the author's research.

One hour a month is not much time. Yet it can make a big difference in your community. That is why I think every family should do something nice for a neighbor or their neighborhood. You can ask other families to join you. Just think about the difference you can make!

**Highlight** the restated claim.

# Paraphrasing and Quoting

When you use information from a source, you must paraphrase or quote the source.

**Paraphrasing** is rewording or retelling information using your own words in a logical order, while maintaining the meaning of the text.

Sentence from source: *Police studies show that crime rates can drop more than 10 percent when people build trusting relationships with their neighbors.*

Getting to know your neighbors can help reduce ◄ ・・・・・ **Paraphrasing**
crime in your community.

**Quoting** is copying text exactly as it was written in a source, putting the text in quotation marks, and naming the author.

Latoya Smith wrote, "Experiences that develop ◄ ・・・・・・ **Quoting**
trust among neighbors can lead to happier, cleaner,
and safer communities."

**Plagiarizing** is using exact words from a text as your own without giving the author credit.

Avoid plagiarizing by paraphrasing or identifying the source.

**RESEARCH**

**COLLABORATE** Read "A Helping Hand." Identify a fact from the article. Then work with your partner to paraphrase and quote the fact. Write your paraphrase and quote on a separate sheet of paper.

COLLABORATE  Read the article and answer the questions.

# From Trash to Treasured Neighbors

by Marcia Cho

April 8—When nine-year-old Jerod West began cleaning up the streets, his neighbors started to notice.

"I looked out my window and saw a boy picking up trash," said resident Pam Cook. "I went out to thank him and ended up joining him. Soon, other neighbors came out to help."

That was three years ago. Now cleaning up the neighborhood has become an annual event known as the Spring Clean.

"Now we are friends as well as neighbors, and we help one another," said Herman Juárez. "Jerod's efforts made us all want to take care of our neighborhood—and become better neighbors."

**1.** Quote a sentence from the article.

_____

_____

**2.** Paraphrase the last paragraph by retelling the information. Maintain meaning and logical order without plagiarizing.

_____

_____

# Add MEDIA!

Writers add information and interest to their writing by including different **media**, or formats for sharing information. Writers of opinion speeches might create multimedia texts by including images and videos to persuade their audience.

**Images**, such as photographs and drawings, help readers visualize the topic. During an opinion speech, you might include images to inform and persuade your audience about your topic.

**Videos**, or recorded images, bring a topic to life with movement and sound. If information in a video supports your claim, you can include this piece of digital media as evidence in your speech. Playing a video that you found during research or creating one yourself can make your speech more persuasive.

**COLLABORATE** With your partner, discuss what types of media could support your claim or make your speech more persuasive. Follow your classroom's usual rules and procedures for partner discussions. For example, take turns speaking or assign roles. Then, conduct research to identify and gather examples. Takes notes on your research, and describe how the media could strengthen your speech.

---

### Media That Could Support My Claim and Persuade the Audience

Media Idea 1: _____

Type of Media: _____

Source or URL: _____

How this could strengthen my speech:




---

Media Idea 2: _____

Type of Media: _____

Source or URL: _____

How this could strengthen my speech:

# Revise

**Relevant Details** Reread your opinion speech with your partner. Have you developed a coherent speech by including

☐ reasons that directly support your claim?

☐ relevant facts and details from your research?

☐ media that strengthen your speech?

## Revise for Relevant Details

The writer of the speech about doing something nice in one's neighborhood noticed that, in his first draft, his evidence did not support his claim. He wanted to improve the clarity and coherence of his speech by including information directly related to the topic. He revised his speech to make it more engaging by adding a relevant factual detail from his research.

It can make neighborhoods safer, too. ~~According to one study, the number of neighborhood recycling programs has increased by 20 percent since 2005.~~

For example, studies show that crime rates can drop more than 10 percent in communities where people get to know their neighbors and look out for one another.

# Edit

**Conventions** Read your opinion speech again.
Have you used correct writing conventions?

☐ spelling

☐ punctuation

☐ singular and plural nouns

☐ common and proper nouns

☐ linking words that connect reasons to the claim

## Peer Review

**COLLABORATE** Listen to another group practice its speech. Confirm that you understood the main claim and supporting reasons by briefly paraphrasing what you heard. Discuss how the other group could make the speech more persuasive. Give helpful feedback about the presentation.

# Time to Celebrate!

**COLLABORATE** With your partner, plan your presentation and decide who will say which part of the speech. Then present your opinion speech to the class, using conventions and tone that are appropriate for an important speech. To communicate ideas effectively, remember to make eye contact, enunciate clearly, and speak at an understandable rate and volume. After your presentation, allow time for classmates to ask questions. Remember to listen actively and answer politely. Write about the questions asked.

# Reflect on Your Project

**My TURN** Think about the opinion speech you wrote. Which parts of your speech are the strongest and most persuasive? What could you improve? Write your thoughts.

## Strengths

## Areas of Improvement

# Reflect on Your Goals

Look back at your unit goals.
Use a different color to rate yourself again.

# Reflect on Your Reading

Synthesize information to explain what you enjoyed most about the texts you read in this unit.

_____

_____

_____

_____

_____

_____

# Reflect on Your Writing

How did writing a historical fiction story help you improve your skills as a writer?

_____

_____

_____

_____

_____

_____

# Events

## Essential Question

How do communities change over time?

▶ **Watch**

"Changing Communities"

**TURN and TALK**

What kinds of events can change a community?

## Spotlight on Biography

### READING WORKSHOP

**Primary Source:** Daniel Burnham

*The House That Jane Built* ..................... Biography
by Tanya Lee Stone

**Primary Source:** Sojourner Truth

from *Frederick Douglass* ..................... Biography
by Josh Gregory

**Infographic:** Think Big

from *Milton Hershey* ..................... Biography
by Charnan Simon

**Time Line:** Changing the World with One Idea

*Green City* .....................**Narrative Nonfiction**
by Allan Drummond

**Poem:** Thank You for Understanding

*Grace and Grandma* .....................Drama
by Rich Lo

### READING-WRITING BRIDGE

- Academic Vocabulary • Word Study
- **Read Like a Writer • Write for a Reader**
- Spelling • Language and Conventions

### WRITING WORKSHOP

- Introduce and Immerse • Develop Elements     **Opinion Essay**
- Develop Structure • Writer's Craft
- Publish, Celebrate, and Assess

### PROJECT-BASED INQUIRY

- Inquire • Research • Collaborate

# Independent Reading

You will read several biographies, a work of narrative nonfiction, and a drama in this unit.

You may want to read with the purpose of learning about people you find interesting. You might choose other biographies, autobiographies, or drama.

As you read independently, try using some fix-up strategies. Fix-up strategies help you to get "unstuck" when you do not understand something. Try different fix-up strategies for different kinds of reading.

## Fix-Up Strategies

| | |
|---|---|
| ☐ Reread | Reread a sentence, a word, or a part of the text to find meaning. |
| ☐ Ask Questions | Ask questions as you read and look for the answers in the text. Remember what you have read. |
| ☐ Make a Connection | Use what you know to make a connection between the text and a personal experience or memory, what you have read in another text, or what you know about the world. |
| ☐ Make Predictions | As you read, think about what might happen next. |
| ☐ Stop and Think | Stop reading every so often and summarize in your head what you have read. |
| ☐ Adjust Your Reading Rate | Adjust your rate of reading to the difficulty of the text. Slow down for difficult or unfamiliar text. |

# Independent Reading Log

| Date | Book | Genre | Pages Read | Minutes Read | My Ratings |
|------|------|-------|------------|--------------|------------|
|      |      |       |            |              | ☆☆☆☆☆ |
|      |      |       |            |              |            |
|      |      |       |            |              |            |
|      |      |       |            |              |            |
|      |      |       |            |              |            |
|      |      |       |            |              |            |
|      |      |       |            |              |            |
|      |      |       |            |              |            |

# Unit Goals

Shade in the circle to rate how well you meet each goal now.

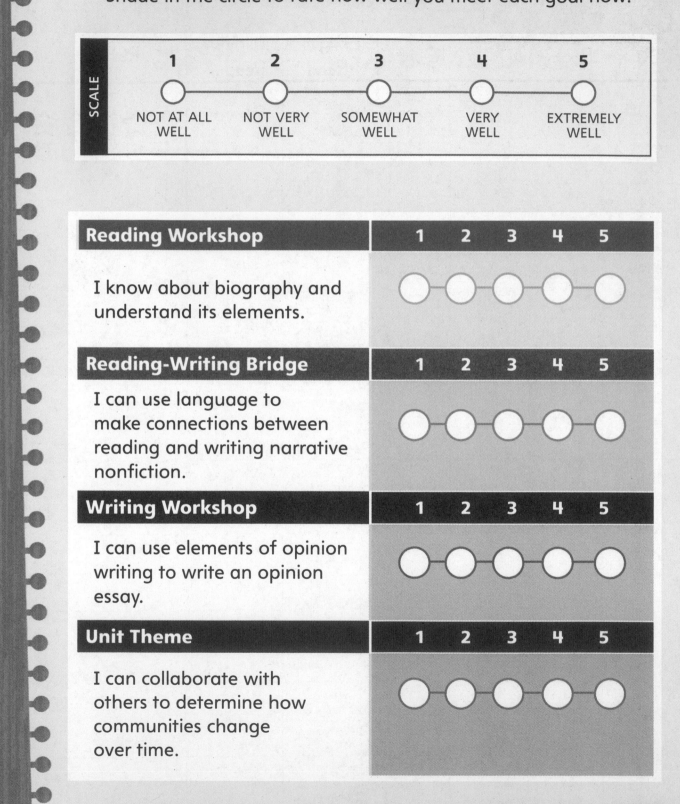

**SCALE**

| 1 | 2 | 3 | 4 | 5 |
|---|---|---|---|---|
| NOT AT ALL WELL | NOT VERY WELL | SOMEWHAT WELL | VERY WELL | EXTREMELY WELL |

## Reading Workshop
| | 1 | 2 | 3 | 4 | 5 |
|---|---|---|---|---|---|

I know about biography and understand its elements.

## Reading-Writing Bridge
| | 1 | 2 | 3 | 4 | 5 |
|---|---|---|---|---|---|

I can use language to make connections between reading and writing narrative nonfiction.

## Writing Workshop
| | 1 | 2 | 3 | 4 | 5 |
|---|---|---|---|---|---|

I can use elements of opinion writing to write an opinion essay.

## Unit Theme
| | 1 | 2 | 3 | 4 | 5 |
|---|---|---|---|---|---|

I can collaborate with others to determine how communities change over time.

# Academic Vocabulary

Use these words to talk and write about this unit's theme, *Events*: *benefit*, *generation*, *advice*, *consumer*, and *familiar*.

**TURNandTALK** Read the words and definitions. Make a connection between two words. What other connections can you make?

**benefit** [n.]—something that helps a person or thing

**generation** [n.]—a group of individuals born and living at the same time

**advice** [n.]—an opinion or suggestion offered about a situation

**consumer** [n.]—a person who buys goods

**familiar** [adj.]—common, well-known

*Benefit* and *consumer* are connected because

_____

_____.

*Generation* and *familiar* are connected because

_____

_____.

*Consumer* and *advice* are connected because

_____

_____.

INTERACTIVITY

# DANIEL BURNHAM

People need places to play, and they deserve to live in a beautiful area with plenty of parks. Those were the beliefs of Daniel Burnham.

Burnham was a builder and city planner. He lived in Chicago, Illinois, which is on the shores of Lake Michigan.

In the early 1900s, Burnham drew up a plan to make most of Chicago's shoreline into parks. He convinced city leaders to follow the plan. Today most of Chicago's shoreline is parkland. Many thousands of people use the parks every year.

Here are some of Burnham's quotes about parks and the value of nature.

"First in importance is the shore of Lake Michigan. It should be treated as park space to the greatest possible extent."

"A city . . . must provide for the health and pleasure of the great body of workers."

Here are quotes from other people about Chicago's lakefront park:

"[A part of the lakefront should be] Public Ground... to Remain Forever Open, Clear and Free of any Buildings, or Other Obstruction whatever."

— Chicago leaders, 1836

## Weekly Question

### How can one person improve a community?

**Turn and Talk** Which quote from Daniel Burnham best shows how he wanted to help his community? Discuss your opinion with your partner. Give reasons for the quote you chose.

Chicago

*Lake Michigan*

lakefront parkland

"The lakefront by right belongs to the people."

"[The lake is] a living thing, delighting man's eye and refreshing his spirit."

"The Chicago Lakefront Trail is one of the city's modern marvels."
— Writer and cyclist Luke Seemann, 2016

GENRE: BIOGRAPHY

## Learning Goal

I can learn more about biography and analyze text structure in a biography.

**Spotlight on Genre**

# Biography

**Biography** is a type of narrative nonfiction. It is the story of a real person's life that is written by another person.

Most biographies have a text structure that follows **chronological**, or time, order.

- Time-order words, such as *before*, *then*, and *later*, help readers understand the order of events in a person's life.
- Chronological order can also help readers identify events that cause the person to change over time or find solutions to problems.

Look for dates to identify the order of events.

**TURN and TALK**  With a partner, discuss an event in the life of a person in a story you have read. Use the Narrative Nonfiction Anchor Chart to determine if the story was a biography. Take notes on your discussion.

**My NOTES**

# Narrative Nonfiction Anchor Chart

## Purpose

To recount a true event or series of events

## Types of Narrative Nonfiction

⊚ **History:** about past events

⊚ **Biography:** about someone's life (not the author's life)

⊚ **Autobiography:** about the author's life

⊚ **Memoir:** about one time or event in the author's life

⊚ **Newspaper article:** about current events

⊚ **Journal or diary:** about daily events in the author's life

**Tanya Lee Stone** has enjoyed writing ever since she was young. Today she is best known for her books about remarkable people who might be unknown to readers. For example, you may not have heard of Jane Addams. After you read *The House That Jane Built*, she is someone you will likely remember!

# The House That Jane Built

## Preview Vocabulary

As you read *The House That Jane Built*, pay attention to these vocabulary words. Notice how they provide clues about the life of Jane Addams.

| | |
|---|---|
| community | donate |
| convince | generous | transformed |

## Read

A text's structure can help you make predictions by showing when and why events happened. Preview the text and predict what it will be about. Follow these strategies the first time you read this **biography**.

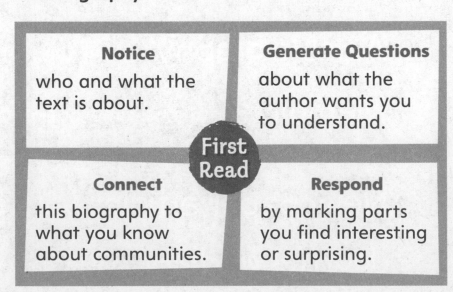

**Notice** who and what the text is about.

**Generate Questions** about what the author wants you to understand.

**First Read**

**Connect** this biography to what you know about communities.

**Respond** by marking parts you find interesting or surprising.

# The House That Jane Built

## A Story About Jane Addams

by

**TANYA LEE STONE**

illustrated by

**KATHRYN BROWN**

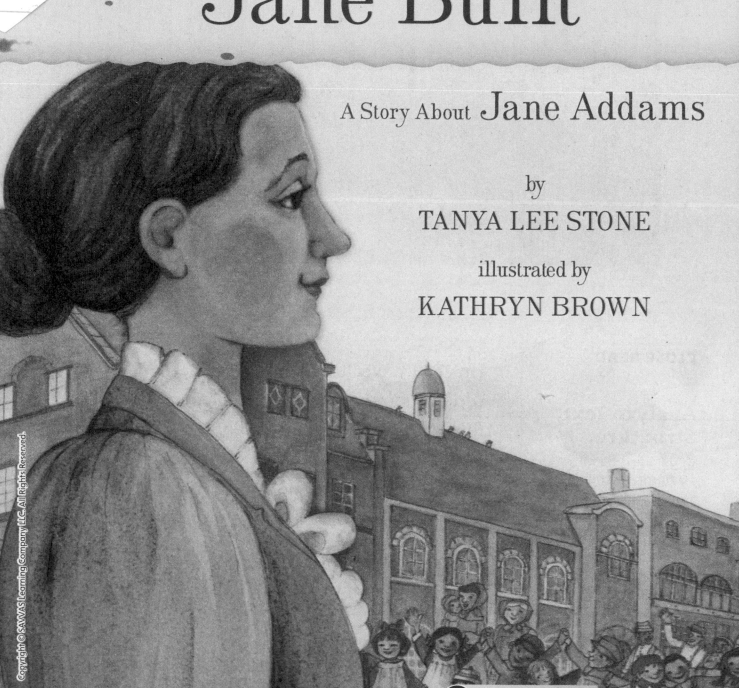

AUDIO

ANNOTATE

**CLOSE READ**

## Analyze Text Structure

<u>Underline</u> a detail in paragraph 1 that helps you recognize that this biography has a time-order text structure.

1   In 1889, a wealthy young woman named Jane Addams moved into a lovely, elegant house in Chicago, Illinois. But instead of moving into a lovely, elegant neighborhood, she picked a house that was smack in the middle of one of the filthiest, poorest parts of town.

2   Why would a wealthy young woman do this when she could have lived anywhere?

3    Jane was just six years old when she went
     on a trip with her father and noticed that not
     everyone lived like her family did. She vowed
     that one day she would live "right in the midst
     of horrid little houses" and find a way to fix
     the world.

4    Jane was a strong soul from the start. And
     she was brave. When she and her stepbrother
     George were young, they would sneak away
     at night to explore in nearby caves. Once, Jane
     lowered George over a cliff on a rope to spy on
     an owl in its nest.

**CLOSE READ**

## Correct or Confirm Predictions

Highlight a detail in
paragraph 3 that could
help you correct or
confirm a prediction
you made about what
this biography of Jane
Addams would focus on.

## Vocabulary in Context

Use context clues within the sentence to determine the meaning of *collection* in paragraph 5.

Underline the context clues that helped you determine the word's meaning.

5    Jane was smart. She read and read from her father's book collection, which doubled as the town library. Most girls did not go to college then, but Jane's father believed women should be educated. She went to Rockford Female Seminary and graduated at the top of her class.

6    But when school was over, she wasn't sure what to do with her life. That same summer, her father died.

7    Jane was lost.

8    About two years later, she and her friends traveled to Europe. They went to the theater, the opera, and many beautiful places. But then Jane saw something in London she couldn't forget: people in ragged clothes with outstretched hands, begging a cart vendor to buy his leftover rotten fruits and vegetables that hadn't sold at market. The spoiled food was all they could afford.

9    What could she do to help? Long after her trip was over, the question stuck in her mind. She remembered how she felt when she was six.

**CLOSE READ**

**Analyze Text Structure**

Underline details in paragraphs 8 and 9 that help you recognize that the biography has a time-order text structure.

## Correct or Confirm Predictions

Highlight details in paragraphs 10 and 11 that help you correct or confirm a prediction you made about how events in London led to the events that happened later in Chicago.

**community** a group of people living in the same area

10   Jane traveled back to London to learn about a place she had heard was helping the poor in a brand-new way. At Toynbee Hall, the idea was to have rich and poor people live together in the same community and learn from each other. Instead of simply serving soup, for example, people could take cooking classes. Other skills were taught as well.

11   Toynbee Hall was the first settlement house. It was called a settlement house because the well-off people who worked there during the day didn't go back to their own homes at night. Instead, they "settled" in and lived at Toynbee Hall, right in the same neighborhood as the needy.

12   Jane now knew what to do.

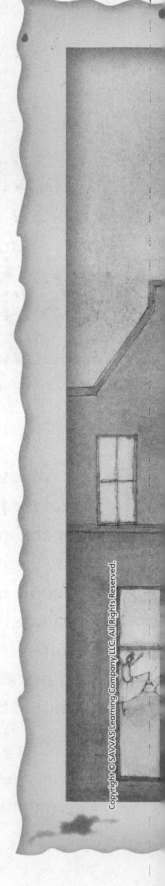

**Analyze Text Structure**

Underline a sentence in paragraph 14 that helps you recognize that the text is structured chronologically.

13    She told her friend Ellen Gates Starr about her plan to build a settlement house in Chicago. It was "as if a racehorse had burst out of the gate, free at last to pour every ounce of energy into running."

14    There was a glittery side to Chicago, with its mansions, fancy shops, and sparkling lakefront. But there was a gritty side, too. One million people lived in Chicago in 1889. Most were immigrants—people who came from other countries. They came for a better life, but they didn't speak English. That made it hard to find good jobs. Many needed help.

15  Jane found the perfect house. It had big rooms with high ceilings and marble fireplaces. And it was in one of the worst neighborhoods in the city. Garbage lay rotting in the streets, piled high. Large families were crammed into tiny, ramshackle houses with no running water. The smell from back-lot outhouses hung in the air. Rough boys ran the streets, stirring up trouble because they had nothing to do.

## Correct or Confirm Predictions

Highlight details in the paragraph that help you correct or confirm any predictions you made about problems the text would describe.

## Analyze Text Structure

Authors may include multiple text structures within an informational text to emphasize important ideas.

Underline details that describe the interaction between Jane and Helen Culver. How do these details help you recognize that the text has a cause-and-effect structure?

16    The house had belonged to Charles J. Hull, and he had left it to a wealthy cousin named Helen Culver. At first, Jane paid rent, but after she told Helen what she had in mind, Helen gave her the house for free. In thanks, Jane named it Hull House.

17    Jane moved in on September 18, 1889. The very first night, she was so busy and excited that she forgot to lock a side door before going to sleep. But no one broke in. She decided to leave Hull House unlocked from then on so people would know they could come in at any time.

18    People who didn't have enough to eat or had no shoes on their feet or had just lost a job began to find their way to Hull House.

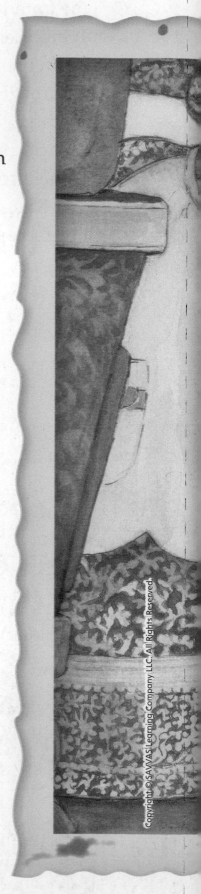

## Correct or Confirm Predictions

Highlight details in the two paragraphs that correct or confirm any predictions you made about problems Jane would try to solve.

19  Of course, it wasn't always peaceful. Once, a couple of boys threw rocks at the house and broke a window.

20  Instead of getting upset, Jane took it as a sign to give the neighborhood kids something to do. She had her own way of looking at things.

21   Another time, Jane discovered a man in the house looking for something to steal. He tried to jump out a window to escape, but she showed him the door so he wouldn't get hurt. When he broke in a second time, she asked him why. He said he was out of work and had no money. Jane told him to report back the next morning. When he did, she gave him a job.

### CLOSE READ

## Analyze Text Structure

Underline words and phrases that help you explain the order of events in the biography.

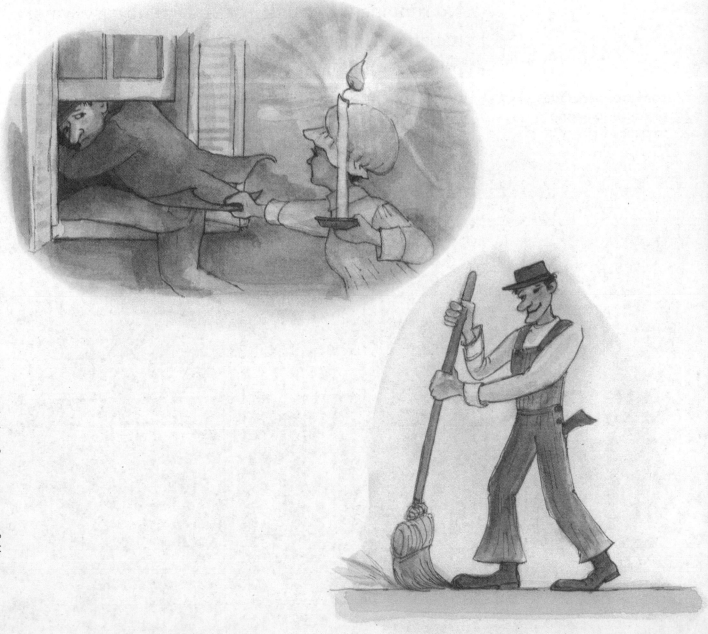

## Vocabulary in Context

<u>Underline</u> a context clue beyond the sentence that helps you determine the meaning of *tackled* in paragraph 23.

**donate** give as a way to help others

**convince** persuade or cause someone to believe

22    Jane spent her own money running Hull House, and asked other well-off people to donate, too. She did not want to be paid for working there. Even when people gave her gifts, she gave them away. Her friends teased Jane about this. One friend gave her new underwear with her initials just so Jane couldn't pass them on. But she did!

23    Any problem Jane discovered, she tackled. No running water in houses meant no easy way to bathe. This led to sickness. So Jane put in a public bath. People flocked to it, which helped her convince city officials they needed to build more public baths.

24   No safe place for children to play? Jane talked a wealthy man into giving her the lot he owned near Hull House. Workmen tore down the shabby buildings and turned the lot into a playground. It was the first one in Chicago!

25   Little kids home alone because their parents had to work fourteen hours a day? Jane started a morning kindergarten and after-school clubs. She also set up afternoon classes for older kids who had to go to work during the school day.

**CLOSE READ**

## Analyze Text Structure

<u>Underline</u> details that help you recognize that paragraphs 24 and 25 have a problem-and-solution text structure.

## Correct or Confirm Predictions

Highlight details in paragraph 26 that correct or confirm any predictions you made about how people helped Hull House grow.

**generous** giving or showing kindness toward others

26   Jane did not do all this alone. Ellen Gates Starr was her partner from the start. Many other smart, generous people moved into Hull House and helped. They taught literature, art, English, math, science, and cooking.

27   Soon there was not just one building, but two. Then three, and four, and more. By 1907, Hull House had grown into thirteen buildings, including a gymnasium, coffee house, theatre, music school, community kitchen, and an art gallery.

28 By the early 1920s, more than nine thousand people a week visited Hull House. The house that Jane built brought all kinds of people together and helped those in need. It changed a bad neighborhood into a great and strong community. Hull House transformed the lives of all who stepped inside.

29 Today, every community center in America, in large part, has Jane Addams to thank. With all that she did, both inside and outside the house that Jane built, her childhood wish to help fix the world came true.

**CLOSE READ**

## Analyze Text Structure

<u>Underline</u> details in paragraphs 28 and 29 that help you recognize how the biography is structured.

**transformed** changed or made very different

# Develop Vocabulary

In biographies, authors use specific words to explain the main idea, or the most important idea in the text. These words help identify what the author wants the reader to know about the subject.

**My TURN** Add a vocabulary word from the word bank to complete each sentence. Then use the word in a sentence about the text.

## Word Bank

community          donate          generous          transformed

---

<u>Community</u> means "a group of people living in the same area."

Sentence: Jane helped people in her community.

---

_____means "showing kindness toward others."

Sentence:

---

_____means "changed or made very different."

Sentence:

---

_____means "give as a way to help others."

Sentence:

# Check for Understanding

**My TURN** Look back at the text to answer the questions.

**1.** How can the reader tell that *The House That Jane Built* is a biography?

**2.** What is the author's purpose for including the question in paragraph 2? How does it connect to the rest of the biography?

**3.** How are events from Jane Addams's youth related to her later decision to build Hull House? Cite text evidence.

**4.** Based on text evidence, what were some of Jane Addams's personality traits? Analyze how these traits helped her create Hull House.

# Analyze Text Structure

A biography usually has one overall text structure. An author might include other text structures to emphasize key ideas. To **analyze text structure**, look for words that help you recognize the text structure. Then think about how the structure helps you understand the text.

1. **My TURN** Go to the Close Read notes in *The House That Jane Built* and underline parts that help you analyze text structure.

2. **Text Evidence** Use some of the parts you underlined to complete the chart.

| Text Evidence | Text Structure | How Structure Helps Me Understand the Text |
|---|---|---|
| paragraph 1: "In 1889" | time order | It helps me know when an important event in Jane's life happened. |
| paragraphs 8 and 9: | | |
| paragraph 16: | | |
| paragraph 25: | | |

# Correct or Confirm Predictions

Readers review elements of a text to correct or confirm **predictions**, or educated guesses, they made. After reading, readers use the text's details, pictures, and structure—such as cause and effect—to correct inaccurate predictions or confirm accurate ones.

1. **My TURN** Go back to the Close Read notes and highlight evidence to correct or confirm predictions you made about the text.

2. **Text Evidence** Use some of your highlighted text to complete the chart.

| Prediction Before Reading | Details | Correct or Confirm the Prediction |
|---|---|---|
| I predicted that this biography would focus on: **a house that Jane Addams built to help people.** | "… she would live 'right in the midst of horrid little houses' and find a way to fix the world." | Confirmed. The focus of the biography is how Jane created Hull House and helped people in a community. |
| I predicted that Jane's efforts to help in the neighborhood would: | | |

# Reflect and Share

**Talk About It** Jane Addams helped many people by finding creative solutions to serious problems. Consider other texts you have read this week. What creative solutions did people use to solve problems?

- - - - - - - - - - - - - - - - - - - - - - - - - - - - - - -

**Ask and Answer Relevant Questions** During discussions, it is important to ask questions that are relevant, or related, to the topic. You should also answer questions about your topic and explain your ideas in more detail.

- ◎ Ask questions to clarify other people's statements.
- ◎ Answer questions to clarify your own statements.
- ◎ Ask questions to encourage other people to share ideas.
- ◎ Answer questions to add more details about your own ideas.

Use these sentence starters to guide your questions to make sure they are relevant:

What did you mean when you said . . .?

What do you think about . . .?

- - - - - - - - - - - - - - - - - - - - - - - - - - - - - - -

## Weekly Question

How can one person improve a community?

# Academic Vocabulary

**Related Words** are words that share roots or word parts. These words can have different meanings based on how the word is used, such as *explore*, *explorer*, and *exploration*.

**My TURN** For each sentence below,

1. **Use** print or digital resources, such as a dictionary or thesaurus, to find related words.

2. **Add** an additional related word in the box.

3. **Choose** the correct form of the word to complete the sentence.

| Word | Related Words | Sentence |
|---|---|---|
| benefit | benefiting<br>beneficial<br>_____ | One _____ of living near the park is the baseball field. |
| generation | generate<br>generational<br>_____ | You will _____ more speed by riding downhill. |
| advice | advise<br>adviser<br>_____ | She is a great _____ because she always tells me the right things to do. |
| consumer | consume<br>consumerism<br>_____ | The bear is a _____ because it eats other animals for food. |
| familiar | familiarity<br>unfamiliar<br>_____ | I like this _____ story because I already know the ending. |

# r-Controlled Vowels

**r-Controlled Vowels** *ir, er, ur, ear* can all spell the vowel sound you hear in the word *turn*. The letter *r* immediately after the vowel changes, or controls, the sound of the vowel.

**My TURN** Read each sentence from *The House That Jane Built*. Read and write the word or words that contain an *r*-controlled vowel on the line. Then underline the *r*-controlled letters in the word.

1. By the early 1920s, more than nine thousand people a week visited Hull House. _____

2. Rough boys ran the streets, stirring up trouble because they had nothing to do. _____

3. Jane traveled back to London to learn about a place she had heard was helping the poor in a brand new way.

   _____

# High-Frequency Words

**High-frequency words** are common words used in reading and writing. Memorize them so you can read them quickly. Read these high-frequency words: *system, brought*. Try to identify them in your independent reading.

# Read Like a Writer

Authors use descriptive language to help readers picture a scene.

**Model !**  Read the sentence from *The House That Jane Built*.

> But instead of moving into a lovely, elegant neighborhood, she picked a house that was smack in the middle of one of the filthiest, poorest parts of town.

*descriptive adjectives*

1. **Identify** Tanya Lee Stone uses opposite descriptions for the purpose of describing the neighborhoods.

2. **Question** How do these descriptive adjectives help me picture the neighborhoods?

3. **Conclude** The descriptive words *filthiest* and *poorest* help me picture the neighborhood in which Jane chose to do her work.

Read the text.

> . . . people in ragged clothes with outstretched hands, begging a cart vendor . . .

**My TURN**  Follow the steps to analyze the text. Describe the author's use of descriptive language to achieve a specific purpose.

1. **Identify** Tanya Lee Stone uses the descriptive adjectives

_____ .

2. **Question** How do the descriptive adjectives help me picture the people that Jane saw in London?

3. **Conclude** The descriptive words help me picture

# Write for a Reader

Descriptive adjectives help your writing come alive!

Writers use descriptive language for the specific purpose of helping readers picture people, settings, and events. Descriptive adjectives add specific details so readers can visualize what the writer is describing.

**My TURN** Think about how Tanya Lee Stone's use of descriptive language in *The House That Jane Built* helped you picture what she was describing. Now make your writing more detailed by using descriptive adjectives to help readers picture what you are describing.

1. List several descriptive words that describe your favorite animal.

_____

_____

2. Write a paragraph that describes your favorite animal. Use some of the words from your list. Underline all of the descriptive adjectives in your writing. Then briefly describe how your use of descriptive language allows you to achieve the purpose of helping readers picture the animal.

_____

_____

_____

_____

_____

_____

# Spell *r*-Controlled Vowels

***r*-Controlled Vowels *ir, er, ur, ear*** can all spell the vowel sound you hear in the word *term*.

**My TURN** Read the words. Sort them by the spelling of the *r*-controlled vowel.

## SPELLING WORDS

| certainty | swerve | thirsty |
| earn | termite | thirteen |
| return | third | thirty |
| search | | |

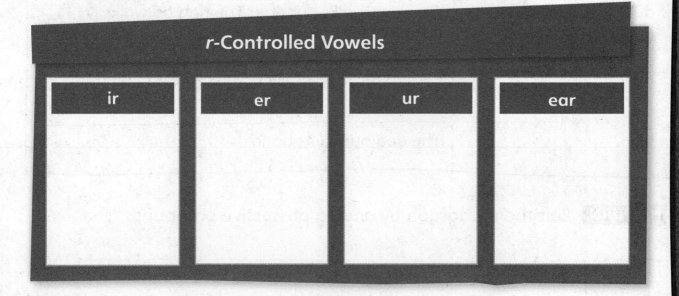

*r*-Controlled Vowels

| ir | er | ur | ear |
|----|----|----|-----|
|    |    |    |     |

# High-Frequency Words

Write the following high-frequency words on the lines.

system _____

brought _____

# Possessive Pronouns

Pronouns are words that take the place of nouns. Some pronouns show who or what owns, or possesses, something. This kind of pronoun is called a **possessive pronoun**.

| Possessive Pronouns | Examples |
|---|---|
| my, mine | This is <u>my</u> coat. This coat is <u>mine</u>. |
| your, yours | I like <u>your</u> story. The best story is <u>yours</u>. |
| her, hers | I borrowed <u>her</u> hat. That hat is <u>hers</u>. |
| his | Marco returned <u>his</u> bike. The bike is <u>his</u>. |
| our, ours | Grandpa walks <u>our</u> dog. The dog he walks is <u>ours</u>. |
| their, theirs | I voted for <u>their</u> project. The project I voted for is <u>theirs</u>. |
| its | The dog buried <u>its</u> bone. |

**My TURN** Edit the paragraph by adding possessive pronouns.

I walk _____ neighbor's dog. _____ name is Toby. Sometimes _____ mom joins us. _____ dog treats are Toby's favorite. I wish Toby was _____ .

# Opinion Essay

An **opinion essay** states a writer's point of view on a certain topic. The purpose of an opinion essay is to help a reader take a side on a matter or to get the reader to do something. A good opinion essay is supported with strong reasons.

Copyright © SAVVAS Learning Company LLC. All Rights Reserved.

**Learning Goal**

I can use elements of opinion writing to write an opinion essay.

**My TURN** Choose an opinion essay that you have read and use it to fill in the chart.

| | | |
|---|---|---|
| The **introduction** includes a clear statement of opinion. |  | What is the writer's **opinion**? |
| The **body** provides the writer's **reasons**. Reasons include facts and examples. The reasons should be convincing. |  | What **reasons** does the writer provide to support the opinion? |
| The **conclusion** may restate or summarize the writer's opinion. It could also persuade the reader to take some kind of action. |  | How does the writer **end** the essay? |

**253**

# Topic

Look for the topic at the beginning of an opinion essay.

A **topic** is the subject or issue an author chooses to write about. An opinion essay allows writers to share their feelings or point of view about a topic and persuade readers to share the same opinion.

Some possible topics for an opinion essay include

- a book or movie review
- a particular subject with different viewpoints, such as recycling

**My TURN** Think about a book review or opinion essay you have read. Then fill in the chart about the topic.

| What is the topic of the essay? |
|---|
| |

| What words or phrases does the writer use to show his or her opinion or point of view about this topic? | Why is this topic important to the writer? |
|---|---|
| | |

# Point of View and Reasons

Effective writers support their **point of view**, or opinion, with **reasons**. If writers want to be convincing, they need strong reasons, or explanations, that tell why readers should agree with their opinion. Finding strong reasons usually involves research. **Reasons** may include

- facts, or information that can be proved to be true
- numbers, such as statistics or data
- the findings of others
- examples that are relevant and based on facts
- details, or descriptions that explain the facts

**My TURN** Read an opinion essay from your classroom library. Use it to fill in the chart. Discuss your findings with a partner.

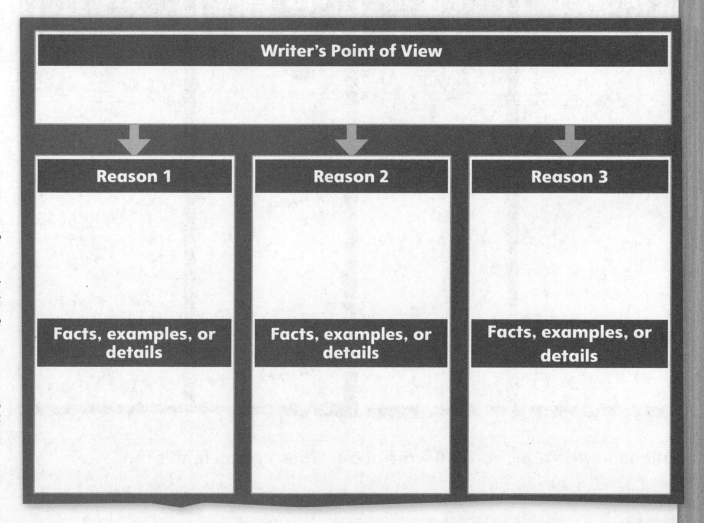

**Writer's Point of View**

| Reason 1 | Reason 2 | Reason 3 |
|---|---|---|
| **Facts, examples, or details** | **Facts, examples, or details** | **Facts, examples, or details** |

# Brainstorm Topics and Focus on Opinion

Writers of opinion essays **brainstorm topics** that they feel strongly about. As they brainstorm, they focus on their **opinion** about each topic.

Remember, your **purpose** is to convince readers to feel the same way you do. Consider what your audience would find persuasive.

**My TURN** Brainstorm topics related to the idea at the top of each column.

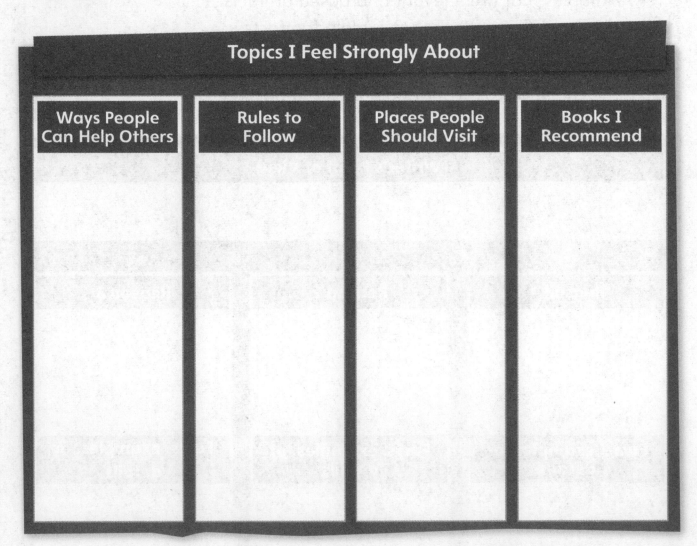

| Topics I Feel Strongly About | | | |
|---|---|---|---|
| Ways People Can Help Others | Rules to Follow | Places People Should Visit | Books I Recommend |
| | | | |

Highlight the topic you will write about. Then complete this sentence:

I believe that _____.

# Plan Your Opinion Essay

Taking a side for or against your topic can help you plan your opinion essay. Think about the reasons you will give to support your opinion. Decide which reasons are the most convincing.

**My TURN** Use the organizer to map your opinion essay. Share your opinion and reasons with an adult or with your Writing Club. Ask questions about reasons you do not understand in others' essays. Compliment good ideas.

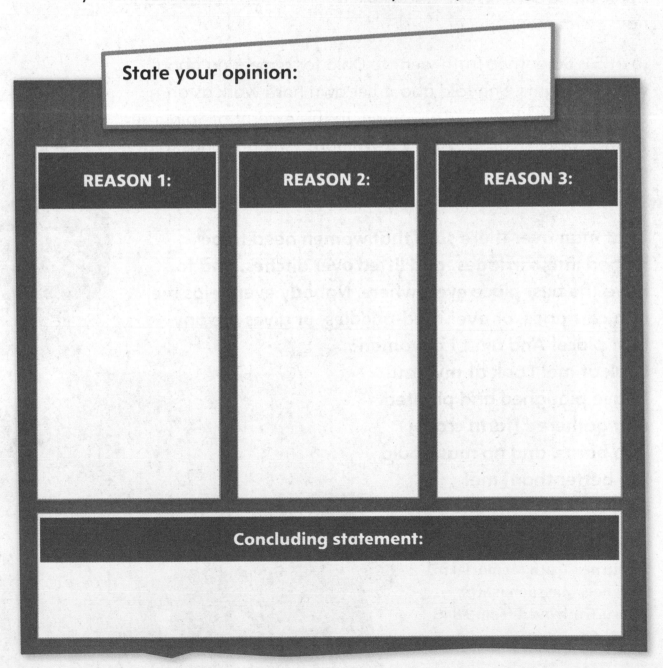

State your opinion:

REASON 1:

REASON 2:

REASON 3:

Concluding statement:

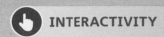 **INTERACTIVITY**

# Sojourner TRUTH

Sojourner Truth was born in New York in 1797. She was an enslaved person for many years, but in the 1820s she ran away to gain her freedom. As the years passed, she worked hard to end slavery. She also worked for women to have equal rights with men.

In 1851, Sojourner Truth went to Ohio for a meeting about women's rights. She told about her own hard work as an enslaved person and as a woman. In this excerpt of Sojourner Truth's speech, called "Ain't I a Woman?" she responds to a man who claimed that women were treated so well that they did not need equal rights.

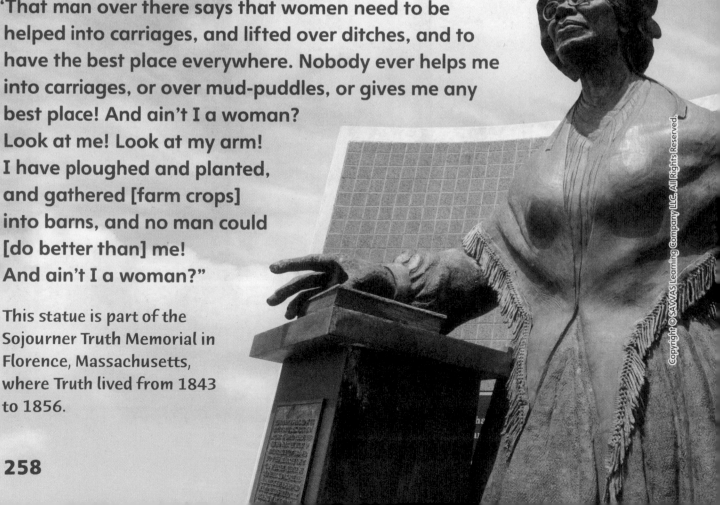

**"That man over there says that women need to be helped into carriages, and lifted over ditches, and to have the best place everywhere. Nobody ever helps me into carriages, or over mud-puddles, or gives me any best place! And ain't I a woman? Look at me! Look at my arm! I have ploughed and planted, and gathered [farm crops] into barns, and no man could [do better than] me! And ain't I a woman?"**

This statue is part of the Sojourner Truth Memorial in Florence, Massachusetts, where Truth lived from 1843 to 1856.

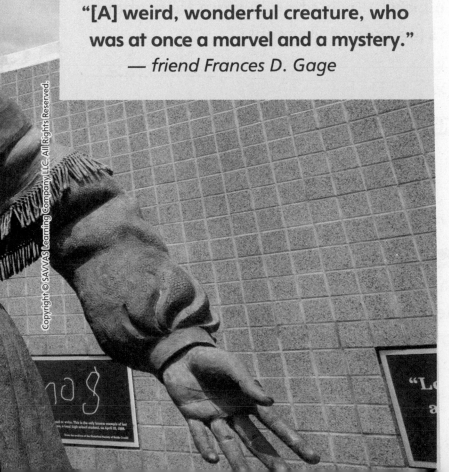

People who knew Sojourner Truth said these things about her:

"There was both power and sweetness in that great warm soul and that vigorous [strong] frame."
— *Antislavery author Harriet Beecher Stowe*

"Wise, unselfish, brave, and good"
— *Women's rights leader Lucy Stone*

"[A] weird, wonderful creature, who was at once a marvel and a mystery."
— *friend Frances D. Gage*

## Weekly Question

**How can personal stories change society?**

**Quick Write** Sojourner Truth told people what her life as a woman was like. How might stories such as hers help people change the way they think? How can the way people think change society? Freewrite your ideas.

## Spotlight on Genre

# Biography

A **biography** tells the story of a real person's life, written by another person. A biography may cover a person's whole life or only parts of it. The author of a biography conducts research to gather information about the person. A biography usually includes

- A **sequence of true events**, especially key events from the subject's life, including challenges, problems, and successes
- **Photographs** or other **historical documents**
- A third-person **point of view,** or outside perspective

**Establish Purpose** The **purpose,** or reason, for reading a biography is often to learn facts about a person's life or for enjoyment.

Whose life story would you like to read about in a biography?

My **PURPOSE** _____

_____

_____

**TURN and TALK** With a partner, discuss different purposes for reading *Frederick Douglass*. For example, after previewing the text, you may want to find out what role Douglass played in the abolitionist movement.

# Biography
## Anchor Chart

★ The subject is a real person.

★ The setting is a real time and a real place, and there are often multiple settings.

★ Events are told as a narrative and based on facts gathered from sources.

★ The narrative is written from a third-person point of view.

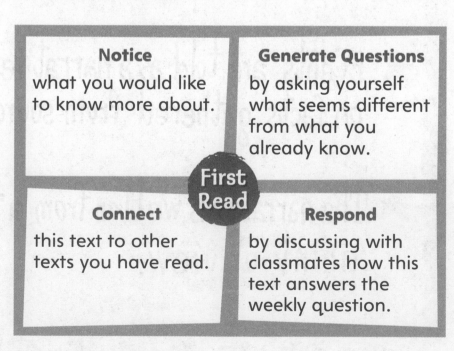

**Josh Gregory** has written nearly 200 books for young people, including many biographies. He has written about historical figures and athletes. His book about Steve Jobs—the developer of many well-known digital technologies—has been very popular.

*from*

# Frederick Douglass

## Preview Vocabulary

As you read *Frederick Douglass*, pay attention to these vocabulary words. Notice how they give you clear ideas about the sequence of events.

> slavery    abolitionist
>
> violence    equality    influential

## Read

Before you begin, look at the headings, images, and captions and establish a purpose for reading. The following strategies can help you when you read a **biography** the first time.

**Notice**

what you would like to know more about.

**Generate Questions**

by asking yourself what seems different from what you already know.

**First Read**

**Connect**

this text to other texts you have read.

**Respond**

by discussing with classmates how this text answers the weekly question.

Genre  Biography

*from*

# FREDERICK DOUGLASS
## by Josh Gregory

 AUDIO

 ANNOTATE

## Background
Frederick Douglass faced many hardships growing up enslaved in Maryland. As a young man, he escaped from slavery and began a new life with his wife, Anna Murray, in New Bedford, Massachusetts. In this excerpt, we learn how Douglass became a national leader who worked to end slavery and gain equal rights for all people.

263

# Spreading a Message

1    In Massachusetts, Douglass began to build a
new life with Anna. They soon started a family,
eventually having five children. To support
them, Douglass worked a variety of odd jobs.
It was sometimes difficult to find work. Even
though slavery was illegal in the North, black
people living there were still not always treated
fairly. Many white people would not hire them
for jobs.

## Joining the Movement

2    As a free man, Douglass was able to read
whatever he wanted, whenever he wanted. He
began subscribing to abolitionist newspapers.
In them, he read about the ways people were
working to end slavery completely. He also
started attending local abolitionist
meetings, where people shared their
ideas for ways to help.

The Douglasses arrive
in New Bedford.

Police and proslavery whites break up an abolitionist meeting as Douglass delivers a speech.

3    At these meetings, Douglass became friends with important abolitionist leaders such as William Lloyd Garrison. They wanted Douglass to share his story with others. At first, he was unsure. He did not want to draw too much attention to himself. But one day in 1841, he stood up and spoke to a crowd in the town of Nantucket. The audience was awed by his remarkable tale and his impressive way with words.

## Speaking Out

4    Douglass was still afraid of being caught. However, he knew that his life story and speaking skills could help spread the abolitionist cause. He toured the northern states, giving speeches about his experiences as a slave. He became famous for his passionate arguments against slavery. Though he was sometimes met with harsh treatment from proslavery whites, he never gave up.

**CLOSE READ**

## Identify Main Idea and Key Details

Underline evidence that Douglass risked his safety to speak out against slavery.

265

## Make Inferences

Highlight details that help you make inferences about how Douglass's books and speeches affected people's feelings about slavery.

**violence** acts that cause great harm, such as damage or injury

## Sharing His Story

5    In 1845, Frederick published the first of his three autobiographies. The book became a best seller. In it, Douglass included detailed descriptions of the violence and mistreatment he had experienced while a slave. The book was the first time many readers were exposed to the true horrors of slavery.

## Traveling Abroad

6    Because he included the names of his former owners in his book, Douglass was more afraid than ever that they would find him. To avoid being captured, he traveled to Europe. There, he continued giving speeches and gathering support for the effort to end slavery. He made many friends and was amazed at how well people treated him overseas.

Abolitionists in Europe did everything they could to support Douglass after hearing his story.

### Finally Free

7   Though he was successful in Europe, Douglass knew he needed to return home. He wanted to be with his family and continue fighting to end slavery. To help, his European supporters raised the money he needed to pay his former owners for his freedom. This made him legally free. An escaped slave could be captured and returned to slavery. A free person could not. In 1847, he returned home, able to speak and write without fear.

## Vocabulary in Context

The word *raised* can mean "lifted up" or "collected funds." Use context clues within the sentence to determine the meaning of the word *raised* in the text.

Underline the context clues that support your definition.

After returning home, Douglass went right back to work spreading his message about the evils of slavery.

### Identify Main Idea and Key Details

Underline sentences that help you identify how this feature relates to the main idea of the biography.

# THE ABOLITIONIST MOVEMENT

Frederick Douglass was only one of many people working to end slavery in the United States. From the earliest days of the nation, people spoke out against this horrible practice. Here are some of the most famous of them.

## William Lloyd Garrison

An early supporter of Douglass, William Lloyd Garrison began publishing the antislavery newspaper *The Liberator* in 1831. Garrison was known for his controversial political opinions. While many abolitionists argued only for slaves' freedom, Garrison also argued for equality for African Americans.

**equality** the right for all people to be treated the same

## Harriet Tubman

After escaping slavery when she was about 29 years old, Harriet Tubman dedicated herself to helping others do the same on the Underground Railroad. Slave owners offered rewards for her capture, while abolitionists praised her heroic deeds.

**CLOSE READ**

## Make Inferences

Highlight details that help you make an inference about how the actions of Tubman, Truth, and Brown helped to end slavery.

## Sojourner Truth

Like Frederick Douglass, Sojourner Truth was a former slave who became famous for her powerful antislavery speeches. Later in life, she dedicated herself to the cause of women's rights and provided advice to recently freed slaves.

## John Brown

Unlike most abolitionists, John Brown believed that violence was the only way to end slavery. In October 1859, he and an armed group of followers took about 60 people hostage in Harpers Ferry, Virginia, which is now part of West Virginia. Brown hoped to inspire slaves to join him in rebellion. However, his plan was unsuccessful. He was convicted of treason, or betraying the country, and hanged.

## Identify Main Idea and Key Details

Underline details about the beliefs important to Douglass's work to help you identify the main idea.

# A National Leader

8   After returning to the United States, Douglass decided to start his own abolitionist newspaper. Called *The North Star*, its first issue was published on December 3, 1847. Unlike other similar newspapers, it was owned, written, and edited by African Americans. It included everything from news articles to poems and book reviews. Douglass himself wrote many of the paper's articles.

## Freedom and Equality for All

9   In addition to wanting to end slavery, Douglass believed in equality for all Americans. In *The North Star*, his other writings, and his speeches, he often discussed the importance of equal rights for women. He also wrote often about the necessity of education for all Americans.

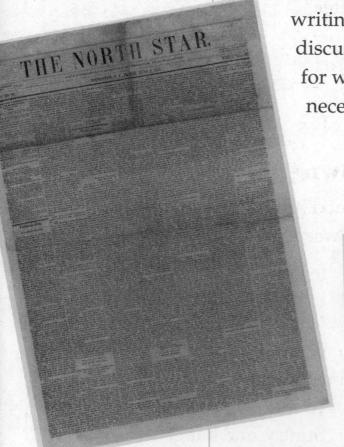

*The North Star* was named for the bright star in the night sky that escaped slaves used as a guide toward freedom.

# A Spectacular Speech

On July 5, 1852, Frederick Douglass delivered one of the best-known speeches of his career. He spoke at a Fourth of July celebration in Rochester, New York. In front of a crowd of about 500 people, he pointed out that Independence Day did not mark freedom for African Americans. It only stood for the freedom of the nation's white residents. He called for the country to embrace its founding principles of freedom and equality by ending slavery.

**CLOSE READ**

**Make Inferences**
Highlight details that help you make inferences about why Douglass's speech in Rochester is one of his most famous.

# A Timeline *of* Frederick Douglass's Life

## 1817–1818

Frederick Augustus Washington Bailey is born on a plantation in Maryland.

## 1838

Frederick escapes from slavery and takes the last name Douglass.

**CLOSE READ**

## Vocabulary in Context

Use context clues in paragraph 10 to determine the meaning of the word *conflict*.

Underline the context clues that support your definition.

## The End of Slavery

10   In the 1850s, the national debate over slavery became more and more heated. Many people in the northern states wanted abolition. However, plantation owners in the southern states did not want to give up their source of free labor. Finally, the Civil War broke out between the North and the South in 1861. Douglass hoped that the conflict could bring an end to slavery once and for all.

## 1845

Douglass publishes his first autobiography and travels to Europe.

NARRATIVE

OF THE

LIFE

OF

FREDERICK DOUGLASS,

AN

AMERICAN SLAVE.

WRITTEN BY HIMSELF.

BOSTON:
PUBLISHED AT THE ANTI-SLAVERY OFFICE,
No. 25 CORNHILL.
1845.

## 1865

The 13th Amendment abolishes slavery in the United States.

11    During the Civil War, Douglass encouraged free black men to join the military and fight against the South. He even met with President Abraham Lincoln to discuss the way black soldiers were treated. He wanted to make sure they received fair payment for their services.

12    The North defeated the South in 1865. Later that year, Congress approved the 13th Amendment to the U.S. Constitution, which officially ended slavery throughout the country.

**CLOSE READ**

## Make Inferences

Highlight facts that help you make an inference about how Douglass worked with other leaders to improve the lives and treatment of African Americans.

Douglass's meeting with Abraham Lincoln during the Civil War was just the start of his government leadership.

Copyright © SAVVAS Learning Company LLC. All Rights Reserved.

## Identify Main Idea and Key Details

Underline evidence that Douglass was an important leader to help you identify the main idea.

## More to Do

13   Even after slavery was abolished, Douglass kept fighting for equality. He argued for the importance of voting rights and other fair treatment for African Americans and women. Beginning in the early 1870s, he was appointed to several positions in the U.S. government. Among them were marshal in the District of Columbia and U.S. minister and consul general to Haiti. These positions made him the first African American to hold high rank in the government.

## Remembering a Hero

14   In 1895, at about the age of 77, Frederick Douglass died of heart failure. Around the world, people celebrated the life of this great man. With strength and determination, he had risen up from slavery to become one of the nation's most influential figures. He is remembered as a hero who fought bravely to end slavery and promote equality. His work continues to inspire people to this day.

**CLOSE READ**

### Identify Main Idea and Key Details

Underline sentences that help you identify the main idea of the biography.

**influential** having a great effect on someone or something

Douglass greets supporters after taking office as marshal of the District of Columbia.

# Develop Vocabulary

The author of a historical biography uses specific words that help readers understand the main idea and key details. You can use this newly acquired vocabulary to discuss the fight against slavery in America.

**My TURN** Write the word from the word bank next to its definition. Then use the vocabulary word in a sentence about the text.

**Word Bank**

slavery     abolitionist     equality     influential

| Vocabulary Word | Definition | Sentence Featuring the Word |
|---|---|---|
| equality | the right for all people to be treated the same | Douglass believed in equality for all Americans. |
| | a person who believes that slavery should be stopped | |
| | having a great effect on someone or something | |
| | a system in which some people are owned by others | |

# Check for Understanding

My **TURN** Look back at the text to answer the questions.

1. What characteristics help you recognize that the text is a biography?

2. What is the most likely reason that the author included the section titled "The Abolitionist Movement" in this biography?

3. Why was Douglass at risk when he spoke in public against slavery? Cite relevant text evidence to support your response.

4. Which evidence from the text can be used to prove that Douglass was an influential leader of the abolition of slavery?

# Identify Main Idea and Key Details

The **main idea** is the most important idea about the topic.
The **key details** explain or support the main idea. You evaluate the
key details in a text to identify the main idea.

1. **My TURN** Go to the Close Read notes in *Frederick Douglass* and
   underline evidence that helps you identify the main idea and key
   details that support it.

2. **Text Evidence** Complete the graphic organizer. Use some of the
   key details you underlined to identify the main idea of the text
   and important supporting evidence.

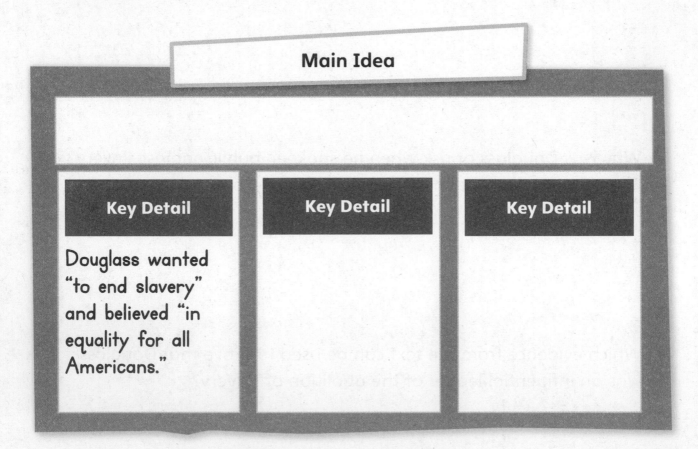

**Main Idea**

| **Key Detail** | **Key Detail** | **Key Detail** |
| --- | --- | --- |
| Douglass wanted "to end slavery" and believed "in equality for all Americans." | | |

**How do the key details support the main idea?**

_____

_____

# Make Inferences

Readers **make inferences**, or figure out information that is not stated directly in a text. They look for clues in the text and combine this text evidence with what they already know to support their understanding.

1. **My TURN** Go back to the Close Read notes in *Frederick Douglass* and highlight parts that help you make inferences.

2. **Text Evidence** Use some of your highlighted evidence to make inferences that support your understanding of the text.

| Key Detail | What I Read | What I Know | My Inference |
|---|---|---|---|
| the reason Douglass joined the abolitionist movement | "black people living there were still not always treated fairly" | When people are treated unfairly, they try to find a way to be treated better. | Douglass likely joined because he wanted all people to be treated fairly. |
| how Douglass's work affected people's feelings about slavery | | | |
| how other abolitionists fought against slavery | | | |

# Reflect and Share

**Write to Sources** In *Frederick Douglass*, you learned about a formerly enslaved person who became a leader in the struggle to abolish slavery. Consider this text and other texts you have read this week. What personal qualities helped people meet their goals? Choose one person, and use examples from the text to write and support your response.

**Interact with Sources** Writers interact with sources by taking notes that will help them answer questions. Before you begin writing, think about questions that could guide your notes about the texts.

- What qualities of the person do I want to focus on?
- What text details show how the person met goals?
- How did personal qualities help the person succeed?

Write key details from the texts that help answer these questions. Use this text evidence to support an appropriate response. Write your response on a separate sheet of paper.

## Weekly Question

How can personal stories change society?

# Academic Vocabulary

**Synonyms and Antonyms** Words that have the same or similar meanings are **synonyms.** For example, *enormous* and *huge* are synonyms. Words that have opposite meanings are **antonyms.** *Huge* and *tiny* are antonyms.

**My TURN** For each word below,

1. **Read** the definition.

2. **Identify** a synonym and antonym.

3. **Use** each synonym and antonym in a sentence and **explain** each meaning.

4. **Use** a print or online dictionary or thesaurus as needed.

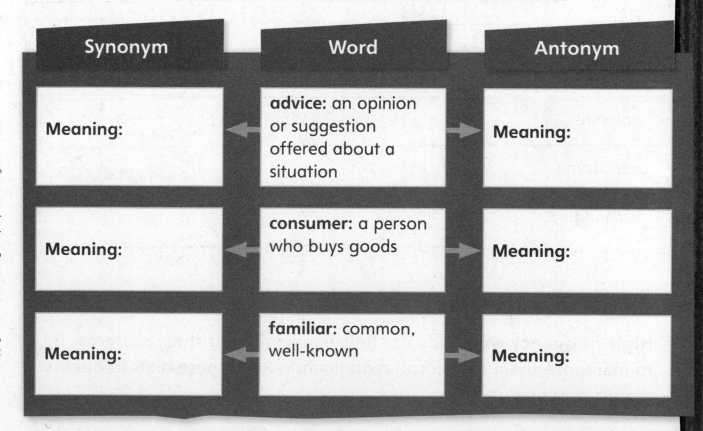

| Synonym | Word | Antonym |
|---|---|---|
| Meaning: | **advice:** an opinion or suggestion offered about a situation | Meaning: |
| Meaning: | **consumer:** a person who buys goods | Meaning: |
| Meaning: | **familiar:** common, well-known | Meaning: |

# VCCCV Syllable Pattern

**VCCCV Syllable Pattern** words have three consonants between vowels. Two of the consonants could be blends (like *nd*, *fl*, *cl*, *st*), two letters whose sounds are blended together. Two of the consonants could be digraphs (like *ch*, *th*, *sh*, *ph*), two letters that spell one sound. A word with the syllable pattern VCCCV would not be divided between either a blend or a digraph. When you know where to divide the syllables in a VCCCV pattern word, you will be able to read it.

**My TURN** Read each VCCCV syllable pattern word. Then write the two syllables in each word.

| VCCCV Pattern Words | First Syllable | Second Syllable |
|---|---|---|
| conflict | | |
| farther | | |
| hamster | | |
| dolphin | | |
| handsome | | |
| exchange | | |

# High-Frequency Words

**High-frequency words** do not follow regular word study patterns. Try to memorize them so you can read fluently. Read these high-frequency words: *common*, *though*.

# Read Like a Writer

Authors use graphic features such as illustrations to provide additional information that will deepen a reader's understanding of key ideas.

**Model !**  Read the sentence from *Frederick Douglass*.

> Though he was sometimes met with harsh treatment from proslavery whites, he never gave up.

*illustrated major event*

**1. Identify** The illustration that goes with this text shows police and proslavery whites breaking up an abolitionist meeting as Frederick Douglass delivers a speech.

**2. Question** How does this illustration help me understand the text?

**3. Conclude** It helps me understand the harsh treatment Frederick Douglass had to face as he worked to end slavery.

Read the sentence.

> Beginning in the early 1870s, he [Douglass] was appointed to several positions in the U.S. government.

**My TURN** Follow the steps to analyze graphic features. Describe how the author uses illustrations to help readers.

**1. Identify** The illustration near paragraph 13 shows _____

_____ .

**2. Question** How does this illustration help me understand the text?

**3. Conclude** It helps me understand _____

_____ .

# Write for a Reader

Writers use graphic features such as illustrations for specific purposes. Often they include illustrations to help readers better understand a major event in a text.

Ilustrations help readers picture what words describe!

**My TURN** Think about how the illustrations in *Frederick Douglass* helped you better understand the major events in the text. Now think about how you could use illustrations to help readers understand major events in a person's life. On the lines, write three major events in the life of a person you would like to write about. Draw one of the events on a separate sheet of paper. Below your drawing, briefly explain how this graphic feature achieves the purpose of helping readers understand the event.

1. _____
   _____
   _____

2. _____
   _____
   _____

3. _____
   _____
   _____

# VCCCV Syllable Pattern

**VCCCV Syllable Pattern** Some words have three consonants in the middle. If two consonants form a blend or a digraph, divide the word before or after the blend or digraph. For example, the word *complete* would divide like this: com / plete; the word *instant* would divide like this: in / stant. Knowing where to divide a word with a VCCCV syllable pattern will help you spell it correctly.

**My TURN** Sort the words by the number of letters in their first syllable. Then alphabetize each list, using the third letter, or beyond, as needed.

---

**SPELLING WORDS**

| | | |
|---|---|---|
| surprise | sample | employ |
| pilgrim | inspect | exclaim |
| subtract | contrast | athlete |
| control | | |

---

**Two Letters**

_____

_____

_____

_____

**Three Letters**

_____

_____

_____

_____

_____

_____

_____

_____

# High-Frequency Words

Write the following high-frequency words on the lines.

common _____

though _____

# Contractions

A **contraction** is a word made by putting two words together. When words are joined in a contraction, an apostrophe replaces a letter or letters. Pronouns can be used with linking verbs or helping verbs to make contractions. For example:

| | |
|---|---|
| I am = I'm | we are = we're |
| he is = he's | they will = they'll |

| Pronoun | Verb | Contraction |
|---|---|---|
| I, he, she, we, you | will | I'll, he'll, she'll, we'll, you'll |
| he, she | is | he's, she's |
| you, we, they | are | you're, we're, they're |

**My TURN** Edit this draft by replacing each underlined pronoun and verb with a contraction.

Amir put on his coat. "<u>I am</u> ready," he told his brother.

"If we do not go now, <u>we will</u> be late," his brother said.

"<u>We are</u> late!" Amir said. "Now <u>they will</u> be upset."

"<u>You are</u> the one <u>who is</u> always late," his brother said.

# Develop the Topic

The **topic** in an opinion essay is the subject or idea the writer is discussing in the essay. Writers usually have strong feelings about topics they choose. A writer might take either side—for or against the idea.

| **My Topic:** School sports are just as important as classes. | |
|---|---|
| **Ideas that support my position on the topic:** | **Ideas that do not support my position on the topic:** |
| • Children need exercise to stay healthy. <br> • Sports help children focus in class. | • Children get enough exercise at home. <br> • Children need more time learning in the classroom. |

By thinking about both sides of an issue, writers can **describe** and **develop** a topic. Writers can better **explain** to readers the importance of the topic. They can **convince** readers to accept their point of view.

**My TURN** Use the organizer to draft a topic for your own opinion essay.

| **My Topic:** | |
|---|---|
| Ideas that support my position on the topic: | Ideas that do not support my position on the topic: |
| | |

# Develop an Opinion

An **opinion** is your **point of view** on a topic. An opinion essay presents a point of view on a topic. Effective writers state their opinions clearly. The opinion statement is the focus of the essay.

**Examples:** Students should not have a lot of homework.

Dogs should be allowed to swim at the town lake.

I think *Charlotte's Web* is the best book about animals.

I think cats make better pets than dogs.

**My TURN** Read the following paragraph from an opinion essay. Underline the writer's opinion.

When you go to a restaurant, the first thing you get is a menu. You can order a salad or a grilled cheese sandwich. You can even order a milk shake! But at the school cafeteria, you just get what they serve that day. In my opinion, students should be able to order off a menu for school lunch.

**My TURN** Write an opinion statement as you develop a draft for your opinion essay.

Make an opinion statement clear with the words *should* or *should not*.

# Distinguish Between Fact and Opinion

A **fact** is information that is known to be true and can be proved. You can check facts by reading, observing, or asking an expert.

An **opinion** is someone's belief or way of thinking about something. Opinions cannot be proved true or false, but they can be explained or supported. Words such as *feel*, *think*, *best*, and *worst* might signal opinions.

| Facts | Opinions |
|---|---|
| School begins at 8:00 A.M. | School starts too early. |
| The willow is a type of tree. | The willow is the most beautiful tree. |

**My TURN** On the lines provided, write **F** for sentences that are facts and **O** for sentences that are opinions.

_____ Mars is the fourth planet from the sun.

_____ Students need more time for lunch.

_____ Banana bread is delicious.

_____ School recess is a half hour.

_____ Dogs are nicer than cats.

_____ George Washington was a general.

_____ Earth is the most fascinating planet.

_____ Houston is a city in Texas.

**My TURN** As you develop your draft in your writing notebook, identify sentences that are facts and those that are opinions. If you have too many opinions, research facts to support your opinion.

# Develop Reasons

**Reasons** support a writer's opinion. In an opinion essay, the writer usually gives at least two or three reasons. Then each reason is supported with facts. You can use resources such as books and reliable sites on the Internet to find facts that support your reasons.

**My TURN** Read the information in the chart. Then answer the question.

| **Opinion Statement:** Our playground needs more trees. | |
|---|---|
| **Reasons:** <br> • Trees are beautiful. <br> • Trees are healthy for people. <br> • Trees are good for the environment. | **Facts to Support Reasons:** <br> • Some trees bloom. <br> • Trees provide shade and cool the ground. <br> • Trees also make oxygen. |

Which reason do you think best supports the opinion statement? Explain.

_____

_____

| **How to Develop Reasons** |
|---|
| • Create a list of reasons that support your opinion. <br> • Before you write, arrange the reasons in order of importance. <br> • Do research to find facts to support your reasons. |

**My TURN** In your writing notebook, organize a reason-and-fact chart before you start your own opinion essay.

# Develop Supporting Facts

Writers give **supporting facts** to back up their reasons for an opinion essay. Writers might also provide **details** or **examples** to support their facts.

**My TURN** Read this passage from a book review. Draw a box around the opinion statement. Underline two reasons that support the opinion and highlight supporting facts for each reason.

> The most interesting book I have read this year is *Firefighters in Action*. I like it because the author uses personal stories.
>
> The book explains the firefighters' different jobs. For example, Captain Owen describes his battle in the air. He flies an air tanker through thick smoke. Fire Chief Ann Ramirez describes working on the ground. One time she had to battle a fire on a steep slope and worry about slipping!
>
> Another reason the book is great is because there are photographs on every page. The photos show what a forest looked like before and after a fire. Even after the fire, I can see some trees standing and new seedlings were already growing.

**My TURN** Identify facts from one of your own drafts. Make sure you have included details or examples that develop each fact. Share your facts and details with your Writing Club.

Use the library and reliable Web sites to find facts.

# THINK BIG

People can change their communities for the better when they think big. Big ideas make life better for everyone.

## BIG IDEA: COMMUNITY GARDENS

Many cities encourage community gardening. The gardens produce food, create beauty, and give people a sense of pride about where they live. They also bring people together to work, play, and learn.

Around **15 percent** of the world's food is grown in urban areas, such as backyards, rooftop gardens, or community gardens.

## BIG IDEA: SUPERMARKETS IN FOOD DESERTS

"Food deserts" are areas in a community without stores that sell healthy foods, such as vegetables and fruits. In some communities, grocery stores are few. Community leaders often work to open new supermarkets in food deserts.

About **23.5 million** people live in food deserts.

About **2.2 percent** of all U.S. households are more than ten miles away from a supermarket.

## Weekly Question

### How do big ideas change communities?

**Illustrate** On a separate sheet of paper, illustrate, or draw, to show how you might help change your community for the better.

**Learning Goal**

I can learn more about biography and explain the author's purpose in a biography.

## Spotlight on Genre

# Biography

A **biography** is a type of narrative nonfiction that tells a story about a person's life. Narrative elements add interest to real (nonfiction) information about a person's life. Authors can have more than one **purpose**, or reason, for writing a biography. For example, an author may want to write a biography to **entertain** readers with engaging stories and to **inform** readers about events in the subject's life.

**TURNandTALK** Think about two biographies you have read. With a partner, compare the authors' purposes for writing the biographies.

**Be a Fluent Reader** Fluent readers of biographies read with accuracy. Accuracy means reading with few or no mistakes.

When you read text aloud,

- sound out letters in unfamiliar words.

- reread a sentence if you do not know the meaning of a word or idea.

# Elements of Biography Anchor Chart

The author of a biography tells the story of a real person's life.

| Narrative Element | Purpose |
|---|---|
| Story Structure | Tells the events of a person's life in time order |
| Point of View | Told from a third-person point of view and gives facts and details about the person's life |
| Theme | Teaches a lesson about life by telling about a person's struggles and triumphs |

**Charnan Simon** was the editor of a children's magazine and the author of more than 100 books for young readers. She had a passion for bringing history and science to life through her stories. Charnan Simon died in 2014.

*from*
# Milton Hershey

## Preview Vocabulary

As you read *Milton Hershey*, pay attention to these vocabulary words. Notice how they provide clues to the author's purpose.

| | | |
|---|---|---|
| succeed | determined | |
| impressed | eventually | imagined |

## Read

Before you begin, read the title to identify the subject of the **biography**. Then follow these strategies as you read the text the first time.

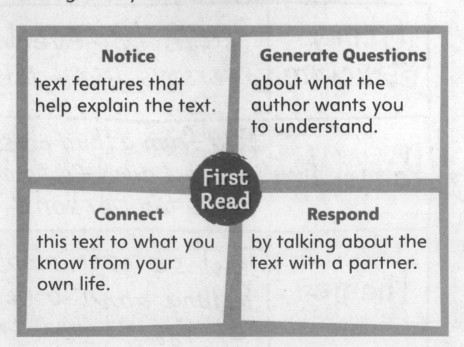

**Notice** text features that help explain the text.

**Generate Questions** about what the author wants you to understand.

**First Read**

**Connect** this text to what you know from your own life.

**Respond** by talking about the text with a partner.

*from*

# MILTON HERSHEY

## CHOCOLATE KING, TOWN BUILDER

### BY CHARNAN SIMON

 AUDIO

 ANNOTATE

Ask and
Answer
Questions
Highlight details about
trying hard. Use these
details to help you ask
a question about the
author's purpose for
including an old saying
in the text.

**succeed** do well or
achieve a goal

**determined** committed
or firmly decided

# "If at First You Don't Succeed..."

1    Have you ever had a really wonderful idea, but you couldn't make it work? No matter how hard you tried, it just never turned out the way you wanted it to. There is an old saying, "If at first you don't succeed, try, try again." This can be difficult advice to follow. When you keep failing, you want to give up.

2    One man who knew all about trying and failing was Milton Snavely Hershey. He tried to set up his own business many times. Each time he failed miserably. He lost all of his own money and the money of his friends and family. But Milton was stubborn. He knew he had a good idea, and he was determined to make it work.

3    Today, we can all be grateful for Milton Hershey's stubbornness. His good idea was the Hershey Chocolate Company. Thanks to Milton's hard work and determination, we have Hershey's candy bars, chocolate syrup, cocoa, and other treats to sweeten up our world!

**Vocabulary in Context**

Use a context clue beyond the sentence to determine the meaning of the word *philanthropist* in the text feature.

<u>Underline</u> the context clue that supports your definition.

4    Milton Hershey made a lot of money from his chocolate company. He wanted to use his money in a worthwhile way. Instead of spending it all on himself, he used his money to help other people.

5    Milton Hershey built an entire town called Hershey, Pennsylvania. In this town he built homes, schools, and churches. He also built theaters, swimming pools, a sports arena, and an amusement park.

6    Perhaps most importantly, Milton Hershey started a school for disadvantaged children. Milton knew what it was like to be young and penniless. He had no children of his own, but that didn't stop him from wanting to help other children. He gave his entire personal fortune to the school that is named after him. Today, the Milton Hershey School serves more than one thousand boys and girls.

## PHILANTHROPIST

Milton Hershey was a philanthropist. A philanthropist is a person who helps others by giving them money and other things they need. A philanthropist doesn't expect to receive anything in return.

7    Milton Snavely Hershey was born in the little
town of Derry, Pennsylvania, on September
13, 1857. Milton's family had lived in the rolling
hills of central Pennsylvania for more than one
hundred years. His great-grandfather built the
farmhouse, called The Homestead, in which
Milton was born.

8    Milton didn't live in the comfortable stone
farmhouse for long, however. His father,
Henry, was a dreamer. Henry couldn't seem
to settle down to any one job or place to live.
He moved his family many times during
Milton's childhood.

**CLOSE READ**

## Explain Author's Purpose

<u>Underline</u> details that help you connect information about where Hershey was born with where he later built his factory and town. Explain how these details relate to the author's purpose and message.

**Explain Author's Purpose**

Underline details that help you explain the author's purpose for including information about Hershey's education.

9    All of this moving made it hard for Milton to get an education. By the time he was thirteen years old, he had attended six different schools. But Milton's father loved books and reading. He wanted his son to keep going to school. Milton's mother Fanny, however, was more practical. She thought it was time for her son to learn a trade.

10    Milton's mother and father came to an agreement. Milton would leave school and become a printer's apprentice. An apprentice is a young person who is learning a trade from a skilled person. In Milton Hershey's day, an apprentice usually lived with the person he worked for. Milton's mother was pleased that her son would be learning a trade. His father was happy that Milton would be surrounded by writing and newspapers.

Young Milton attended this one-room schoolhouse called the Derry Church School.

11    Unfortunately, Milton wasn't a very good printer's apprentice. After two years, Fanny Hershey found another job for her son. Milton would learn to make candy in Joe Royer's Ice Cream Parlor and Garden in Lancaster, Pennsylvania.

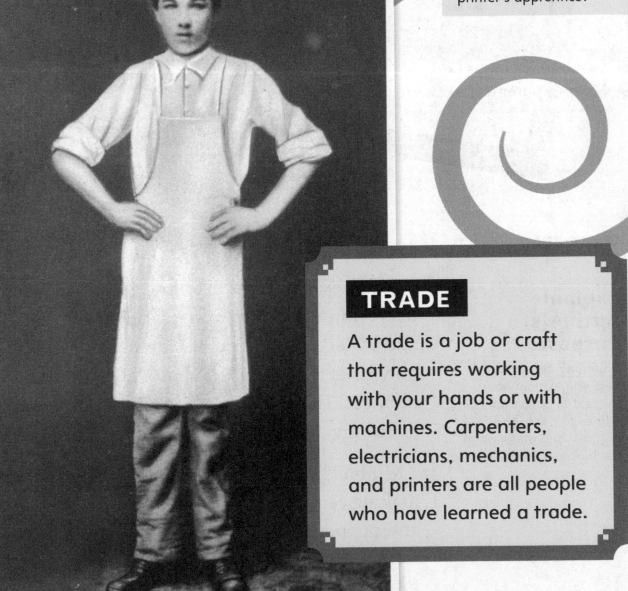

**CLOSE READ**

## Ask and Answer Questions

Highlight a detail that can help you answer this question to deepen your understanding of the text: What is the author's purpose for including the information about Hershey failing as a printer's apprentice?

### TRADE

A trade is a job or craft that requires working with your hands or with machines. Carpenters, electricians, mechanics, and printers are all people who have learned a trade.

Henry and Fanny Hershey, Milton's parents

**CLOSE READ**

**Explain Author's Purpose**

Underline details that help you explain how the text in paragraph 13 relates to the author's purpose and message of the biography.

12   Milton liked candy making from the beginning. It was a tricky business, since there were no exact recipes to follow. Joe Royer taught his young apprentice to start with sugar, then add water and flavorings. He showed Milton how to let the mixture boil until just the right moment. Then, together, Joe and Milton poured the candy out onto a big marble counter to cool.

13   Milton learned that he had a special knack for making candy. Customers liked his caramels and peppermints and fudge. After a few years, Milton decided he had learned all he could from Joe Royer. It was time to start his own candy business.

14     Luck was with Milton. His caramel candies—made with fresh milk—were a great success. An Englishman was so impressed with the candies, he ordered a huge supply to be shipped to England. Milton knew the milk would keep his candy fresh even after weeks on an ocean liner.

15     Before he knew it, Milton had more business than he could handle. He borrowed money from the Lancaster National Bank to buy more candy-making equipment. Milton had no trouble paying back the loan.

## Ask and Answer Questions

Highlight details in paragraphs 14 and 15 that help you ask a question about how Hershey's business became successful. Then use these details to answer your question and deepen your understanding of how Hershey's success relates to the author's message.

**impressed** affected in a favorable way

## Explain Author's Purpose

Underline a sentence that helps you explain the author's purpose for describing different types of caramels in the biography.

16   Business kept booming. Everyone seemed to be eating the caramels Milton was making in his Lancaster Caramel Company. There were so many to choose from! McGinties, Jim Cracks, and Roly Polies for the children. Lotuses, Paradox, and Cocoanut Ices for adults. Melbas, Empires, and Icelets for people who liked their candies made with skimmed milk instead of smooth, rich cream. And all of the different shapes and flavors were invented by Milton Hershey himself.

Lancaster Caramel Company, about 1889, where Milton achieved his first great success.

As a result of the company's success, Milton was named one of Lancaster's Most Important Citizens in 1889.

17    Soon Milton had to expand. He built factories in other Pennsylvania cities. He started a branch in New York City, and another in Chicago. He shipped his caramels all over the country—and soon, all over the world. People everywhere—Japan, China, Australia, and Europe—loved Milton's caramels.

18    The Lancaster Caramel Company made Milton Hershey a rich man. But it wasn't caramels that made him famous. In 1893, Milton had an idea that would make "Hershey" a household name around the world.

**CLOSE READ**

## Vocabulary in Context

Readers use context to determine the meaning of multiple-meaning words. They look at words within the sentence and in nearby sentences to define the words.

The word *branch* can mean "a small limb of a tree" or "one location of a business." Use context clues within and beyond the sentence to determine the meaning of *branch* in paragraph 17. Underline the context clues that support your definition.

### Ask and Answer Questions

Highlight details that help you ask a question about how Hershey overcame the challenges of making chocolate. Then use these details to answer your question and deepen your understanding of how overcoming challenges relates to the author's purpose and message.

**eventually** finally or after a long time

# "I Want to Make Chocolate"

19  It all started when Milton visited the World's Columbian Exposition in Chicago. Milton was fascinated by an exhibition of chocolate-making equipment from Germany. He studied the machinery for hours. Then he made up his mind. He would buy the equipment, ship it to Lancaster, and start making chocolate himself.

20  Making chocolate was harder than it looked. Milton and his candy makers tried one recipe after another, until they found just the taste they wanted. Eventually, Milton's factory was making 114 different kinds of fancy chocolates. Then, in 1900, Milton Hershey made a big decision. He didn't want to run both a caramel factory and a chocolate factory. From then on, he would only make chocolates.

# WORLD'S COLUMBIAN EXPOSITION

The 1893 World's Columbian Exposition in Chicago was held to celebrate the 400th anniversary of Christopher Columbus's arrival in North America. It was a giant world's fair, with exhibits from around the globe. More than 27,000,000 people visited the exposition.

## Explain Author's Purpose

<u>Underline</u> details that help you explain the author's purpose for including the "World's Columbian Exposition" text feature.

**Ask and Answer Questions**

Highlight details about Pennsylvania. Use those details to ask and answer a question about why Hershey was determined to build his factory there.

21    On August 10, 1900, Milton Hershey sold the Lancaster Caramel Company for $1 million. He immediately began plans to build a huge new chocolate factory. This factory would be located out in the farmland near Milton's birthplace in Derry, Pennsylvania.

22    Building a factory in the middle of the cornfields made sense to Milton Hershey. There was plenty of land to build on. There was plenty of fresh water. And there were plenty of cows to provide good, fresh milk for making delicious chocolates.

Milton decided to build his chocolate factory in the farm country near his hometown.

23    Not everyone agreed with Milton. His wife, Kitty, told him he ought to have his head examined. Everyone knew that factories belonged in cities! Besides, she would ask, where would the factory workers live—in a barn?

24    But Milton Hershey had thought of that, too. He promptly began to build a town for his workers. There would be comfortable houses with gardens. There would also be schools, churches, and stores. There would be a post office and a trolley car for transportation. It would be a wonderful town—and it would eventually be named Hershey, Pennsylvania.

**CLOSE READ**

**Explain Author's Purpose**

<u>Underline</u> details about Hershey's solution for a problem related to his factory workers. How do these details help you explain the author's purpose and message?

Kitty Hershey, around the time she married Milton (1898)

## Ask and Answer Questions

Highlight details that help you generate a question about transportation in Hershey, Pennsylvania. Use text evidence to answer the question and gain information about the town of Hershey.

# TROLLEY CARS

Trolley cars, or streetcars, are a sort of passenger train that roll along rails in city streets. The cars are run by overhead power lines.

25    It all happened just the way Milton Hershey said it would. The Hershey Chocolate Company was soon bigger than anyone could have imagined. And Hershey, Pennsylvania, grew into a thriving town with two main streets— named Chocolate and Cocoa Avenues!

Many of the streets of Milton's town were given names that refer to chocolate.

The first houses in Milton's town were built on Trinidad Avenue.

### CLOSE READ

## Explain Author's Purpose

Underline details the author includes about Hershey's success. Use these details to help you explain the author's purpose and message within the text.

**Fluency** Read paragraph 25 aloud with a partner to practice reading with accuracy. When you come to an unfamiliar word, pause and try to sound it out.

**imagined** believed or thought was possible

# Develop Vocabulary

In biographies and other narrative nonfiction, authors use vivid words to describe a person's actions, beliefs, and interactions. These words help create a complete picture in readers' minds.

**My TURN** Add a vocabulary word from the word bank to complete each sentence. Then use the word in a sentence about Milton Hershey.

## Word Bank

**succeed**     **determined**     **impressed**     **imagined**

## Milton Hershey

Determined means "committed."
Sentence: Hershey was determined to start a chocolate company.

_____ means "do well."
Sentence:

_____ means "believed."
Sentence:

_____ means "affected in a favorable way."
Sentence:

# Check for Understanding

**My TURN** Look back at the text to answer the questions.

**1.** How do you know that *Milton Hershey* is a biography?

**2.** Why does the author include a section about the World's Columbian Exposition in the biography?

**3.** Why should Milton Hershey be remembered for more than making candy? Construct a logical argument using details from the text.

**4.** Connect the saying "If at first you don't succeed, try, try again" to Hershey's story. Cite text evidence.

# Explain Author's Purpose

An **author's purpose** is his or her reason for writing a text. An **author's message** is the specific idea that the author wants readers to understand after reading the text. You can use text details to explain the author's purpose and message within a text.

1. **My TURN** Go to the Close Read notes in *Milton Hershey*. Underline parts that help you explain the author's purpose and message.

2. **Text Evidence** Use some of the parts you underlined to complete the chart.

| What the Text Says | How the Text Relates to Author's Purpose | How the Text Relates to Author's Message |
|---|---|---|
| "Milton learned that he had a special knack for making candy. . . . It was time to start his own candy business." | The author wants to tell readers how Hershey started his own candy business. | The author wants readers to understand that Hershey was ambitious and hard working. |

Explain the author's purpose and message within the biography:

# Ask and Answer Questions

Readers can **ask and answer questions** about the author's purpose and message within a text. Asking, or generating, questions during reading and then answering those questions after reading will help you deepen your understanding and gain information about the text.

1. **My TURN** Go back to the Close Read notes and highlight evidence that helps you ask and answer questions about the text.

2. **Text Evidence** Use some of your highlighted evidence to ask and answer questions about the text during and after reading.

| Highlighted Text | My Question | Answer to My Question |
|---|---|---|
| "There is an old saying, 'If at first you don't succeed, try, try again.'" | What is the author's purpose for including this saying in the text? | The author wants readers to understand that Hershey did not succeed at first, but he kept trying until he was successful. |
| | | |

# Reflect and Share

**Write to Sources** Milton Hershey followed his dream of building the Hershey Chocolate Company. Consider the biographies you have read so far in this unit. How did the subjects of the biographies achieve their goals? What challenges did they face? Write a response about the character traits that helped the subjects of two biographies achieve their goals and overcome challenges.

- - - - - - - - - - - - - - - - - - - - - - - - - - - - - - - - - - - - - - - - - -

**Use Text Evidence** When writing a response to a text, use text evidence to support your ideas.

- ◎ Look for key words or sentences that explain the person's goals and challenges.
- ◎ Look for character traits and connections across texts.

Locate evidence that supports your ideas about the shared character traits of the subjects of two biographies, and take notes. Organize your notes, and develop the ideas. Then write your response on a separate sheet of paper.

- - - - - - - - - - - - - - - - - - - - - - - - - - - - - - - - - - - - - - - - - -

**Weekly Question**

How do big ideas change communities?

# Academic Vocabulary

**Learning Goal**

I can develop knowledge about language to make connections between reading and writing.

**Context Clues** are the words and sentences around a word that give clues to a word's meaning. Some common context clues are synonyms and antonyms. A **synonym** is a word with the same or similar meaning as another word. An **antonym** is a word with the opposite meaning.

**My TURN** For each pair of sentences below,

**1. Read** the sentences.

**2. Identify** the context clue for the boldfaced vocabulary word.

**3. Tell** whether the context clue is a synonym or an antonym.

| Sentences | Context Clue | Type of Context Clue |
|---|---|---|
| One **benefit** to the project is working as a team. It is an advantage to have many minds thinking about the project. | advantage | synonym |
| The younger **generation** is skilled with technology. People in that age group began using technology when they were very young. | | |
| She gave great **advice**. Her guidance helped me decide exactly what to do. | | |
| The **consumer** bought everything the seller had on sale. | | |
| I thought the music sounded **familiar**, but the band was new to me. | | |

# Latin Suffixes

**Latin Suffixes -able, -ible, -ation** can be added to the ends of some words. The suffixes -able or -ible change a verb into an adjective. The suffix -ation changes a verb to a noun. When a verb ends with the letter e, the e is often dropped when adding the suffix.

The suffixes -able and -ible are spelled differently, but they are read, or pronounced, the same. In the suffix -ation, the letter a spells the long a sound. The letters tion spell the sound you hear in the word shun.

**My TURN** Read each word. Complete the chart.

| Word | Base Word | Suffix | Part of Speech |
|------|-----------|--------|----------------|
| inspiration | inspire | -ation | noun |
| advisable | | | |
| reversible | | | |
| starvation | | | |
| inflatable | | | |

# High-Frequency Words

**High-frequency words** are words that you will see often in texts. Read these high-frequency words: *language*, *clear*.

# Read Like a Writer

An author's attitude toward a subject is **tone**. Authors' words create a tone that contributes to the author's **voice**, or personality.

**Model !**  Read the sentence from *Milton Hershey*.

> Today, we can all be grateful for Milton Hershey's stubbornness.

*author's word choice*

1. **Identify** Charnan Simon uses the word *grateful* to describe how people should feel about Hershey's stubbornness.

2. **Question** How does word choice reveal tone and voice?

3. **Conclude** It suggests a positive tone that reveals the author's belief that stubbornness can sometimes be a good trait.

Read the sentence.

> Business kept booming.

**My TURN**  Follow the steps to analyze the sentence. Describe how word choice contributes to tone and voice.

1. **Identify** The author describes business as _____.

2. **Question** How does word choice reveal tone and voice?

3. **Conclude** The author's word choice suggests _____
   _____.

# Write for a Reader

**Word choices may be positive, negative, or neutral.**

Choose words carefully to create a particular tone, or attitude, toward the subject you are writing about. Think about how the tone will show your writer's voice.

**My TURN** In *Milton Hershey*, Charnan Simon chooses specific words to show she admires Hershey. Now you will choose words to create a particular tone that contributes to voice.

1. Think of a person you admire. Write the person's name and explain why you admire the person.

   **Person:** _____

   **Why I Admire This Person:** _____

   _____

2. Write a paragraph about the person you admire. Choose words that reveal your attitude toward the subject. Then underline the words in your paragraph that show your tone. Finally, briefly describe how your use of language in this paragraph shows your tone and contributes to your writer's voice.

   _____

   _____

   _____

   _____

   _____

   _____

# Spell Words with -able, -ible, -ation

When the word parts *-able*, *-ible*, and *-ation* are used as suffixes added to base words, they sometimes require spelling changes. For example, to add the suffix *-ation* to *civilize*, drop the final e before adding the suffix.

**My TURN**   Sort the words according to those that drop the final e when adding the suffix and those that do not drop a final e. If a word does not fit either category, write it in the *Other* column.

**SPELLING WORDS**

| | | |
|---|---|---|
| anticipation | flexible | terrible |
| civilization | likable | usable |
| convertible | movable | visible |
| dependable | | |

| Drop the Final *e* | Do Not Drop the Final *e* | Other |
|---|---|---|
| | | |
| | | |
| | | |

# High-Frequency Words

High-frequency words are common words that appear frequently in text. Write the following high-frequency words on the lines.

language _____

clear _____

# Prepositions and Prepositional Phrases

A **preposition** is the first word in a group of words called a **prepositional phrase**. A prepositional phrase ends with a noun or pronoun called the **object of the preposition**. The preposition shows a relationship between the noun or pronoun and the other words in a sentence.

| Type of Preposition | Examples of Prepositions | Prepositional Phrases |
| --- | --- | --- |
| **Location and Direction** | across, against, around, at, behind, below, beyond, by, down, far, from, in, inside, near, on, outside, over, to, toward, under, within | The fence **behind** the shed is white.<br>The picture was hung **below** the clock.<br>We walked **toward** the classroom. |
| **Time** | after, at, before, during, until | I have math class **after** lunch.<br>School ends **at** 3:00. |
| **Description** | in, for, with, without | The man **with** the dog is Mr. Sanchez.<br>This apple is **for** you. |

**My TURN** Edit this draft by adding prepositions that make sense. Then underline the prepositional phrase.

We went to the chocolate factory _____ the school year began. The factory is _____ my grandmother's house. A shop _____ the factory has a giant chocolate statue _____ the counter.

# Compose an Introduction

The **introduction** of an opinion essay focuses on what the essay is about. The introduction

- identifies the topic.
- states the writer's opinion, or point of view, about a topic.
- may include persuasive language.

**Learning Goal**

I can use elements of opinion writing to write an opinion essay.

### A New Park for Oakville

The city of Oakville is known for its natural spaces. Oakville has nature trails, forest preserves, and two parks. We need to build another park in the southwest part of the city to make Oakville the best place to live.

The topic is Oakville's natural spaces.

The opinion is that another park should be built.

Persuasive language helps to convince others.

**My TURN** Compose the introduction of your opinion essay in your writing notebook. Use this checklist as a guide for focusing your introduction.

## MY INTRODUCTION

- ☐ gives the topic of my essay.
- ☐ states my opinion, or point of view, about the topic.
- ☐ includes persuasive language.

# Organize Supporting Reasons

An opinion essay includes reasons and examples that support the writer's opinion. The **supporting reasons** help to convince or persuade readers to think the way the writer does. Writers organize their reasons in different ways, depending on the purpose they are trying to achieve.

| Organizational Structure | Purpose |
|---|---|
| *most* important reason to *least* important reason | to grab the reader's attention right away |
| *least* important reason to *most* important reason | to provide a strong ending |
| similar reasons grouped together | to establish a clear and even flow of ideas |

**My TURN** Organize the supporting reasons for building a park in Oakville. Number reasons from most important (1) to least important (3).

_____ A park will offer a place for people to walk their dogs.

_____ A park in the southwest part of Oakville will be the very first natural space for the people who live in that area.

_____ A park will make it easier for people to exercise, which will improve their health.

**My TURN** In your writing notebook, list and organize supporting reasons for your opinion about the topic.

# Organize Supporting Facts

Writers include facts to support their opinions. **Supporting facts** convince readers to share the writer's opinion. In an opinion essay, one or more facts should support each reason.

**My TURN** Work with a partner. For each reason given in the chart, write the number of the fact that best supports the reason.

**Facts:**

1. The park district estimates that 77 percent of the population exercises when a park is nearby.

2. No public spaces currently allow dogs.

3. Oakville's population in the southwest has doubled, but the residents have no park.

## Building a Park in Oakville

| | | |
|---|---|---|
| **Reason:** A park will offer a place for people to walk their dogs.<br><br>**Fact #:** _____ | **Reason:** A park in southwest Oakville will be the first natural space for people who live in that area.<br><br>**Fact #:** _____ | **Reason:** A park will make it easier for people to exercise, which will improve their health.<br><br>**Fact #:** _____ |

**My TURN** Decide how to organize the supporting facts for your opinion essay. Use this structure as you continue to compose your draft.

# Compose a Conclusion

The final paragraph of an opinion essay is the **conclusion**. Clear and coherent conclusions do not include new information but restate information in a new way.

> If we want Oakville to remain known for its natural spaces, we need to build another park now. It will provide a terrific place for our new and longtime residents to get together. Please write a letter to our mayor and ask her to approve this project.

The writer restates the topic and opinion.

The writer restates an important reason in a new way.

The writer asks the audience to support the opinion and take action.

**My TURN**  Answer these questions about your opinion essay. Use your answers to help you compose a coherent conclusion for your essay.

1. What is your topic and opinion?

2. Which reason or fact in your essay is the most persuasive?

3. How could you ask your audience to agree with you or take action?

# Use Technology

Authors might use **technology** to share their writing with readers. Using a computer and word-processing software to type a draft can make it easier to interact and collaborate with others.

Typing an electronic draft instead of writing a draft on paper can be helpful for the following reasons:

- It is easier to share with others through e-mail.
- Many copies can be printed out quickly to share with others.
- It is neater and clearer for others to read.
- There is more space around the text to write notes.

**My TURN** Use a computer to type a draft of your opinion essay. Then, share your draft with your Writing Club. Follow rules for working together. This includes printing copies for everyone in your Writing Club, taking turns reading one another's essays, and offering suggestions. Discuss how this collaborative process was helpful.

**My TURN** Identify a topic, purpose, and audience. Then select any genre, and plan a draft by brainstorming your ideas.

**Double-check your essay on the screen before you print it out.**

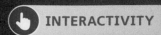 INTERACTIVITY

# CHANGING THE WORLD
## with One Idea

Many people think of Sir Tim Berners-Lee as a modern day world-changer. Berners-Lee was born in London in 1955, the son of two computer scientists. Working with computers came easily to Berners-Lee. After a few years planning computer software, he began working on a new idea. He was inspired to find a way to link information.

**1990** Tim Berners-Lee develops a computer program. The program makes it possible to link files of information in one file to other files.

**1992–93** The first public e-mail server becomes available. Before then, most computer users did not have e-mail.

**1990**   **1991**   **1992**   **1993**

**1991** Berners-Lee invents the World Wide Web (WWW). The Web allows all computer users to find information through linking pages.

Berners-Lee developed a computer program that could store information in files and also connect to other files. These connected files, known as hypertext, led Berners-Lee to develop the World Wide Web. Learning changed forever with an amazing source of information on computers, phones, and other Internet devices.

**This time line shows important technology changes in the 1990s.**

**1994** **1995**

**1994–95** The first browser for home use becomes available. A browser lets a computer user find and look at information on the Internet.

## Weekly Question

**How can a leader's experiences inspire change?**

**Annotate** Adding notes or comments to a text to improve understanding is annotating. Underline parts of the time line that you think most clearly answer the weekly question. Share your ideas with a partner and take notes on your discussion.

# Narrative Nonfiction

**Narrative nonfiction** is writing that tells about a real event or series of events. Narrative nonfiction includes these elements:

- **Facts** and **details** that inform the reader about one or more events
- **Narrative elements,** such as vivid descriptions of people, places, and events, that make the text read like a story
- A **chronological**, or time order, text structure

**Establish Purpose** The purpose, or reason, for reading narrative nonfiction may be for enjoyment or to gain knowledge about a particular person, event, or time in history.

Narrative nonfiction describes real events!

**My PURPOSE** _____

_____

_____

**TURN and TALK** With a partner, discuss different purposes for reading *Green City*. For example, you may want to know how the people worked together to help their community. Set your purpose for reading this text.

# ELEMENTS OF
# NARRATIVE
# NONFICTION
## ANCHOR CHART

- a **STORY STRUCTURE** with time-ordered sequence

- **CHARACTERS** who are real people

- **FACTS** and **DETAILS** about real-life events

- a **THEME**, or message, the author wants to share

**Allan Drummond** is an award-winning author and illustrator who enjoys writing about how people can work together to solve problems and change their communities. He explores this theme in the text you are about to read as well as in his most recent children's book, *Pedal Power: How One Community Became the Bicycle Capital of the World.*

# Green City

## Preview Vocabulary

As you read *Green City*, pay attention to these vocabulary words. Consider what they suggest about how the sequence of events unfolds.

> destroyed      opportunity
>
> sustainability    reclaimed    constructed

## Read

Before you begin, look at the illustrations to identify the order of events. Follow these strategies when you read this work of **narrative nonfiction** the first time.

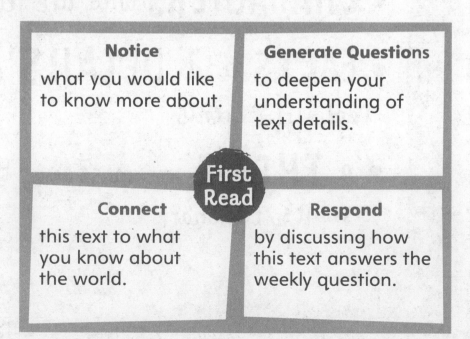

**Notice** what you would like to know more about.

**Generate Questions** to deepen your understanding of text details.

**First Read**

**Connect** this text to what you know about the world.

**Respond** by discussing how this text answers the weekly question.

# Green City

## How One Community Survived a Tornado and Rebuilt for a Sustainable Future

### by Allan Drummond

 AUDIO

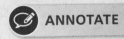 ANNOTATE

## Distinguish Viewpoint

<u>Underline</u> details that help you identify the author's viewpoint, or opinion, about the tornado's effect on people in Greensburg. Your own opinion may differ from that of the author. Consider these differences as you read the text.

**destroyed** completely ruined

1    I remember the night when a tornado destroyed Greensburg in nine minutes flat.

2    All of my things, our house, *everything* was blown thousands of feet into the air.

3    When it was all over and we climbed out of our shelter in the basement, everyone's past had been swept away.

4    Suddenly the entire town of Greensburg had no future.

5   Eleven people died because of the storm.

6   It took twelve people to lift a truck off Mr. Schmidt's house.

7   It was like a huge bomb had gone off. Our school was destroyed just two weeks before graduation.

8   The hospital, nine churches, the water tower, the drugstore with its soda fountain, the grocery store, the two hotels, the three banks, the theater, and everything else—just gone.

**CLOSE READ**

**Make Connections**
Highlight details that help you make a connection between buildings in Greensburg and your town. Explain how the buildings that had been in Greensburg were similar to and different from buildings where you live.

9   The trees were shredded to nothing. Not a bird in sight.

10   The only buildings left standing were the courthouse, the historic S.D. Robinett building, and Greensburg's giant grain elevator complex.

11 And looking at the town from high up, it was clear that nothing was left. Some people were asking, "What good is Greensburg anymore?" After all, we'd only been a little town in the middle of endless cornfields.

12 Down on the ground there was a gigantic mess to clean up.

13 The very next day we met in a huge emergency tent set up amid rubble outside the courthouse. Five hundred people were there, along with TV news teams, emergency crews, and volunteers.

14 With almost no buildings left, the only thing that remained of Greensburg was the people.

15 It seemed like the end of our town.

16 But some people saw the whole situation as an opportunity for a fresh start.

17 Soon the big question for everyone became "What do we want to be now?"

CLOSE READ

## Distinguish Viewpoint

Underline details that help you identify two viewpoints about the situation in Greensburg. Explain which viewpoint you would take.

**opportunity** a chance for a good experience or improvement

## Vocabulary in Context

The author uses the word *flocked* to describe the action of volunteers.

Use context clues within and before the sentence to determine the meaning of *flocked* as it is used in paragraph 20.

Underline the context clues that support your definition.

18   Everyone set to work.

19   The president flew in and declared Greensburg a disaster area.

20   So many volunteers flocked to the town we had to build a whole trailer park for them!

GOD BLESS GREENSBURG

Thanks to ♥ ALL ♥ VOLUNTEERS

21    Donations came from all over Kansas, the United States, and the world.

22    The government sent experts to help us.

23    And there was a whole lot of rubble to clear out—more than 388,000 tons.

24    We had to move out of town and find somewhere to stay during the big cleanup.

25    By the summer, we were living in our own small city of three hundred trailer homes outside Greensburg.

26    Life was not easy, and there were disagreements. Some people moved away and never came back.

27    Out there, living close to the weather, we realized how hot Kansas really could be.

28    We had to drive everywhere.

29    And there was always the chance that our trailers would be blown away by the wind.

30    We kept dreaming of what Greensburg and our new homes would look like.

31    We did a lot of talking about how to build again.

32    Sure, we all agreed on tornado-proof houses. And houses that we could keep cool in the summer and warm in the winter without using more fuel than necessary would be great. The word *green* kept coming up at every meeting.

33    "Isn't green just a color of paint?" asked Bob Dixson.

34    Then Daniel Wallach spoke up. "Green is basic common sense," he declared. "Don't use up more than you need. It's sustainability! The Kansas farmers' way!"

35    Mr. Wallach opened an office and called it Greensburg GreenTown.

36    "Not just green houses, a whole green city!" he said.

CLOSE READ

## Distinguish Viewpoint

Underline details that help you explain how your viewpoint on sustainability compares to Daniel Wallach's viewpoint.

**sustainability** a way of doing or making something that does not harm the environment and uses resources wisely

37    The whole idea of a green city had everyone excited, and some people got really creative. Lana and John Janssen reclaimed the kitchen cabinets and tiles from the remnants of their old house.

38    Daniel Wallach suggested the Silo Eco-Home, with rounded walls like the grain elevator complex that survived the storm.

39    Jill and Scott Eller started work on an amazing wind-resistant geodesic dome home made from wooden panels.

40 Bob Dixson designed a super-strong, super-insulated wood frame for his home.

41 Sixteen sustainable, affordable houses, called the Prairie Pointe Townhomes, would be built for Greensburgers right on Main Street.

42 But these were difficult times, and not everyone had the money to keep going.

# Going Green

Daniel Wallach lived in nearby Macksville when the tornado hit. As an expert on community projects he was able to give good advice right from the start when people began talking about rebuilding green.

Only five days after the storm, Daniel Wallach wrote down his ideas for Greensburg GreenTown. This would be an office where homeowners and businesses that were thinking about rebuilding green could learn all about it.

A month later the office was open, and it became a place where people could share information about the latest ideas in green building and living.

When the news spread that Greensburg was aiming to rebuild green, people in the United States and around the world got very excited. Greensburg became famous when newspapers and TV stations used the words "Green City" to describe the project.

Bob Dixon took a little while to come around to green ideas. But later on, as mayor of Greensburg, he became well known as a leader of the town's green initiative.

MAIN STREET

**Make Connections**

Highlight details that help you connect the family's experience of rebuilding their home to a personal experience that required hard work.

**Vocabulary in Context**

In the text, the author uses the word *solar* to describe pipes used in sustainable homes.

Use context clues within and before the sentence to determine the meaning of *solar*.

Underline the context clues that support your definition.

43   My family was lucky, and for the next two years we worked hard to build our home in as sustainable a way as possible.

## Building a Sustainable House

1. A house loses heat through its windows. The cold north side of a house gets little or no sun, so the windows should be smaller here. The rooms that aren't used much during the day should be put on the cold side.

2. The sunny south side of a house can have large windows to allow the light and warmth of the sun into the dwelling.

3. Solar pipes made of shiny metal with a clear cover on top can be set into the roof to bring sunlight down into dark areas, reducing the need for electric light during the day.

4. Plenty of insulation in the walls, roof, and floor of a house acts like a warm blanket, keeping the heat inside. All this insulation keeps the house cool in summer, too.

5. Solar panels generate electricity from the sun.

6. Water use can be reduced with special faucets and toilets.

7. Reclaimed materials can be used to build new floors and walls.

8. Sometimes appliances and cabinets can be reclaimed, too.

9. Rainwater can be collected from the roof and used to water the garden.

10. Some types of plants require less water.

11. Light-colored sidewalks and paths are much cooler to walk on than dark ones. They reflect the heat of the sun.

44   The town's businesses were rebuilding green, too—new offices for start-up companies, and a retail center.

45   The 5.4.7 Arts Center arrived by truck and was put together by University of Kansas architecture students.

46   On the outskirts of town we built a wind farm big enough to power the whole community.

47   The banks made sure their new buildings were as eco-friendly as possible.

48   So did the Best Western hotel and, beside it, the Kiowa County Memorial Hospital.

49   Our new hurricane-proof water tower was constructed next to the new, green Big Well Museum.

50   We knew our school had to be at the very center of it all. The plans looked exciting.

51   For three years we only had small trailers for classrooms.

52   But we became experts in environmental science.

## Distinguish Viewpoint

Underline a detail that reveals the author's viewpoint on how the townspeople changed as they waited for the school to be rebuilt. Do you share this viewpoint? Explain.

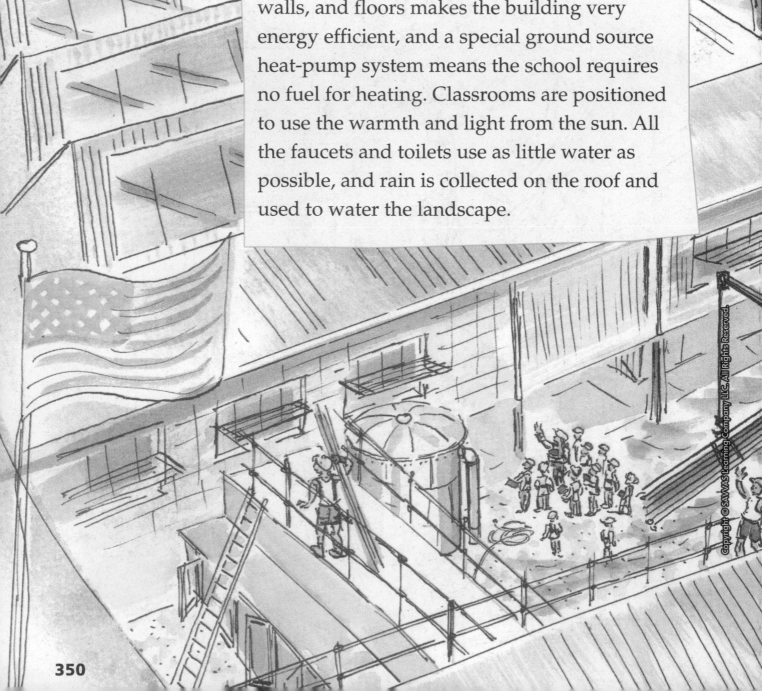

## Make Connections

Highlight details that help you connect some ways that the green school in Greensburg compares or contrasts to your school.

## The Kiowa County School Leads the Way in Green School Design

The Kiowa County School was designed to be the greenest building in the whole town. It was built from scratch. Reclaimed and recycled materials were used wherever possible, and the school has a wind turbine to generate electricity. Insulation in the roof, walls, and floors makes the building very energy efficient, and a special ground source heat-pump system means the school requires no fuel for heating. Classrooms are positioned to use the warmth and light from the sun. All the faucets and toilets use as little water as possible, and rain is collected on the roof and used to water the landscape.

53   Our new school was going to be one of the greenest in the United States.

**CLOSE READ**

## Distinguish Viewpoint

<u>Underline</u> details that help you infer the author's viewpoint on Greensburg's plan to build a green school.

## Make Connections

Highlight details that help you connect the text to your own experiences. Compare experiences when you worked hard to solve a problem to the experiences of people in Greensburg.

54    It took a few years for everything to come together, but now look! Greensburg is Green City.

55    We moved into our new houses and Greensburg has come back to life.

56   I still remember the night when the tornado destroyed our town in nine minutes flat.

57   Back then it really did seem like the end for Greensburg. Our town and our future were shattered.

58   But we *did* rebuild into one of the greenest towns in America.

59   That's official—the president even said so on TV.

60   By thinking and building green, we've given Greensburg its future. We planned for the future, because the future is green. Just ask the experts!

**CLOSE READ**

## Distinguish Viewpoint

<u>Underline</u> details that help you compare the author's viewpoint on the importance of green building and living to your own viewpoint on the topic.

# Develop Vocabulary

In narrative nonfiction, authors choose words that best describe an event or series of events. These words help readers connect events described in the text to their own lives.

**My TURN** Add each vocabulary word from the word bank to the chart. Then connect the word to an experience of your own. Finally, use the word in a sentence about experiences in Greensburg.

## Word Bank

| reclaimed | opportunity | constructed | destroyed |
|-----------|-------------|-------------|-----------|

| Word | Personal Experience | Experience in Greensburg |
|------|--------------------|--------------------------|
| **destroyed** <br> completely ruined | My little brother destroyed my model airplane. | The tornado destroyed many buildings in Greensburg. |
| a chance for a good experience | | |
| took back to reuse | | |
| built or made | | |

# Check for Understanding

**My TURN** Look back at the text to answer the questions.

1. What details help you understand that *Green City* is a narrative nonfiction text?

2. Why do you think the author chose to narrate the Greensburg events himself?

3. Why does the author use Daniel Wallach to explain sustainability? Cite text evidence.

4. What do you think is the theme, or message, of the text? Cite text evidence.

# Distinguish Viewpoint

An author's **viewpoint** is a way of looking at or thinking about something. Readers consider the opinions, details, and examples that support the author's viewpoint. Then readers compare the author's viewpoint with their own.

1. **My TURN** Go to the Close Read notes in *Green City* and underline parts that help you understand the author's viewpoint. Then distinguish this viewpoint from your own.

2. **Text Evidence** Use some of the parts you underlined to complete the chart.

| Text Evidence that Reveals Author's Viewpoint on . . . | How My Viewpoint Compares with Author's Viewpoint |
|---|---|
| a tornado destroying Greensburg "...everyone's past had been swept away. Suddenly the entire town of Greensburg had no future." | I agree with the author that the people of Greensburg must have felt like they lost their past and their future when the tornado destroyed their town. |
| how the townspeople changed as they waited for the school to be rebuilt | |
| rebuilding Greensburg | |

# Make Connections

**Making connections** between what you read and your personal experiences helps you better understand a text. To make these connections, think about what happens in a text and find similar examples in your own life.

1. **My TURN** Go back to the Close Read notes and highlight parts that help you make connections.

2. **Text Evidence** Use some of the highlighted text to make connections between the text and your personal experiences.

| Experiences of People in Greensburg | Experiences in My Life |
|---|---|
| **Being Creative**<br>"reclaimed the kitchen cabinets and tiles"; "Silo Eco-Home"; "geodesic dome" | **Being Creative**<br>When I got to redo my bedroom, I was excited and made drawings that showed my ideas. |
| **Working Hard** | **Working Hard** |
| **Solving Problems** | **Solving Problems** |

# Reflect and Share

**Write to Sources** In this unit, you have read about people who helped improve lives in their community or society. Based on these texts, which person was most successful in improving the lives of other people? Write your opinion and include evidence to support it.

**Use Text Evidence** When you write your opinion, you must support it with evidence from the text. To find the best text evidence, ask yourself if the evidence

- contains facts, reasons, or examples
- supports your opinion
- will help convince others of your opinion

On a separate sheet of paper, write an introductory sentence that states your opinion. Then support your opinion with evidence from the text. Use linking words and phrases, such as *because* and *for example*, to connect your opinion to reasons that support it. End your paragraph with a sentence that restates your opinion.

## Weekly Question

How can a leader's experiences inspire change?

# Academic Vocabulary

**Analogies** are a type of figurative language. They compare two items that have something in common. To write an analogy, compare something unfamiliar to something familiar to link words and ideas.

**Learning Goal**

I can use language to make connections between reading and writing.

**My TURN** For each analogy below,

1. **Identify** the relationship between the underlined words.

2. **Write** the missing word on the line.

3. **Explain** the comparison in the analogy.

Benefit is to positive as harm is to _____negative_____.

A benefit is positive. Harm is negative. *Positive* is an adjective that describes benefit. *Negative* is an adjective that describes harm.

Generation is to age group as hammer is to _____.

_____

_____

Advice is to suggestion as fact is to _____.

_____

_____

Consumer is to seller as customer is to _____.

_____

_____

Familiar is to family as unknown is to _____.

_____

_____

# Homographs

**Homographs** are words that are spelled the same but have different meanings. Two words that are homographs may or may not have the same pronunciation. The word *wind* in paragraph 29 of *Green City* means "moving air" and is pronounced with a short *i* sound. The word *wind* may be pronounced with a long *i* sound and mean "to curve or twist." Often the context tells you the meaning and pronunciation. You can also use a print or digital dictionary.

**My TURN** Reread paragraph 27. Identify a word that has a homograph and explain its meaning in the text. Then, use a print or digital dictionary to find a different meaning for the word's homograph. Finally, use the homograph in a sentence of your own.

> **Homograph in text:** _____
>
> **Meaning in text:** _____
>
> **Meaning of homograph:** _____
>
> **Your sentence:** _____

# High-Frequency Words

**High-frequency words** appear often in text. Read these high-frequency words: *equation, among*. Memorize these words to recognize them.

# Read Like a Writer

Authors write for a specific purpose—to entertain, inform, or persuade. How the author organizes ideas is called text structure. Text structure supports the author's purpose and helps readers understand important ideas in a text. One type of text structure is sequence, or time order.

**Model !** Read the sentence from *Green City*.

> Suddenly the entire town of Greensburg had no future. ▶······ **Time-order word**

1. **Identify** The author uses a time-order text structure to show how quickly the storm created damage.

2. **Question** How does this text structure support the author's purpose?

3. **Conclude** It supports the author's purpose of informing readers about the storm's devastating effects on the town.

Read the sentence.

> The very next day we met in a huge emergency tent set up amid rubble outside the courthouse.

**My TURN** Follow the steps to analyze the sentence. Describe how the text structure supports the author's purpose.

1. **Identify** The author uses a time-order text structure to discuss

_____ .

2. **Question** How does this text structure support the author's purpose?

3. **Conclude** It supports the author's purpose of _____

_____ .

# Write for a Reader

Use time-order words to organize the event sequence in your text!

Writers use text structure to organize information for readers. Putting events in time order helps readers understand the sequence of events in a text.

**My TURN** Think about how Allan Drummond used a time-order text structure to tell about the rebuilding of Greensburg in *Green City*. Consider how you can use a time-order text structure to contribute to your own purpose for writing.

1. Think about how a flower grows from a seed. List at least four time-order words you could use to describe the process.

   _____

   _____

2. Write a few sentences describing how a flower grows from a seed, using some of the time-order words you listed.

   _____

   _____

   _____

   _____

3. Explain how using time-order text structure contributes to your purpose for writing.

   _____

   _____

   _____

# Homographs

**Homographs** are words that are spelled the same but have different meanings. Many homographs are pronounced differently.

**My TURN** Read the words. Sort them into alphabetical order. If two words start with the same few letters, you can alphabetize to the second, third, or fourth letters. You might even alphabetize to the fifth letter! Remember to alphabetize based on the first letter that is different between the two words.

**SPELLING WORDS**

| | | |
|---|---|---|
| transplant | minute | research |
| consult | digest | incline |
| finance | upset | construct |
| content | | |

_____     _____

_____     _____

_____     _____

_____     _____

# High-Frequency Words

Memorize high-frequency words so you recognize them instantly. Write the following high-frequency words on the lines.

equation _____

among _____

# Comparing with Adjectives

Adjectives are describing words. You can use adjectives to compare. To compare two people, places, groups, or things, you usually add *-er* to an adjective. These are called **comparative adjectives.** To compare three or more people, places, groups, or things, you usually add *-est*. These are called **superlative adjectives.**

**One thing:** My dad has a new car.
**Two things:** My mom's car is newer than my dad's car.
**Three or more things:** Grandpa's car is the newest car in the family.

**Some Comparing Adjectives**

| One | Two/Comparative | Three or more/ Superlative |
|-----|-----------------|----------------------------|
| green | greener | greenest |
| great | greater | greatest |
| high | higher | highest |
| few | fewer | fewest |

**My TURN** Edit this draft by correcting incorrect comparative and superlative adjectives.

Grandma and her neighbor Jean each planted green beans.

Grandma's beans grew highest than Jean's beans, but Grandma's

plants had fewest beans. Another neighbor, Ben, brought beans

home from the store. His beans were green than Grandma's or

Jean's. I told Grandma that she had the great beans of all.

# Revise Drafts by Adding Linking Words

**Learning Goal**

I can use elements of opinion writing to write an opinion essay.

In an opinion essay, writers use **linking words** and phrases to connect their opinion and reasons. Linking words add coherence, or tie ideas together. They make your writing clearer.

| Examples of Linking Words and Phrases | |
|---|---|
| also | for example |
| because | therefore |

Notice how this writer added linking words and phrases, in blue, to connect reasons to an opinion.

Our activity center built a swimming pool because swimming is great exercise. Swimmers use all their body parts. For example, they use their arms and legs to move forward. They also use their stomach muscles to help them move in a straight line.

**My TURN** Fill in each blank with a linking word or phrase from the chart.

I think owning a pet is good _____ it teaches responsibility. _____ pets have to be fed every day. They _____ need fresh water daily. Pets love to go on walks. _____ pet owners will be motivated to walk too.

**My TURN** Revise a draft of your opinion essay by adding linking words and phrases to connect your opinion and reasons.

# Revise Drafts by Adding Details

Opinions that are not well supported are not very convincing. To support an opinion, writers need **details**. Details add coherence because they tie ideas together. They add clarity because they further explain ideas. Details in opinion essays may include facts, examples, or explanations.

**My TURN**  Read the paragraph. Look at the added details, in blue, that support the reasons for the opinion. Then complete the chart.

I think our school should stay open late. Students who stay late can complete homework. They can concentrate better and get help from teachers. Students could also learn fun things. For example, students could learn how to play the guitar.

| Opinion: I think our school should stay open late. | | |
|---|---|---|
| **Reason** | **Supporting Detail** | **How the Detail Supports the Reason** |
| Students who stay late can complete homework. | | |
| Students could also learn fun things. | | |

**My TURN**  Revise a draft of your opinion essay by adding details for coherence and clarity.

# Edit for Capitalization

Writers follow standard rules of English conventions, including **capitalization**. The name of a particular person, place, or thing is a proper noun. Proper nouns begin with a capital letter.

- Capitalize **official titles** of people.

  Mrs. Nora Brown          Dr. Parker

  Mayor Castro             Uncle Tony

- Capitalize the names of **holidays**.

  Thanksgiving        Memorial Day        Presidents' Day

- Capitalize **geographical names**.

  United States       Houston             New Mexico

  Magnolia Road       Mustang Park        Pacific Ocean

**My TURN** Edit the following paragraph for correct capitalization.

The best vacation I had was when we went to south padre island. I was so excited to spend time with aunt lucy at our family reunion. We watched the sunrise over the gulf of mexico. We hope to come back next labor day.

**My TURN** Edit one of your own drafts for capitalization. Look for titles of people, holidays, and geographical names.

If it were a holiday, Capitalization Day would be a proper noun.

# Peer Edit

Exchanging writing with a partner and making comments is **peer editing**. Reading peers' opinion essays helps your peers know whether their reasons are convincing. You might also find problems or errors in the essays. Remember to share ideas and suggest corrections politely. For example, first name something the writer did well, and then mention something he or she could fix. Pointing out both strong and weak points in your partner's essay helps you develop social communication skills.

**My TURN** Work with a partner. Read each other's opinion essay and politely discuss how to make the reasons stronger. Use the checklist to help you.

## CHECKLIST FOR PEER EDITING

☐ Does the writer state an opinion clearly?

☐ Do strong reasons support the opinion?

☐ Does the writer add details that support the reasons?

☐ Are the reasons listed logically?

☐ Does the writer use linking words to connect the opinion to reasons?

**My TURN** Answer these questions about your partner's opinion essay.

What is the strongest part of the opinion essay?

_____

_____

What part of the essay needs improvement?

_____

_____

# Use Peer and Teacher Suggestions

After you have had a peer edit your draft, a teacher may edit it too. Then it is time to **revise** your opinion essay. When you revise, include both peer and teacher suggestions to your final copy. The revisions will make your writing clear and coherent.

Before you revise, ask yourself: Did my teacher or a peer suggest that I

- revise my opinion statement?
- add more reasons and supporting details?
- add linking words and phrases?
- reorder or combine my reasons logically?
- delete weak reasons or details?

**My TURN** Revise your draft one last time for coherence and clarity. Add reasons or details suggested by your peer or teacher. Reorder paragraphs if needed. Then rewrite your opinion essay on your own paper.

**My TURN** Answer these questions about your revision. Then explain to the Writing Club how your final essay is improved.

What changes did you make to your essay?

1. _____

2. _____

3. _____

Why did you make these changes?

_____

_____

_____

# THANK YOU
## for Understanding

## TOGETHER

"Oh, Buddy! Buddy!

Where can you be?"

My new little pup

Had found his way free.

Quickly mom came,

and soon sister too.

The neighbors called out,

"What can we do?"

The doors swung open

And people came out.

We searched down the street,

Together we'd scout.

Mom pointed and called,

"Look there in the shade!"

I ran over and saw him,

asleep where he'd played.

# WANTED: A FRIEND

Walking into school one day,

My feet would hardly move.

Being new was painful—

I hoped you'd all approve.

You came to me at recess,

said you were new once too.

"It's hard to leave your friends,"
    you said,

"But, you will find some new."

At first, I'd felt so all alone,

But then, you changed it all.

You took me by the hand and said,

"Let's go and play some ball!"

## Weekly Question

**How do people support each other in difficult times?**

**Freewrite** What kind of support did the speaker in each poem receive? When has someone supported you during a difficult time? When have you supported someone else? Write your ideas.

# SILENT BOND

My feelings were hurt,

My heart was not light.

But you gave me comfort,

And held me so tight.

# Drama

Learn to recognize the literary elements of drama. A **drama** is a story written to be acted out for an audience. A drama is also called a **play**.

The text structure of drama is different from other genres. In a drama, the action of the story is organized into

- **Acts:** major divisions of the action
- **Scenes:** smaller divisions of the action
- **Lines:** words spoken by characters or stage directions related to the setting and action

Actors perform a drama for an audience!

**TURN and TALK**  Discuss with a partner how a drama is similar to and different from a biography. Use the Drama Anchor Chart to compare and contrast the genres. Take notes on your discussion.

**My NOTES** _____

_____

_____

_____

_____

_____

# Drama Anchor Chart

**Purpose:** To entertain or tell a story

**Structure:** Acts and scenes performed by actors in front of an audience

**Elements:**

- **Cast of Characters:** List of characters in the drama
- **Setting:** Time and place of the story
- **Dialogue:** words the actors say
- **Stage Directions:** descriptions of how to move or act out dialogue

**Rich Lo** is a writer and artist who lives in Chicago, Illinois. His family emigrated from China in 1964 to live in the United States. Rich Lo has written two children's books and illustrated a third one. One of his books tells about his experiences growing up in China.

# Grace and Grandma

## Preview Vocabulary

As you read *Grace and Grandma*, pay attention to these vocabulary words. Notice how they provide clues to what the drama is about.

| heritage | immigrants |
|---|---|
| interview | permission | arrival |

## Read

Before you begin, skim the text to identify the characters. Follow these strategies when you read this **drama** the first time.

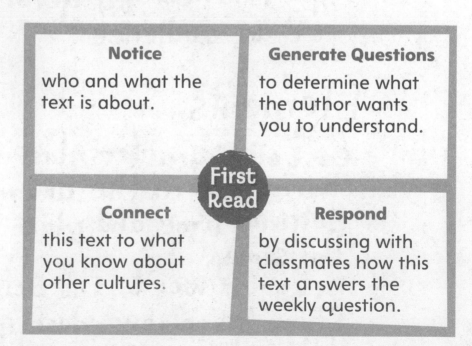

**Notice**
who and what the text is about.

**Generate Questions**
to determine what the author wants you to understand.

**First Read**

**Connect**
this text to what you know about other cultures.

**Respond**
by discussing with classmates how this text answers the weekly question.

# Grace *and* Grandma

*by* Rich Lo

 AUDIO

 ANNOTATE

## Identify Play Elements

<u>Underline</u> words that help you identify all of the characters who will appear in the play. Use this text evidence to discuss this element of the drama.

**heritage** family or cultural history and traditions that are passed down through the years

---

### Characters

DAD

GRACE LIU, Age 8

GRANDMA MEI

MOM

WENDI ZHANG, Age 8

1 *Setting: Chicago, Illinois, in the year 2006*

## Scene 1

2 *It's Monday afternoon.* GRACE *has just come home from school and is talking to* DAD *in the kitchen of their home.*

3 **DAD** (*to* GRACE): How was school today, Grace?

4 **GRACE:** It was good—except for Chinese class. As usual.

5 **DAD:** Shhh! Don't let your grandmother hear you say that!

6 **GRACE** (*lowering her voice*): I don't know why I have to take Chinese.

7 **DAD:** Yes, you do know why. Everyone in our family speaks Chinese. It's an important part of our heritage.

8 **GRACE:** But you hardly ever speak Chinese at home! Except when you're saying something you don't want me to understand. You know, like, "Let's make Grace go to bed early tonight so we can have some peace and quiet."

9 **DAD** (*laughing*): If you understand that, you must be learning *something* in Chinese class.

10 **GRACE:** I don't understand the words. I hear my name, and then I can guess the rest from the look on your face.

11 **DAD:** That means you're pretty bright. Bright enough to learn Chinese. When you do, Mom and I won't be able to keep secrets from you anymore.

12 **GRACE:** That'd be nice, but . . . Chinese is so hard. Our teacher is strict, too. Really, Dad, what's the point? I'm an American! I don't speak Chinese with any of my friends. We all speak English! Chinese is what the older Chinese people speak.

13 **GRANDMA MEI** (*entering the room*): Older, eh?

14 **GRACE** (*hugging* GRANDMA MEI): I didn't mean it that way, Grandma! I just—

15 **GRANDMA MEI:** It's all right, Grace. I know I'm no spring chicken. (*She laughs.* GRACE *looks confused.*)

16 **DAD:** *Spring chicken* means someone young, like a chicken that just hatched in the spring.

## Monitor Comprehension

Highlight words that you could reread to monitor your comprehension of which characters are speaking in this scene.

## Identify Play Elements

Underline details that help you identify the setting of scene 2.

## Vocabulary in Context

**Idioms** are phrases or expressions whose meaning cannot be understood from the ordinary meaning of the words that form them.

Underline the idiom in paragraph 18 to identify it. Then underline the context clue within the sentence that helps you explain its meaning. Finally, use the idiom in an original sentence.

17 *It's dinner time on the same day.*

18 **GRANDMA MEI:** That was one of the first phrases I learned when I came to this country. I was a spring chicken back then, just like you are now, Grace. Back then, I didn't want to learn English any more than you want to learn Chinese.

19 **GRACE** (*frowning*): But you *had* to learn English to live here. I don't have to learn Chinese to live here! I just want to speak English. I'm going to go do my *English* homework.

20 (GRACE *picks up her backpack and heads to her room.*)

## Scene 2

21 *It's early Monday evening of the same day.* MOM *has just come home from work. She joins* GRACE, DAD, *and* GRANDMA MEI *at the dinner table.*

22 **MOM** (*speaking excitedly*): Guess what happened at work today?

23 **DAD:** Hmm. You discovered a cure for the common cold?

24 **GRANDMA MEI:** We already have the cure. It's Chinese hot and sour soup, from Great-Grandma Ni Ni's recipe.

25 **DAD:** True, true. Okay, so what happened?

26 **MOM:** I met a woman whose family just moved from China. Her daughter is starting at your school next week, Grace. She's just a month younger than you.

27 **GRACE:** What's her name? Does she speak English?

28 **MOM:** Wendi Zhang, and yes. Her mom says Wendi started learning English when she was 2!

29 **GRANDMA MEI:** I'm not surprised. In China, people think it's very important to learn English.

30 **MOM:** Wendi's grandfather came to America around the same time you did, Mei! Wendi's dad was born here in Chicago.

31 **GRACE:** I thought you said Wendi just moved here.

32 **MOM:** Yes. Her dad went to China to become a teacher. Then he got married, and now the family has come to live in America. You'll help Wendi find her way around school, won't you?

33 **GRACE:** Okay, I guess so, but I have a lot to do tomorrow! I don't see why someone else can't—

**CLOSE READ**

**Monitor Comprehension**

Highlight dialogue that can help you ask and answer a question to monitor your comprehension of who Wendi is.

**Identify Play Elements**

Underline stage directions that help you understand how the actors speak and move in the scene.

34 **MOM** (*in a serious tone*): Wendi shares your heritage, Grace. I thought you'd be excited!

35 **GRACE:** Why should I care about my heritage? (*Pulls back her chair from the dining room table.*) I'm not hungry anymore. May I go to my room?

36 (MOM *nods, and* GRACE *leaves the table and goes to her room.*)

37 **MOM:** What's the matter with her?

38 **DAD:** I don't know. Every time we mention the word *China* lately, she turns into a storm cloud.

39 **GRANDMA MEI** (*laughing*): She doesn't seem to like the word *heritage*, either! Oh, well. Let's not allow this pasta to go to waste. (*She takes the pasta* GRACE *left on her plate.*)

## Scene 3

40 *It's later on Monday evening.* GRACE *is lying on her bed, doing homework.* GRANDMA MEI *knocks on her door and peers around the corner. She's carrying leftover spaghetti and salad on a tray.*

41 **GRANDMA MEI:** Mind if I come in for a moment, Grace?

42 **GRACE** (*sitting up*): Of course not.

43 **GRANDMA MEI:** I brought you some leftovers. The pasta is cold, but I know you like it that way!

44 **GRACE** (*laughing*): True! I guess you've seen me eating straight from the refrigerator! Thanks, Grandma. I'm sorry about how I acted before. I was rude.

45 **GRANDMA MEI:** It's okay. I think I know a little bit about how you're feeling. When I came to this country, in 1939, I was the same age you are now. I didn't want to come here. I wanted to stay in China. There I didn't have to think about being Chinese all the time. Everyone there was Chinese! So I just felt like a *person*. But here, being Chinese made me stand out.

46 **GRACE:** What do you mean?

**CLOSE READ**

## Vocabulary in Context

The word *straight* can be an adjective that means "without a curve" or a adverb that means "directly."

Use context clues within the sentence to determine the meaning of the word *straight* in paragraph 44.

Underline the context clues that support your definition.

## Identify Play Elements

Underline dialogue that contains questions that another character answers in the scene.

**immigrants** people who come to live in another country

**47 GRANDMA MEI:** When my family came to America, we had a difficult time at first. There was so much we had to learn—and so many questions we had to answer.

**48 GRACE:** I don't understand. Why was it so hard?

**49 GRANDMA MEI:** Well, it's complicated. All ships carrying Chinese immigrants had to land at a place called Angel Island, so that's where my family went. We were frightened. It was all so new to us.

**50 GRACE:** What happened there?

**51 GRANDMA MEI:** We stayed in a crowded building. We had to sleep on bunk beds. I didn't even know what a bunk bed was! I remember they gave us oatmeal for breakfast—I thought it was the worst thing I'd ever tasted! I wanted rice and eggs, like we had at home.

**52 GRACE:** I don't understand. Why did you have to stay at Angel Island?

ANGEL ISLAND

San Francisco

San Francisco Bay

53 **GRANDMA MEI:** The law said that all Chinese immigrants had to go to Angel Island. We were all assigned numbers. When they called my number, I had to go to an interview. At the interview, American officials asked us a lot of questions. I remember they asked me strange things like, "How many windows are in your house in China?"

54 **GRACE:** Why would they need to know *that*?

55 **GRANDMA MEI:** They wanted to make sure we were who we claimed to be. If I said there were 10 windows in our house, and my mother said there were 16 windows in our house, they might think we weren't really related to each other. Of course, I was only 8. I didn't even know how many windows were in our house, but I knew I wanted permission to stay in the U.S.

**CLOSE READ**

## Monitor Comprehension

Highlight sentences you can reread to monitor your comprehension of how Grandma Mei's dialogue informs the audience about the interview in this scene.

**interview** a formal meeting where one or more persons questions another person

**permission** formal or official approval to do something

**Vocabulary in Context**

Use context clues within the sentence to determine the meaning of the phrase *settled into* in paragraph 59.

Underline the context clue that supports your definition.

56 **GRACE:** But they let you stay in America anyway, right?

57 **GRANDMA MEI:** Yes. We were at Angel Island for two long weeks. We waited and answered questions and more questions. And we got medical exams. Finally, we were allowed to come to Chicago. We were so excited. Can you imagine?

58 **GRACE:** That's quite a story. You went through a lot to become an American, Grandma.

59 **GRANDMA MEI:** Well, it happened a long time ago. We settled into our new lives here, and after a while we started to feel at home. I'm just telling you all this now because—

60 **GRACE:** Grandma, I know why you're telling me. It's part of my heritage.

61 **GRANDMA MEI:** I know you don't like that word, but yes, that's partly why. We went through a great deal to make our home here. I'm proud and happy that you consider yourself American. But I want you to be proud of your background, too.

62 **GRACE:** I am, Grandma! It's just that sometimes it seems as though everyone wants me to be more Chinese than American.

63 **GRANDMA MEI** *(quietly)*: We just don't want you to forget that you're both.

64 **GRACE:** I know.

65 **GRANDMA MEI:** I told you about Angel Island for another reason, too. Remember that girl who's starting at your school tomorrow—the one who just moved here from China?

66 **GRACE:** Wendi. Did she have to stay at Angel Island, too?

67 **GRANDMA MEI:** No! Wendi didn't have to go through Angel Island, but coming to live in a new country is always difficult. America is a land of opportunity, but it's still hard in many ways. Take it from me!

68 **GRACE:** You're right, Grandma. I promise I'll help Wendi feel at home in Chicago. It'll be fun! I wonder if she's ever eaten American food before.

69 **GRANDMA MEI:** Probably. American fast food is all over China now, but she's never had Chicago pizza! And as we both know—

70 **GRACE and GRANDMA MEI** *(together)*: Chicago pizza is the BEST!

**Monitor Comprehension**
Highlight stage directions that help you infer the characters' feelings.

## Identify Play Elements

Underline details that help you identify how the setting of scene 4 is different from the setting of other scenes.

## Vocabulary in Context

**Idioms** are phrases or expressions whose meaning cannot be understood from the ordinary meaning of the words that form them.

Underline the idiom in paragraph 76 to identify it. Then underline the context clue in paragraph 78 that helps you explain its meaning. Finally, use the idiom in an original sentence.

## Scene 4

71 *It's Monday, one week later.* GRACE *is outside her school at recess. She is talking to* WENDI *in the schoolyard.*

72 **GRACE:** My mom told me you'd be starting school today. I'm glad you're in my class!

73 **WENDI:** My mother told me about you, too! I almost feel as if I know you already. We are the same in many ways.

74 **GRACE:** Yup! We both have moms who are doctors. And we both have grandparents who moved here a long time ago.

75 **WENDI:** What is *yup*? My English is not as good as yours.

76 **GRACE:** It means "yes." Your English sounds perfect to me! Anyway, I was born here, so I had a head start.

77 **WENDI:** *Head start*? What is that?

78 **GRACE:** It just means I had more time to learn English. I grew up speaking it, but I can't speak much Chinese at all.

79 **WENDI:** I can help you learn Chinese if you like!

80 **GRACE:** That would be great. And I can help you—umm—

81 **WENDI** *(pointing to some students playing a game in the corner of the playground)*: You can help me understand what those children are doing!

82 **GRACE:** Oh, that's a game called Four Square. Let's go check it out!

83 **WENDI:** *Check it out?*

84 (GRACE *smiles, takes* WENDI's *arm, and leads her over to the game.)*

85 **WENDI** *(as she watches the students play)*: I wonder if our grandparents were at Angel Island at the same time. We should have them meet!

86 **GRACE:** That's a great idea. Maybe your family can come over for dinner some night. I'll ask my parents.

87 **WENDI:** Or you can come to our house! This weekend, my grandfather is making a big Chinese feast. He wants to celebrate our arrival in America. I will ask if your family can come!

CLOSE READ

**Monitor Comprehension**

Highlight stage directions that help you monitor your comprehension of the characters' actions in the scene.

**arrival** the act of coming to a place

**Monitor Comprehension**

Highlight dialogue that helps you understand how Grace's feelings have changed from scene 1 to scene 5.

## Scene 5

88 *It's Monday afternoon.* GRACE *has just come home from school. She is talking to* GRANDMA MEI *on the front steps of their apartment building.*

89 **GRANDMA MEI:** Did you meet Wendi Zhang today, Grace?

90 **GRACE:** Yes! She's in my class! She's really nice. She speaks English so well, too! Maybe someday I can speak Chinese that well.

91 **GRANDMA MEI** (*smiling*)**:** There's an old Chinese saying. *Wàn shì kāi tóu nán.* It means "all things are difficult before they are easy." You will learn Chinese if you put your mind to it.

92 **GRACE:** It would be fun to speak Chinese with you, Grandma—and with Wendi, too.

93 **GRANDMA MEI:** I'm glad you have a new friend. She's lucky to have met you! I'm sure she must feel overwhelmed.

94 **GRACE:** She seemed pretty calm for someone who just moved to a new country. I don't think she had to go through the same interview you did, Grandma.

95 **GRANDMA MEI:** Yes, I'm glad she didn't have to remember how many windows are in her old home! Now when are you going to bring her over for pizza?

96 **GRACE:** Oh, that reminds me! Wendi wants to invite us over to her house. She said her grandfather is making a Chinese feast this weekend. It's going to be a party!

97 **GRANDMA MEI:** Wendi's grandfather, eh? He is the one who came to America around the same time I did—is that right?

98 **GRACE:** That's him! I think you two might have a lot to talk about, Grandma. (GRACE *winks*.)

99 **GRANDMA MEI:** I hope you're winking because you have something in your eye, Grace.

100 **GRACE:** Maybe, maybe not!

# Develop Vocabulary

In plays and other works of fiction, authors choose precise words to describe events. These words help readers imagine what is described.

**My TURN** Write the correct vocabulary word from the word bank in the first column, using the synonym or antonym clue provided. Then fill in the missing synonym or antonym and use the vocabulary word in a sentence about the play.

**Word Bank**

immigrants     interview     permission     arrival

| Vocabulary Word | Synonym | Antonym | Sentence |
|---|---|---|---|
| immigrants | newcomers | natives | Many immigrants had to stay on Angel Island. |
| | | denial | |
| | | departure | |
| | questioning | | |

# Check for Understanding

**My TURN** Look back at the text to answer the questions.

**1.** What identifies *Grace and Grandma* as a drama?

**2.** Why does the author have Wendi asking questions about the meanings of words or phrases in paragraphs 75, 77, and 83?

**3.** What can you conclude about how Grandma Mei feels about her Chinese heritage?

**4.** How can you connect the Chinese saying "All things are difficult before they are easy" to Grace's challenges?

# Identify Play Elements

**Play elements** include characters, scenes, settings, stage directions, and dialogue. Identifying how these elements build upon each other will help you better understand the play.

1. **My TURN** Go to the Close Read notes in *Grace and Grandma* and underline parts that help you identify play elements.

2. **Text Evidence** Use some of the parts you underlined to complete the chart.

| Question | Underlined Text Evidence | Play Element |
|---|---|---|
| Who are all the people in the play? | "DAD; GRACE LIU, **age** 8; GRANDMA MEI; MOM; WENDI ZHANG, **age** 8" | characters |
| When and where does scene 2 take place? | | |
| What does Grace ask in scene 3 that causes Grandma Mei to describe her experience at Angel Island? | | |
| What does Grace do in paragraph 98? | | |

Explain how the scenes build upon each other to help you understand the play.

# Monitor Comprehension

While reading a drama, readers **monitor comprehension** to make sure they understand what they read. When their understanding breaks down, readers might reread, use background knowledge, ask questions, or annotate.

1. **My TURN** Go back to the Close Read notes and highlight details that help you monitor your comprehension of the drama.

2. **Text Evidence** Use some of your highlighted details to show how you monitored your comprehension of these details.

| Question | Highlighted Text Details | How I Checked My Understanding |
|---|---|---|
| Who speaks in scene 1? | "DAD", "GRACE", and "GRANDMA MEI" | I reread the characters' names. |
| How are the characters speaking at the end of scene 3? | | |
| What are Grace's actions in paragraph 84? | | |
| In scene 5, how does Grace feel about speaking Chinese? | | |

# Reflect and Share

**Talk About It** In scenes 1 and 2 of the play, Grace does not want to learn Chinese. By scene 5, she changes her mind about learning Chinese. Consider all of the texts you have read in this unit. What are the most effective ways to change someone's opinion about a topic? Use evidence from the play and the other texts to support your opinion.

- - - - - - - - - - - - - - - - - - - - - - - - - - - - - - - - - - - - - - - - -

**Use Text Evidence** When discussing an opinion, it is important to use text evidence to support your ideas.

- ◎ Locate text details that support your opinion.

- ◎ If necessary, identify which part of the text you are using to support your ideas.

- ◎ Quote from the text to support your ideas. Include the scene numbers where your quotes appear.

Make thoughtful comments when discussing your opinion. Use these sentence starters in your discussion:

In my opinion, . . .

In scene 1, . . .

- - - - - - - - - - - - - - - - - - - - - - - - - - - - - - - - - - - - - - - - -

**Weekly Question**

How do people support each other in difficult times?

# Academic Vocabulary

**Parts of Speech** are the categories of words.

- **nouns:** words naming people, places, or things
- **verbs:** words that tell what something or someone is or does
- **adjectives:** words describing nouns
- **adverbs:** words that tell how, when, or where something happens

Words can often be used as more than one part of speech.

**My TURN**  For each sentence below,

**1.** **Underline** the form of the academic vocabulary word. Identify the word's part of speech.

**2.** **Write** your own sentence using a different form of the word. Identify the new part of speech.

**3.** **Use** a print or digital dictionary as needed.

| Sentence | Part of Speech | My Sentence |
|---|---|---|
| The benefit to waking up early is being on time to catch the bus. | | |
| As a consumer, I buy products at the store. | | |
| She knew her mom was cooking stew due to the familiar smell. | | |

# Homophones

**Homophones** are words with the same pronunciation but different meanings and spellings. Some examples include *their–there*, *peace–piece*, and *to–too–two*. Be careful to use the correct word for the context.

**My TURN**  Reread paragraphs 10 and 11 in *Grace and Grandma*. Identify a pair of homophones and explain their meanings in the text. Then, use the homophones in sentences of your own.

Homophones in text: _____ _____

Meaning in text: _____

_____

Your sentences: _____

_____

# High-Frequency Words

**High-frequency words** are commonly used in text. Often they do not follow regular word study patterns. Read these high-frequency words: *government, material*. Try to identify them in your independent reading.

# Read Like a Writer

An **author's message** is an idea the author wants readers to understand. Analyzing word choices can help you identify the message.

**Model** ! Read the passage from *Grace and Grandma*.

> DAD: Yes, you do know why. Everyone in our family speaks Chinese. It's an important part of our heritage.

Word choice emphasizes the message.

1. **Identify** Rich Lo emphasizes his message by using the descriptive adjective *important*.

2. **Question** What does this word show about the author's message?

3. **Conclude** It shows that the author's message is that parts of a person's heritage are worth keeping.

Read the passage.

> GRANDMA MEI: . . . I'm proud and happy that you consider yourself American. But I want you to be proud of your background, too.

**My TURN** Follow the steps to analyze the passage. Describe how the author's word choice helps you understand his message.

1. **Identify** Rich Lo emphasizes his message by using the descriptive word _____.

2. **Question** What does this word show about the author's message?

3. **Conclude** It shows that the author's message is that _____

_____.

# Write for a Reader

Writers share messages with readers. To make sure their message is understood, writers use precise language or descriptive words.

Use descriptive adjectives to emphasize your message

**My TURN** Think about how Rich Lo uses descriptive adjectives to emphasize his message about heritage. Think of a message you want to give readers about the value of friendship. Plan how to use language to make your message understood.

1. What message could you give readers about the value of friendship? What descriptive words could you use to emphasize this message?

_____

_____

2. Write about a character who learns a new skill through friendship. Emphasize your message by using descriptive adjectives.

_____

_____

_____

_____

_____

3. Explain how your use of descriptive adjectives helps make your message clear.

_____

_____

# Spell Homophones

**Homophones** are words that sound alike but have different spellings and meanings. You have to remember how to spell the correct homophone based on how it is used.

**My TURN** Sort the words into homophone pairs. Write each pair on the lines, alphabetizing the words. If a pair of homophones starts with the same two letters, use the third letter in each word to alphabetize the words. Then, on a separate sheet of paper, choose a homophone pair, explain the words' meanings, and use each word in a sentence.

**SPELLING WORDS**

| | | |
|---|---|---|
| ate | sell | deer |
| cell | duel | paws |
| dear | eight | dual |
| pause | | |

_____          _____

_____          _____

_____          _____

# High-Frequency Words

Write the following high-frequency words on the lines.

government _____

material _____

# Adverbs

An **adverb** is a word that can tell how, when, or where something happens. Adverbs tell more about the actions named by verbs. Adverbs can come before or after the verbs they describe. Adverbs that tell how something happens or happened often end in *-ly*.

| Adverbs That Tell | Examples |
|---|---|
| How | carefully, easily, extremely, fast |
| When | again, always, later, never, now |
| Where | behind, far, inside, out, there |

**My TURN** Edit this draft by adding four adverbs to make the paragraph more descriptive.

I was tired. I did not want to go to the store to help my abuela talk to the manager. We had to walk to get there.

I did not understand why she could not learn English. I had learned it. I asked her in English, "Why don't you try to go on your own this time?"

# Use Technology to Publish Written Work

**Learning Goal**

I can use elements of opinion writing to write an opinion essay.

Many authors choose to publish their writing, or make it available for audiences to read. Authors may publish their work in print, such as magazines, or they may use technology to publish it digitally, such as a blog. If they choose to publish using word-processing software, they will need keyboarding skills.

| Importance of Keyboarding Skills | |
| --- | --- |
| **Benefit** | **Explanation** |
| Faster typing | Learning the keyboard improves speed. |
| More accurate typing | Practicing keyboarding skills results in fewer typing mistakes. |
| Higher quality of published work | Follow your teacher's guidelines for typing a final draft with word-processing software. |

**My TURN** Produce a draft of your opinion essay using a computer. Use the checklist to help you focus on your keyboarding skills.

**WHEN I TYPE MY DRAFT,**

☐ I put my name and the date at the top of the page.

☐ I set the title in bold type and center it.

☐ I use the tab key to indent paragraphs.

☐ I press the return key at the end of each paragraph.

☐ I choose a font, or kind of lettering, that is easy to read.

**401**

# Edit for Spelling

To edit your opinion essay for correct spelling, highlight or underline words that might be misspelled. Then follow these steps for each word:

1. **Spell the word as best you can.** Use what you already know about letter sounds and spelling patterns. Recall spelling rules you have learned this year. Look for high-frequency words you know how to spell correctly.

2. **Look up in a print or online dictionary** any word you are not sure how to spell.

3. **Read the definition** to make sure it is the right word.

4. **If you cannot find the word:**

   - Scan the nearby entry words.

   - Look up other possible spellings of the word.

   - Ask for help from peers or adults.

**My TURN** Edit the draft sentences below. Fix the underlined, misspelled words by writing the correct spelling on the line. Remember to use the spelling patterns and rules you have learned as well as the correct spelling of high-frequency words.

1. Brandon is my best <u>freind</u>. _____
2. I am wearing a jacket <u>becuze</u> it is cold. _____
3. You are <u>allways</u> on time for school. _____
4. <u>They're</u> several ways to get to school. _____
5. My favorite part of every meal is <u>desert</u>. _____
6. I wrote my essay on the <u>computur</u>. _____
7. On my birthday, I <u>recieved</u> a lot of great gifts. _____

# Publish and Celebrate

A writer might publish an opinion essay to a particular audience for the following reasons:

- to express thoughts and feelings
- to bring attention to a topic
- to affect the way people think or act
- to change something in the world

**My TURN**  After you publish your opinion essay, complete these sentences about your experience. Write legibly in cursive. Leave spaces between words so your writing is easy to read.

The reasons I chose this topic are _____

_____

_____ .

I organized my opinion essay by _____

_____

_____ .

My opinion essay is persuasive because _____

_____

_____ .

In the future, I would also like to share my opinion on these topics:

_____

_____ .

# Prepare for Assessment

MyTURN Follow a plan as you prepare to write an opinion essay in response to a prompt.

## 1. Study the prompt.

Read the prompt. Underline the kind of writing you will do. Highlight the main idea or topic you will write about.

**Prompt:** Write an opinion essay about whether a third-grader should own a smartphone.

## 2. Brainstorm.

Clearly state your topic and opinion in one sentence. Then the rest of the essay will follow more easily.

## 3. Organize and plan your opinion essay.

Think of several reasons for your opinion. Then think about how to back up those reasons with supporting facts.

## 4. Write your draft.

Start with an introduction. Then organize your supporting reasons and facts. Finally, end with a conclusion that restates your opinion and reason for it.

## 5. Revise and edit your opinion essay.

Use the skills you have learned to make changes and corrections as needed.

Using a graphic organizer can help you organize reasons and facts.

# Assessment

**My TURN** Before you write an opinion essay for your assessment, rate how well you understand the skills you have learned in this unit. Go back and review any skills you mark "No."

|  |  | Yes | No |
|---|---|---|---|
| **Ideas and Organization** | ◐ I can brainstorm and develop a topic and opinion. | ☐ | ☐ |
|  | ◐ I can plan an opinion essay. | ☐ | ☐ |
|  | ◐ I can develop and organize reasons and facts. | ☐ | ☐ |
|  | ◐ I can distinguish between fact and opinion. | ☐ | ☐ |
| **Craft** | ◐ I can revise by adding details to text. | ☐ | ☐ |
|  | ◐ I can write a clear and organized introduction. | ☐ | ☐ |
|  | ◐ I can write a persuasive conclusion. | ☐ | ☐ |
|  | ◐ I can use technology to publish writing. | ☐ | ☐ |
| **Conventions** | ◐ I can use capitalization correctly. | ☐ | ☐ |
|  | ◐ I can edit for spelling. | ☐ | ☐ |
|  | ◐ I can revise by adding linking words. | ☐ | ☐ |
|  | ◐ I can peer edit and incorporate peer and teacher suggestions into my work. | ☐ | ☐ |

## UNIT THEME
# Events

**TURN and TALK** Trait Snapshot
With a partner, look back at the Unit 4 texts. Choose a trait, or characteristic, to describe each person, group, or main character. Find a sentence in the text that supports the trait you selected. Write the sentence and discuss how it relates to the unit theme of *Events*.

**WEEK 3**

## *from* Milton Hershey

**Milton Hershey**

**BOOK CLUB**

**WEEK 2**

## *from* Frederick Douglass

**Frederick Douglass**

**BOOK CLUB**

**WEEK 1**

## The House That Jane Built

**Jane Addams**

BOOK
CLUB

## Green City

**The residents of Greensburg**

_____

_____

BOOK
CLUB

## Grace and Grandma

**Grace**

_____

_____

_____

## Essential Question

**My TURN**

In your notebook, answer the Essential Question: **How do communities change over time?**

BOOK
CLUB

WEEK
6

_Project_

Now it is time to apply what you learned about events in your **WEEK 6 PROJECT: Past and Present.**

# PAST and PRESENT

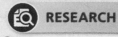
## Activity

All communities change over time. New homes and buildings are built. Older buildings are repaired or removed. Where and how people live changes, too. Create an informational poster about how part of a city or town has changed.

## Research Articles

With your partner, read "From Wood to Stone" to generate questions you have about the inquiry topic. With help from an adult, make a research plan for creating your informational poster.

**1** From Wood to Stone

**2** Yankee Stadium: Then and Now

**3** History in the Making

## Generate Questions

**COLLABORATE** Read "From Wood to Stone." Then generate three questions you have about the article. Share your questions with the class.

1. _____

2. _____

3. _____

# Use Academic Words

In this unit, you learned many words related to the theme of *Events*. Work with your partner to add more academic vocabulary words to each category. If appropriate, use this vocabulary in your informational poster.

| Academic Vocabulary | Word Forms | Synonyms | Antonyms |
|---|---|---|---|
| benefit | benefits<br>benefited<br>beneficial | help<br>asset<br>advantage | problem<br>drawback<br>disadvantage |
| generation | generations<br>generate<br>generated | age group<br>era | individual |
| advice | advise<br>advisor | guidance<br>opinion<br>suggestion | question |
| consumer | consume<br>consumed<br>consumable | buyer<br>user<br>customer | salesperson<br>seller |
| familiar | familiarly<br>familiarity<br>familiarize | usual<br>known<br>ordinary | unusual<br>unknown<br>unfamiliar |

# Inform with Purpose

Writers choose a text structure to organize ideas logically.

**Informational text** informs readers about real people, events, or the natural world. When reading informational text, evaluate details and look for

- text features such as bold and italicized words;
- text features such as images, tables, or graphs;
- the main, or most important, idea in the text;
- facts and details that support the main idea;
- clues to the author's purpose for writing; and
- a specific text structure, or organization of ideas.

 **RESEARCH**

**COLLABORATE** Read "Yankee Stadium: Then and Now" with your partner. Then, answer the questions about the text.

**1.** What is the author's purpose for writing the text?

_____

_____

**2.** How does the author use text features to support the topic?

_____

_____

**3.** How is the information in the article organized? How does this organization help the reader understand the text?

_____

_____

# Plan Your Research

**COLLABORATE** Before you begin researching how part of a city or town has changed, you will need to make a research plan. Use this activity to help you make a plan.

| Research Steps and Example | My Poster |
|---|---|
| **SET A PURPOSE:** What is the purpose, or reason, you are making an informational poster?<br><br>**Example:** The purpose of my poster is to identify and describe wildlife in a park in my state. | The purpose of my informational poster is to<br><br>_____<br><br>_____ |
| **IDENTIFY THE TOPIC:** What will people learn by reading your poster?<br><br>**Example:** My poster will describe the park and identify one bird, one reptile, and one mammal found in the park. | My poster will<br><br>_____<br><br>_____<br><br>_____ |
| **LIST RESEARCH GOALS:** What information will you research to support your topic?<br><br>**Example:** I will research facts and details about a bird, reptile, and mammal that live in the park. I will also find an image of each animal. | I will do research to find<br><br>1. _____<br><br>2. _____<br><br>3. _____ |

Share your research plan with your partner. Add any suggestions to the chart.

# WORLD'S Largest LIBRARY

Libraries contain many types of texts, including multimedia and digital texts. The **Library of Congress** is the national library of the United States. It is also the largest library in the world, with more than 164 million books, photographs, maps, and other documents. The Library of Congress is located in Washington, D.C., but people can explore its collections online.

**EXAMPLE** Molly wants to find historical information and images about wildlife in national parks. She decides to explore the Library of Congress Web site. How can she search the Library of Congress online?

**Search a Topic** Type keywords related to your topic into the "Search Loc.gov" box. Then, click on the magnifying glass to find the information.

https://www.loc.gov/

 LIBRARY OF CONGRESS

All Formats | Search Loc.gov | 🔍

**All Formats**
Audio Recordings
Books/Printed Materials
Films, Videos
Legislation
Manuscripts/Mixed Material
Maps
Notated Music
Newspapers
Periodicals
Personal Narratives
Photos, Prints, Drawings
Software, E-Resources
Archived Web Sites
Web Pages
3D Objects

**Select the Format** The Library of Congress Web site lets you search a variety of formats, or types of sources, in the library's collections. Click on the arrow in the All Formats box and highlight the format you want to search. For example, highlight "Photos, Prints, Drawings" to find images related to your topic.

**COLLABORATE** With your partner, review your research plan and your goals. Use the Library of Congress Web site to identify and gather relevant facts, details, and images for your poster.

Research Goal 1:

Keywords:

Format (Print or Digital Text):

Notes:

Research Goal 2:

Keywords:

Format (Print or Digital Text):

Notes:

Discuss your search results. Do you need to change your keywords? Should you select a different format or type of text?

# Keep Me POSTED!

An **informational poster** tells key information about a topic. Informational posters are a mix of text and images meant to provide important information.

Before you begin developing your informational poster, answer the following questions:

- What is the purpose of your informational poster?
- What is the topic of your poster?
- Which facts and details will you use to support your topic?
- What images about the topic will you include on your poster?
- How will you organize the text and images?

> **COLLABORATE** Read the Student Model. Work with your partner to recognize the characteristics of an informative poster.

## Now You Try It!

Discuss the checklist with your partner. Work together to follow the steps as you create your informational poster.

**Make sure your informational poster**

☐ shows a title that identifies the topic.

☐ states facts and details that support the topic.

☐ includes photos, illustrations, maps, or other images.

☐ displays all text and images with clear organization.

## Student Model

# Wildlife at Big Bend

Big Bend National Park is in western Texas along the border of Mexico. Hundreds of animal species live in Big Bend. Here are some animals you might see during a visit to the park.

## Reptiles

crevice spiny lizard

Big Bend is home to 56 species of reptiles. The diamondback rattlesnake and crevice spiny lizard are two kinds of reptiles that live in Big Bend.

## Mammals

Some of Big Bend's mammals, such as the kit fox and bobcat, avoid the desert heat by sleeping during the day and searching for food at night. Others, such as the blacktail jackrabbit and badger, are active during the day.

blacktail jackrabbit

## Birds

Lucifer hummingbird

More than 450 species of birds have been seen in Big Bend! The tiny Lucifer hummingbird and the Western screech owl make their home in Big Bend.

# Identify Sources

When you use information from a source, identify it as a primary source or a secondary source.

A **primary source** provides firsthand evidence of an event or topic. Examples of primary sources include the following:

- photographs
- speeches
- interviews

- diaries
- letters
- autobiographies

A **secondary source** provides information from someone who does not have firsthand knowledge of an event or topic. Examples of secondary sources include the following:

- textbooks
- encyclopedias

- newspapers
- biographies

 **RESEARCH**

**COLLABORATE** Read "History in the Making." Work with your partner to identify primary and secondary sources referenced in the article. Discuss how you were able to identify the sources.

| Description of Source | Type of Source (Primary or Secondary) | How I Identified the Source Type |
|---|---|---|
|  |  |  |
|  |  |  |
|  |  |  |

Read the article and answer the questions.

# Protecting a Natural Treasure

by Jonathan Garcia

In 1933, Texas established Big Bend State Park to protect land along the Rio Grande River. However, visiting the area was not easy. There were steep mountains and few roads. Between 1934 and 1942, workers built trails and roadways through the park.

Plans were made to make Big Bend a national park. In a 1940 speech, President Franklin Roosevelt said, "We are living under governments that are proving their devotion to national parks . . . I hope, [we] will have another one for us to dedicate, the Big Bend Park away down in Texas, close to the Mexican line." On June 12, 1940, Big Bend became a national park.

**1.** What primary source is in the article? Why is it a primary source?

_____

_____

**2.** Is the article "Protecting a Natural Treasure" a primary or a secondary source? Explain.

_____

_____

# Picture IT!

Add information to digital texts, such as slide shows, by including images, such as illustrations and photographs. Combine words and images to help readers better understand the topic.

Include **illustrations**, such as drawings or other artwork, to capture readers' interest and help them imagine details.

**Wildlife roams freely in a state park.**

Use **photographs** to provide exact details about real people, places, and things.

**Deer are a common sight in state parks.**

**COLLABORATE** With your partner, brainstorm which types of images would best support the topic of your poster. Take notes by recording your ideas and describe how each image would support your topic. Then, conduct research to find or create images for your informational poster.

## Images That Support My Topic

Type of image:

Information the image would provide about my topic:

Source:

Type of image:

Information the image would provide about my topic:

Source:

Type of image:

Information the image would provide about my topic:

Source:

# Revise

**Clarity and Coherence** Reread your informational poster with your partner. Have you included

☐ brief and concise text about the topic?

☐ clear sentences that work together as a whole and are easy for readers to understand?

☐ facts and details that clearly support the topic?

## Revise for Clarity and Coherence

In her first draft, the creator of the poster on Big Bend National Park noticed that the text in her introduction was too long and difficult to understand. She revised her text to improve her sentence structures by adding, deleting, and rearranging ideas for coherence and clarity.

Big Bend National Park is ~~located~~ in ~~an area of~~

western Texas along the border of Mexico. ~~and includes~~

~~miles of U.S. land along the Rio Grande River.~~ ~~In~~
Hundreds of animal species live in Big Bend.
~~Big Bend, there are many types of animals and habitats~~
Here are some animals you might see during a visit to
~~that people can see when they visit the park.~~ ~~Hundreds~~
the park.
~~of animal species live in Big Bend.~~

# Edit

**Conventions** Read your informational poster again. Have you used correct writing conventions?

- [ ] spelling
- [ ] capitalization of proper nouns
- [ ] punctuation, including apostrophes in contractions and possessives
- [ ] commas in compound sentences and items in a series

## Peer Review

**COLLABORATE** Exchange informational posters with another group. As you read, look for characteristics of an informational poster, such as a title and informational text and images. Discuss how the organization of the posters supports the authors' purposes. Suggest edits for coherence and clarity.

# Time to Celebrate!

**COLLABORATE** Decide how you will deliver your informational poster to classmates. Rehearse your presentation, remembering to make eye contact with your audience. Speak clearly at an understandable rate and volume. Then present the poster. After presenting, allow time for questions and comments. Be sure to respond politely.

What questions or comments did classmates have about your poster? Write some of their reactions.

_____

_____

_____

# Reflect on Your Project

**My TURN** Think about your informational poster. Which parts of your poster are the strongest? Which parts could you improve? Write your thoughts.

## Strengths

_____

_____

## Areas of Improvement

_____

_____

## Reflect on Your Goals

Look back at your unit goals. Use a different color to rate yourself again.

## Reflect on Your Reading

What did you learn from the texts that you selected to read for independent reading during this unit?

_____

_____

_____

_____

_____

## Reflect on Your Writing

What did you enjoy most about writing an opinion essay?

_____

_____

_____

_____

_____

_____

# Solutions

## Essential Question

How does the world challenge us?

▶ Watch

**"Our Challenging World"**

**TURN and TALK**

How can people find solutions for the challenges they face?

SAVVAS
realize™

Go ONLINE for
all lessons.

▶ VIDEO

🔊 AUDIO

👆 INTERACTIVITY

🎮 GAME

✏ ANNOTATE

📖 BOOK

🔍 RESEARCH

## Spotlight on Informational Text

### READING-WRITING BRIDGE

- Academic Vocabulary • Word Study • **Read Like a Writer**
- **Write for a Reader** • Spelling • Language and Conventions

### WRITING WORKSHOP

- Introduce and Immerse • Develop Elements          **Poetry**
- Develop Structure • Writer's Craft
- Publish, Celebrate, and Assess

### PROJECT-BASED INQUIRY

- Inquire • Research • Collaborate

# Independent Reading

You will read informational texts, historical fiction, and traditional tales in this unit. Consider what you would like to read for your independent reading. If you decide on an informational text, use its text features to help you understand what you are reading. The boldfaced headings and photo captions highlight the topics as you read. The details in those features will help you explore more information on those topics.

Choose a genre and complete the Connections Box as you read. Consider ways your chosen text connects to what you know from other texts, from your life, and from the world. For example, you might make a connection to society by noticing how events in the text affect people in other countries.

| CONNECTIONS BOX | |
|---|---|
| MY BOOK'S GENRE | How is this text similar to other texts you have read? |
| MY BOOK'S TITLE | How does this text connect with what you know from your life? |
| MY BOOK'S AUTHOR | How does this text connect with what you know about the world around you? |

# Independent Reading Log

| Date | Book | Genre | Pages Read | Minutes Read | My Ratings |
|------|------|-------|-----------|--------------|------------|
|      |      |       |           |              | ☆☆☆☆☆ |
|      |      |       |           |              |            |
|      |      |       |           |              |            |
|      |      |       |           |              |            |
|      |      |       |           |              |            |
|      |      |       |           |              |            |
|      |      |       |           |              |            |
|      |      |       |           |              |            |
|      |      |       |           |              |            |

# Unit Goals

Shade in the circle to rate how well you meet each goal now.

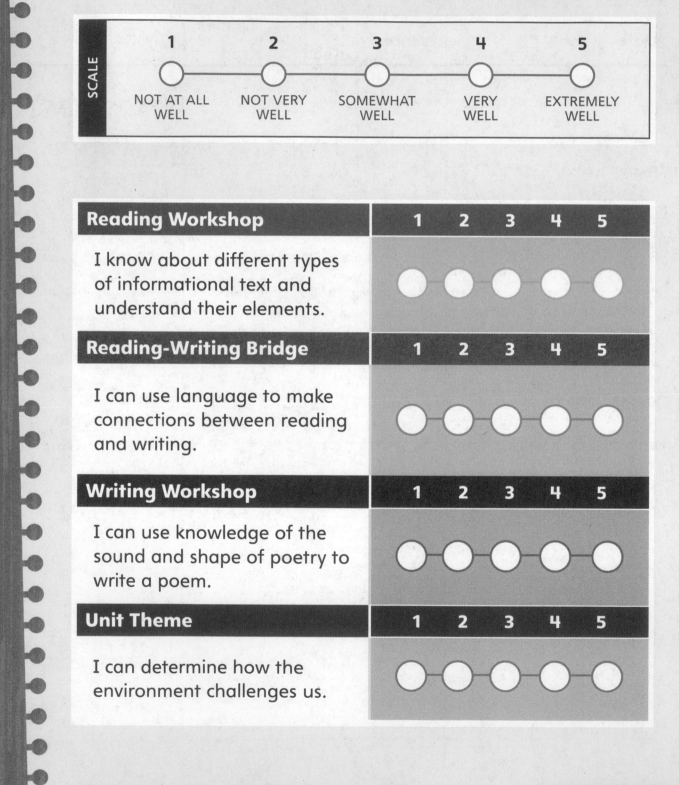

**SCALE**

| 1 | 2 | 3 | 4 | 5 |
|---|---|---|---|---|
| ○ | ○ | ○ | ○ | ○ |
| NOT AT ALL WELL | NOT VERY WELL | SOMEWHAT WELL | VERY WELL | EXTREMELY WELL |

**Reading Workshop**

| | 1 | 2 | 3 | 4 | 5 |
|---|---|---|---|---|---|
| I know about different types of informational text and understand their elements. | ○ | ○ | ○ | ○ | ○ |

**Reading-Writing Bridge**

| | 1 | 2 | 3 | 4 | 5 |
|---|---|---|---|---|---|
| I can use language to make connections between reading and writing. | ○ | ○ | ○ | ○ | ○ |

**Writing Workshop**

| | 1 | 2 | 3 | 4 | 5 |
|---|---|---|---|---|---|
| I can use knowledge of the sound and shape of poetry to write a poem. | ○ | ○ | ○ | ○ | ○ |

**Unit Theme**

| | 1 | 2 | 3 | 4 | 5 |
|---|---|---|---|---|---|
| I can determine how the environment challenges us. | ○ | ○ | ○ | ○ | ○ |

# Academic Vocabulary

Use these vocabulary words to talk and write about this unit's theme, *Solutions*: *analysis*, *threat*, *damage*, *anticipate*, and *pollution*.

**TURN and TALK** Read the words and definitions in the chart. Check the box to show how much you know about each word. Then compare charts with a partner and talk about the words you know.

| Academic Vocabulary | Definition | I do not know this word. | I have seen the word but did not know the meaning. | I know this word and can use it in a sentence. |
| --- | --- | --- | --- | --- |
| analysis | the study of something in great detail | | | |
| threat | something that may cause harm or danger | | | |
| damage | harm done to something so that it is broken or injured | | | |
| anticipate | to expect something to happen | | | |
| pollution | something that makes a place dirty, unsafe, or not suitable to use | | | |

 INTERACTIVITY

# NATURE ROCKS

**1845–1846:** Writer Henry David Thoreau lives alone in a cabin in the woods. Later, he writes a book, *Walden*, about his experiences living in nature.

**1901–1909:** Theodore Roosevelt serves as president of the United States. During his time in office, the United States passes laws to keep many wild areas from being destroyed.

1825    1850    1875    1900    1925    1950

**1872:** Yellowstone National Park becomes the first U.S. national park. The government says that the park is "for the benefit and enjoyment of the people."

## Weekly Question

**How can nature change people's lives?**

**Quick Write** A time line shows events in order. Choose one event on the time line. Write a brief explanation that tells how you think it helped both nature and people.

**1973:** The Endangered Species Act becomes a law. The law protects animals and plants that are in danger of becoming extinct, which means dying out until there are no more left.

1975    2000    2025

**2000s:** Ecotourism becomes popular. Ecotourists go to new places to enjoy nature. They are careful not to disturb plants and animals.

431

Learning Goal

I can learn more about informational texts and analyze text features in an informational text.

**Spotlight on Genre**

# Informational Text

An **informational text** informs or explains by presenting facts. It may include

- An **introduction**, or general idea about a topic
- A **main idea**
- Important **details** to support the main idea
- Information about a **real person**, **place**, or **event**
- **Text features** that clarify or support understanding of the topic

Text features can show important information!

**TURN and TALK** With a partner, discuss a favorite informational text you have read. Use the Text Features Anchor Chart to explain how the author uses print and graphic features to help you understand the text. Take notes on your discussion.

My **NOTES**

_____

_____

_____

_____

_____

_____

# Text Features Anchor Chart

## Purpose
To emphasize, add, or support information

## Types of Text Features

★ photographs

★ section or chapter headings to organize information

★ illustrations, or drawings, to explain or show ideas

★ diagrams, graphs, or tables to provide numerical information

★ bullets or numbers to group information

★ bold or italic fonts to emphasize important words

**Shirin Yim Bridges** was born in Malaysia, spent much of her childhood in China, and moved to the United States to attend college. She has written many informational books on special places, people, and cultures. Her series of history books about real-life princesses from around the world has received national and international awards.

# Deep Down

## Preview Vocabulary

As you read *Deep Down*, pay attention to these vocabulary words. Notice what the words tell you about unusual places on Earth where people live.

| | | |
|---|---|---|
| extreme | | spectacular |
| attracts | region | transport |

## Read

Preview the images in the text. Use these features to make and record predictions about the text. Follow these strategies when you read this **informational text** the first time.

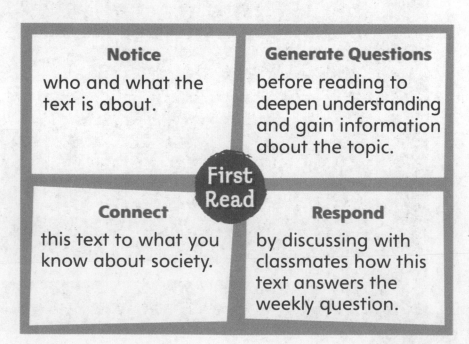

**Notice**
who and what the text is about.

**Generate Questions**
before reading to deepen understanding and gain information about the topic.

**First Read**

**Connect**
this text to what you know about society.

**Respond**
by discussing with classmates how this text answers the weekly question.

# Deep Down
## and Other Extreme Places to Live

BY SHIRIN YIM BRIDGES

 AUDIO

 ANNOTATE

# Life on Earth

## Correct or Confirm Predictions

Highlight a text feature that helps you correct or confirm a prediction you made about the topic of the text.

1   Most people on Earth live where it never gets very hot or very cold. More than half of all people in the world live in or near cities. More than half of all people in the world live within 100 miles of the sea.

2   Many of Earth's people live in quite similar places. When you watch a TV show, the places in which the characters live often don't look very different from where you might live.

3    But if you looked down at Earth from above, you wouldn't see many cities. A lot of Earth is jungle, mountains, deserts, or large areas of snow. What would it be like to live in some of these areas?

4    Let's meet some people living in extreme places.

## Analyze Text Features

Underline details about Earth that the definition of *extreme* helps you understand.

**extreme** far from normal or average

## Life at the Bottom of the Canyon

**Analyze Text Features**

<u>Underline</u> text details that help you explain the author's use of the map to achieve a specific purpose.

**spectacular** wonderful or very beautiful

5    Deep down at the bottom of the Grand Canyon, there is a village called Supai. You can only get to it by foot, horse, mule, or helicopter. The people who live there call themselves the Havasupai. This means "the people of the blue-green water."

6    The blue-green water is the beautiful Havasu Creek that flows through the canyon. There are also four spectacular waterfalls that tumble down into the canyon. The water keeps the land around the village green. Many people call this place a paradise. But living in a place that is so hard to get to has its problems!

### THE HAVASUPAI

**CLAIM TO FAME:** The Havasupai are the people of the blue-green water.

**HISTORY:** Havasupai have been living in the Grand Canyon for more than one thousand years!

**INDUSTRIES:** Farming, hunting, and tourism

# A Remote Paradise?

7    From the air, the Havasupai Creek looks like an emerald snake slithering between dry, red rock. In the past, the Havasupai farmed crops such as corn, squash, and fruit during the spring and summer. In fall and winter, the Havasupai moved higher up the canyon. They would hunt deer for food.

## Correct or Confirm Predictions

Highlight details in the text feature "Supai Village" that help you confirm or correct a prediction you made about the Havasupai's distance from others.

## SUPAI VILLAGE

**LOCATION:** On the Havasupai Reservation, near the southwest corner of the Grand Canyon National Park

**POPULATION:** Around 450 tribal members

**CLAIM TO FAME:** 3,000 feet down at the bottom of the Canyon

**CLOSEST NEIGHBORS:** Three to five hours away by foot, horse, or mule

Farming today on the canyon floor

Supai Village

**Analyze Text Features**

Underline a detail in the text feature "You've Got Mail" that is supported by the photo.

8   As the tribe grew, the Havasupai began to run out of farmland. This was not the only problem. Sometimes the canyon would flood too, damaging crops. They needed to find a new way to survive at the bottom of the canyon.

## You've Got Mail

Letters addressed to Supai are brought by mule train. It is the last U.S. Postal Service mule train left in the country!

# The Blue-Green Water

9    Nowadays, the Havasupai make a living from tourism. The famous canyon attracts more than 20,000 visitors per year. Most visitors make the three-to-five-hour journey to Supai on horseback or mule. The Havasupai now run campgrounds, a café, a trading post, and a lodge.

## Correct or Confirm Predictions

Highlight details that help you correct or confirm a prediction you made about how the Havasupai make a living in the canyon.

**attracts** interests or brings toward

## THE FOUR FALLS

**SUPAI FALLS:** Closest to the village

**NAVAJO FALLS:** ¼ mile beyond Supai Falls

**HAVASU FALLS:** ¾ mile beyond Navajo Falls

**MOONEY FALLS:** 1 mile beyond Havasu Falls. It is the highest of the falls, at 190 feet high.

Havasu Falls is the most photographed of the blue-green falls.

## Analyze Text Features

Underline text evidence that supports your understanding of the extreme weather in the Danakil Depression.

**region** area of land

# Surviving in One of Earth's Hottest Spots

Danakil • Depression

10   In the middle of the Great Rift Valley in Ethiopia is the Danakil Depression. This region looks like a different planet. It is one of the hottest spots on Earth. It is heated from above by the sun and from below by lava flows.

11   You would think that nobody would live here, but it is home to the Afar. The Afar are nomadic people who come to the Danakil Depression every day to mine salt.

## THE DANAKIL DEPRESSION

**CLAIM TO FAME:** Daily temperatures of more than 120°F!

**ALTITUDE:** 300 feet below sea level

**RAINFALL:** Less than 7 inches a year

**CLOSEST CITY:** Mek'ele, 60 miles away

## NOT A COOL BREEZE

Fire winds blow through the Danakil Depression. They are said to feel like a tornado in an oven!

# Afar Gold

12    Ten thousand years ago, the Danakil Depression was part of the Red Sea. The waters have evaporated and left behind salt flats. To the Afar, this salt is like gold. Until recently, blocks of salt called *amolé* were used as money in Ethiopia. Today, northern Afar people still earn money from selling salt.

# Camel Caravans

13    Every day, Afar miners come to the salt flats with around 2,000 camels and 1,000 donkeys. They transport amolé into the cities. The salt blocks are cut by hand. Everybody in the community takes part. The walk from town to the salt flats and back can take six days.

## THE SALT TRADE

**WEIGHT OF ONE SALT BLOCK, OR AMOLÉ:** About 9 pounds

**NUMBER OF BLOCKS PER CAMEL:** 30

**DISTANCE TRAVELED PER DAY:** 15.5 MILES

CLOSE READ

## Analyze Text Features

Underline details in paragraph 13 that are supported by information in the text feature "The Salt Trade."

**transport** carry or move from one place to another

## Vocabulary in Context

The term *shade* can mean "a tone of color." It can also mean "an area where heat and light from sun are blocked."

Use context clues within and before the sentence to determine the meaning of *shade* in paragraph 14.

Underline the context clues that support your definition.

# What Is Life Like in an Ari?

14    The Afar cross the Danakil Depression to mine salt. They then sell it in the cities. The Afar can do this because they bring their homes with them. They pack their houses, called *aris*, onto the backs of their camels. They usually put up their aris around wells. The aris are round, like igloos, and are made from light palm matting. They provide welcome shade in which to cook, eat and sleep.

The Afar live in huts called aris.

## WHAT'S COOKING?

**WHAT THE AFAR USUALLY EAT:** Meat

**WHAT THEY EAT IT WITH:** Thick wheat pancakes

**WHAT THE AFAR DRINK:** Milk

**HOW THE AFAR SAY "WELCOME":** They give their guests a drink of milk!

## HERDING ANIMALS

In addition to mining salt, most Afar herd sheep, goats, cattle, and camels.

## Correct or Confirm Predictions

Highlight details in two text features that help you correct or confirm a prediction you made about where the Sami live.

# Roaming in the Arctic Circle

Arctic Circle

Sami homeland

15    Did you know there are people who use reindeer to pull their sleds? The Sami people do this. In the past, the Sami spent their lives roaming the Arctic. They followed the enormous reindeer herds.

## THE SAMI HOMELAND

**CLAIM TO FAME:** This is the farthest north that human beings live—200 miles north of the Arctic Circle!

**AREA:** 150,000 square miles, about the size of Norway

**COUNTRIES:** Sápmi, the Sami name for this area, spreads across what is now northern Norway, Sweden, Finland, and Russia's Kola Peninsula.

**CLOSE READ**

## Correct or Confirm Predictions

Highlight details that help you correct or confirm a prediction you made about how extreme of a place the Sami homeland is.

### UNDERNEATH THE MIDNIGHT SUN

The Sami live so far north that in the summer the sun never sets!

# The Reindeer Walkers

**Analyze Text Features**

Underline text details that help you explain the author's use of the heading to introduce important information.

16    The Sami call people who herd reindeer *boazovázzi*. This means "reindeer walkers." The herders used to follow the reindeer by foot or on skis. They now use snowmobiles to herd their reindeer.

# An All-in-One Animal

17   Reindeer provide the Sami with meat, hides, and antlers. Most reindeer are allowed to roam free. Some are kept for milking and to pull sleds. Some reindeer can even be saddled like horses!

## CLOSE READ

### Correct or Confirm Predictions

Highlight details that help you correct or confirm predictions you made about the ways the Sami might use reindeer.

## THE MANY USES OF REINDEER

**FOOD:** Reindeer meatballs, reindeer sausage, and smoked reindeer are all very popular.

**MILK:** Reindeer can be milked like cows.

**MEDICINE:** Reindeer antlers are sold to China because many Chinese people believe the antlers have medicinal properties.

**CLOTHING:** Reindeer have hairs that are hollow and filled with air. This trapped air makes reindeer fur very warm.

**TRANSPORT:** Reindeer can be trained to pull sleds; larger species can be ridden like horses.

**TOOLS:** Traditionally, reindeer bones were made into tools, such as needles and knives.

**Analyze Text Features**

Underline details about a lavut in paragraph 18 that are supported by the photo.

# That's Not a Tepee, That's a Lavut

18 When moving with their herds, the Sami still live in cone-shaped tents. These are called *lavuts*. A lavut can stand winds that are 50 miles an hour. The top of each lavut is open to let out the smoke from large fires.

# Can I Please Take a Look at Your Gakti?

19    The lavut is not the only part of Sami life still in use today. The traditional Sami clothing is called the *gakti*. It is still often worn on special occasions. The colors, patterns, and buttons of a gakti are a code. They can tell you whether the person is married and which village he or she comes from.

## Correct or Confirm Predictions

Highlight details in a text feature that help you confirm or correct your prediction about the meaning behind the Sami's use of buttons.

## WHY THE POINTY TOES?

The turned-up, pointy toes of a traditional Sami reindeer-skin boot are designed to hook onto skis.

## ROUND OR SQUARE BUTTONS

Traditionally, square buttons mean a person is married. Round buttons mean a person is not married.

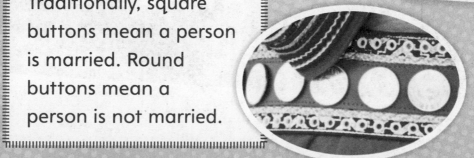

**Analyze Text Features**

Underline text evidence that helps you explain the author's use of a question in the heading to achieve a specific purpose.

# What's It Like Where You Live?

20    Now you've seen some of the extreme places where people live. What do you think might be extreme about your neighborhood? To an Afar child, where and how you live might look pretty different. Many people on this planet have never seen some of the things you probably see every day.

21   Imagine meeting someone from the Sami or Afar tribe. What would seem extreme to them about your normal life?

**CLOSE READ**

## Analyze Text Features

Underline text details that help you explain how the author's use of photos supports the information in paragraph 21.

453

# Develop Vocabulary

In informational texts, authors choose words that accurately describe a topic. These words may be domain-specific words, meaning words that help explain a particular subject.

**My TURN** Use each vocabulary word from the word bank in a sentence that accurately describes people who live in unusual places on Earth.

**Word Bank**

| extreme | spectacular | region | transport |
|---|---|---|---|

The Afar live in an area with extreme heat.

people who live in unusual places on Earth

# Check for Understanding

**My TURN** Look back at the text to answer the questions.

1. What features and characteristics help you identify *Deep Down* as an informational text?

2. Why did the author include maps with the text?

3. Which facts from the text support the idea that the Sami depend on reindeer for their survival?

4. What is the author's viewpoint on people who live in extreme places? Synthesize information from different sections of the informational text in your response.

# Analyze Text Features

Informational texts often include **text features**, such as headings, bold words, charts, maps, sidebars, and photographs. Text features help organize information and support the text.

1. **My TURN** Go to the Close Read notes in *Deep Down* and underline parts that help you analyze text features.

2. **Text Evidence** Use some of the parts you underlined to complete the chart.

| Details from the Text | Text Feature That Supports Text | How the Text Feature Supports the Text |
|---|---|---|
| "at the bottom of the Grand Canyon, there is a village called Supai" | map | The map helps me understand that the Grand Canyon is in the United States. |
| | | |
| | | |

Explain how the author's use of print and graphic features achieves a specific purpose:

# Correct or Confirm Predictions

Readers use text details and evidence from text features to **correct or confirm predictions** about the text.

1. **My TURN** Go back to the Close Read notes and highlight evidence that helps you correct or confirm your predictions.

2. **Text Evidence** Use some of your highlighted text to complete the chart.

| Prediction Before Reading | Text Evidence | Correct or Confirm Prediction |
|---|---|---|
| I predict that the Havasupai live far away from other people. | "CLOSEST NEIGHBORS: Three to five hours away by foot, horse, or mule" | Confirmed. I was right. The Havasupai live far from other people. |
| | | |
| | | |

# Reflect and Share

**Talk About It** Think about the extreme places and events in nature that you have read about this week. How do people survive in extreme places or stay safe when extreme events occur? Discuss the skills and systems that people use to help them survive in extreme places and during dangerous natural events.

**Make Thoughtful Comments** During a discussion, it is important to make thoughtful and related comments.

- ◎ Listen to others' comments, and build on what they say.
- ◎ Make comments that are directly related to the topic.
- ◎ Avoid repeating ideas that have already been shared.

Use these sentence starters when making thoughtful comments:

To survive, people . . .

During dangerous natural events, people . . .

### Weekly Question

How can nature change people's lives?

# Academic Vocabulary

**Related Words** are words that share roots or
word parts. They may have different meanings,
syllabications, and pronunciations. Use a print or
digital dictionary to check.

**MyTURN** For each sentence below,

1. **Use** print or digital resources, such as a dictionary or thesaurus, to find related words and their meanings, syllabications, and pronunciations.

2. **Add** an additional related word in the box.

3. **Choose** the correct form of the word to complete the sentence.

| Word | Related Words | Fill in the Correct Form of the Word |
|---|---|---|
| analysis | analyze<br>analyzed<br>_____ | Dr. Pappas put the cells under a microscope for further _____. |
| threat | threats<br>threaten<br>_____ | My dog may bark when he hears a strange sound, but he poses no _____ to people. |
| damage | damaged<br>damaging<br>_____ | The bike Dad bought was on sale because the seat was slightly _____. |
| anticipate | anticipation<br>anticipated<br>_____ | We knew we would have to wait, but we did not _____ standing in such a long line. |
| Pollution | pollute<br>polluted<br>_____ | No one was allowed to swim in the lake, because the lake water was _____. |

# Vowel Patterns

**Vowel Patterns *au, aw, al, augh, ough*** can all spell the vowel sound you hear in the word *saw*. Sometimes the letters *al* include the *l* sound, but sometimes the letter *l* is silent. Knowing sound-spelling patterns can help you read words with one or more syllables.

| au | laundry, fault, Paul |
|---|---|
| aw | jaw, law, lawn |
| al (with *l* sound) | call, fall, meatballs, salt |
| al (with silent *l*) | talk, walkers |
| augh | caught, taught |
| ough | thought, bought |

**My TURN** Read each single-syllable or multisyllable word. Underline the letters that spell the vowel sound you hear in the word *saw*.

| | | |
|---|---|---|
| brought | daughter | sausage |
| cause | already | launch |
| yawn | stalk | astronaut |
| August | rainfall | also |

# High-Frequency Words

Read these **high-frequency words:** *special, heavy*. Practice saying them aloud.

# Read Like a Writer

Authors use text features to achieve the specific purpose of adding or supporting details in the text. Text features help authors convey key information.

**Model !**  Read the sentence from *Deep Down*.

> **HERDING ANIMALS**
>
> In addition to mining salt, most Afar herd sheep, goats, cattle, and camels.

*sidebar information*

1. **Identify** The text features include a heading and sidebar.

2. **Question** How do they add or support details in the text?

3. **Conclude** The heading gives the main idea for the section. The sidebar tells me more about the Afar.

Read the sentence.

> **UNDERNEATH THE MIDNIGHT SUN**
>
> The Sami live so far north that in the summer the sun never sets!

**My TURN** Follow the steps to analyze text features. Explain how these features help the author achieve her purpose.

1. **Identify** The text features include _____.

2. **Question** How do they add or support details in the text?

3. **Conclude** The heading and sidebar explain _____
_____.

# Write for a Reader

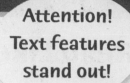

Use text features to help readers better understand ideas. Sidebars with headings, photos and captions, charts, and labeled diagrams are some text features that can provide readers with additional details.

**My TURN** Think about how text features in *Deep Down* give you more details. How can you use text features to give readers more details in an informational text?

1. Think about a subject you know well. Write its name.

_____

2. Write a brief paragraph about the subject.

_____

_____

_____

3. List three text features to include and the information they would give.

_____

_____

_____

4. Explain how the text features you listed would achieve the purpose of helping readers better understand the information.

_____

_____

# Spell Vowel Patterns

**Vowel Patterns *au*, *aw*, *al*, *augh*, *ough*** call all spell the vowel sound you hear in the word *saw*. Knowing how to spell these vowel patterns will help you spell words with this vowel sound.

**My TURN**   Read the words. Sort them by the spelling of the vowel pattern. Write *none* if there is no word for a vowel pattern.

**SPELLING WORDS**

| | | |
|---|---|---|
| fault | awful | fought |
| author | distraught | squawk |
| bought | naughty | sprawls |
| sought | | |

| | |
|---|---|
| au | |
| aw | |
| al | |
| augh | |
| ough | |

# High-Frequency Words

High-frequency words appear often. Write the following high-frequency words on the lines.

special _____

heavy _____

# Comparing with Adjectives

To compare two people, places, groups, or things, you usually add -er to an adjective. These are called **comparative adjectives**. To compare three or more people, places, groups, or things, you usually add -est. These are called **superlative adjectives**.

| Adjective | Comparative Adjective | Superlative Adjective |
|---|---|---|
| It is hot outside today. | It is hotter than it was yesterday. | Today is the hottest day this week. |
| The tree is tall. | The tree is taller than the tree next to it. | The tree is the tallest in the neighborhood. |
| Tori's hair is long. | Tori's hair is longer than Nia's hair. | Tori's hair is the longest of all the girls in her class. |

**My TURN** Edit this draft. Change each underlined adjective to its comparative or superlative form.

Jayden and Dereck are brothers. Jayden is the <u>old</u> brother. They ran a race with their friends. Jayden said he was <u>fast</u> than his brother. In fact, he said he was the <u>faster</u> of all their friends. When the race was over, he turned out to be the <u>slow</u> runner of everyone!

# Poetry

**Poetry** is a creative way to express oneself in writing. The rules for poetry are different from prose, or written language in its ordinary form.

|  | Poetry | Prose |
|---|---|---|
| What is the structure? | Poems may be unstructured or grouped into stanzas. | It has sentences and paragraphs. |
| What does it say? | It tells a story or expresses feelings or ideas. | It usually focuses on a story. |
| Does it use many words? | It often communicates meaning with few words. | It often includes descriptions and complete sentences. |
| Does it use sound devices such as rhyme and rhythm? | Words at the end of lines may or may not rhyme. Poems also may use other sound devices, such as repetition or rhythm. | Sound devices such as rhyme are rarely used. |

**My TURN** Use a poem you have read to answer the questions.

**1.** How many lines and stanzas are in the poem? _____

**2.** What is the poet saying? _____

**3.** Write a phrase that expresses meaning with few words.

**4.** If the poem rhymes, write a pair of rhyming words. Write a word that imitates a natural sound, if there is one.

# What Poetry Sounds Like

Some elements of poetry affect the way it sounds. Read each example and listen to its sound. Then read the explanation.

| Example | Explanation |
|---|---|
| The earth starts to quake. And I can feel the ground shake. | *Quake* and *shake* **rhyme**, or have the same end sound. |
| / / U / U<br>Tall moun tains wob ble.<br>/ / U / U<br>Large build ings top ple. | These lines rhyme and have a **rhythm**, or beat. Tap a pencil as you read aloud. What **rhythm** do you hear? |
| The rocks made a loud noise as they fell. *Crash! Smash!* | With **onomatopoeia**, words sound like their meaning. |
| Nearby neighbors are nice to those in need. | **Alliteration** is the repetition of beginning sounds in nearby words. |

**My TURN** Choose one or more poems you enjoyed reading. Complete the chart using examples from these poems.

| Rhyme | Rhythm |
|---|---|
| | |
| Onomatopoeia | Alliteration |
| | |

# What Poetry Looks Like

The way a poem looks can be important to its mood and meaning.

Most poems use **line breaks:**

- Lines tell you when to pause or stop.
- Lines may be different lengths.
- Lines may or may not have end punctuation.
- Longer poems are often divided into stanzas, or groups of lines.

> The sink drips
> one drop
> at a time.

Some poems are **shapes:**

- Words may twist and turn, or their size and style may vary.
- The shape often connects to the poem's meaning.

**My TURN** Answer these questions.

**1.** How does the poem's shape add to the meaning?

_____

_____

_____

This poem circles round and then falls to the ground.

**2.** How could you rewrite the shaped poem with line breaks?

_____

_____

_____

_____

# Brainstorm Ideas

When authors **brainstorm ideas**, they write down every idea they have without judging whether or not to use the idea. Brainstorming helps authors develop creative and original poetry.

**My TURN** Plan a first draft for your poem by brainstorming. Brainstorm three different topics. Then brainstorm words that sound like their meaning. In the last column, describe the way the poem might look.

| Topic | Sound | Appearance |
|---|---|---|
|  |  |  |
|  |  |  |
|  |  |  |

# Plan Your Poetry

| What is freewriting? | **Freewriting** is writing nonstop for a period of time, without worrying about correct grammar or how the ideas connect. Writers do not need to use complete sentences when they freewrite. |
| --- | --- |
| What is the goal of freewriting? | The goal of freewriting is to let ideas flow and get them down on paper. |
| What do writers do after freewriting? | After freewriting, writers can read what they wrote and choose the best words, phrases, and ideas for their poetry. |

**My TURN** Plan your first draft for your poem by freewriting for five minutes about what you might include. Think about the topic and purpose of your poem and who your audience will be. Then meet with your Writing Club to share and discuss what you wrote. Remember to listen actively by paying close attention as others are speaking.

 INTERACTIVITY

# When Earth Changes...

Our planet is always changing. Volcanoes, earthquakes, and other natural disasters can affect the environment on Earth.

**North America**

**Europe**

**North Atlantic**

**Africa**

**South America**

**South Pacific**

**South Atlantic**

### ANCHORAGE, ALASKA

A 1964 earthquake changed the environment in parts of Alaska. Ocean water flooded dry land, destroying plant and animal habitats.

**LAKE CHAD** At one time, Lake Chad was one of the largest lakes in Africa. About 50 years ago, the lake started to dry up because of drought, meaning there was very little rainfall. Today, many animals in the area struggle to survive.

**TUNGUSKA, RUSSIA** In 1908, some people in Russia saw a huge fireball in the sky. Then they heard an explosion that knocked down about 80 million trees. Today, scientists think the fireball was a space object, such as a comet.

## Weekly Question

**How do changes on Earth affect the environment?**

**Turn and Talk** Choose one of the places shown on the map. Discuss with a partner the changes that affected Earth's environment. Make comments based on information in the text.

Asia

North Pacific

Indian

Australia

**HIMALAYAS** The Himalayas include many of the world's highest peaks. The mountain range was formed when two landmasses slid into each other millions of years ago and pushed up the ground. Even today the mountains continue to rise!

**MOUNT TAMBORA** In 1815, a huge volcano erupted in Indonesia. Volcanic ash drifted all around the Earth, blocking out so much sunlight that the summer of 1816 was one of the coldest in history.

471

## Learning Goal

I can learn more about informational texts and analyze text structure in informational text.

**Spotlight on Genre**

# Informational Text

Text structure is the way an author organizes information. Because **informational text** informs, or gives facts, readers look for patterns and connections among ideas. To identify text structure in informational text, look for

- The **relationship of ideas** within parts of sentences, among sentences in a paragraph, and between and among paragraphs in the entire text
- **Signal words and phrases**, such as *because* and *as a result*, that help you identify how parts of the text relate to one another

Use headings to find information quickly.

**TURN and TALK** Discuss with a partner an informational text that you have read. Use the Informational Text Anchor Chart to help you describe the structure of that text. Take notes on your discussion.

**My NOTES**

# Informational Text Anchor Chart

| Text Structure | Signal Words |
|---|---|
| Time Order | first, next, before, after, finally |
| Compare and Contrast | likewise, similarly, however, on the other hand |
| Cause and Effect | because, consequently, if...then, therefore |
| Problem and Solution | leads to, as a result, thereby |
| Description | most important, for example, in addition |

**Natalie Hyde** grew up in Ontario, Canada. As a child, she loved to collect insects and toads. Today, as an author, she shows her enjoyment of nature by writing children's books about science and the natural world. She still lives in Ontario with her family—and a collection of pets.

from
# Earthquakes, Eruptions, and Other Events that Change Earth

## Preview Vocabulary

As you read the excerpt from *Earthquakes, Eruptions, and Other Events that Change Earth,* notice what these vocabulary words tell about Earth.

| | | |
|---|---|---|
| surface | landforms | |
| processes | damaging | produces |

## Read

Skim the text and make predictions about how natural events (causes) change Earth (effects). Follow these strategies when you read this **informational text** the first time.

| | |
|---|---|
| **Notice** headings and captions that help explain the text. | **Generate Questions** to clarify information. |
| **Connect** the text to what you know about Earth. | **Respond** by marking parts you find interesting or surprising. |

First Read

# Earthquakes, Eruptions, and Other Events that Change Earth

by Natalie Hyde

🔊 AUDIO

✎ ANNOTATE

Natural disasters can be very dangerous for people and animals.

## CLOSE READ

### Analyze Text Structure

<u>Underline</u> sentences that help you recognize a cause-and-effect text structure.

**surface** the outside or outermost part

**landforms** natural features of Earth's surface, such as mountains and valleys

# Planet of Change

1   Earth's surface is always changing. Most of these changes happen slowly. They can take hundreds or even thousands of years. Some changes, however, happen quickly. In fact, Earth's surface can change in a matter of minutes, hours, or days.

### Big changes

2   Natural disasters, such as earthquakes, volcanoes, and tsunamis, can happen without warning. They can change Earth's surface in a big way very quickly. An earthquake's shaking can create large holes or cracks in the land. A volcano's hot lava can create new landforms when cooled. The wall of water from a tsunami can destroy forests, roads, and buildings.

# Layers

3   Earth is not a solid ball. If you were to cut our planet open, you would see it is made up of four layers. The inner core is at the center. It is a solid ball of metal. Around this inner core is the outer core. This layer is liquid metal. The next layer is called the mantle. The mantle is made of solid rock and minerals. The top layer is the crust.

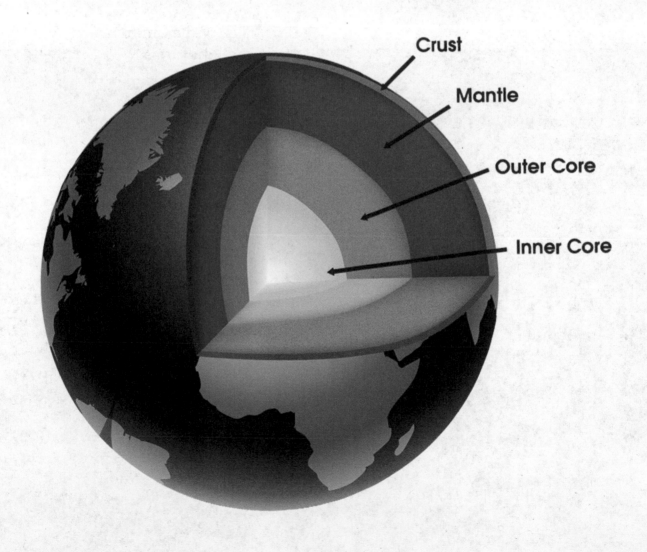

Crust

Mantle

Outer Core

Inner Core

## Synthesize Information

Highlight details in paragraph 4 that help you explain how the crust is different from other layers of Earth.

**processes** series of actions that happen over time

## Rocky crust

4    The crust is the thinnest layer. It is made of rock. This is the layer that we live on. The rocks and minerals in the crust are shaped into landforms. Low landforms fill with water to make lakes, rivers, and oceans. Earth's processes are always at work changing the crust.

Cliffs, hills, and mountains are raised landforms.

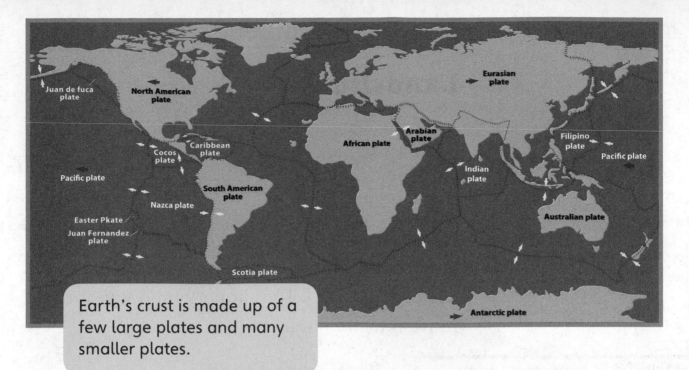

Earth's crust is made up of a few large plates and many smaller plates.

# Earthquakes

5    Earth's crust is divided into plates. A plate is a huge sheet of rock. The plates fit together like big puzzle pieces to form the surface. The plates are moving and rubbing against each other very slowly. Sometimes the edge of one plate is pushed under another plate. This causes an earthquake. During an earthquake, the ground shakes suddenly.

## Moving and shaking

6    Earthquakes happen around the world every day. Most are not strong enough to cause any damage. Some, however, can cause the ground to shake violently. During these strong earthquakes, buildings can crumble and fall, and roads can crack and split.

## CLOSE READ

### Vocabulary in Context

The author uses the word *violently* to describe how the ground moves during some earthquakes.

Use context clues beyond the sentence to determine the meaning of *violently*.

Underline the context clues that support your definition.

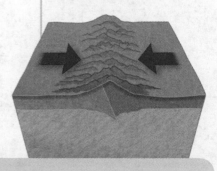

Earth's plates can also push together and can cause the rock to bend and fold. This process can create mountains.

## Analyze Text Structure

<u>Underline</u> details in paragraphs 7 and 8 that help you recognize and describe the text structure on this page.

# Landslides

7    During a landslide, rocks and soil suddenly break loose and slide down hills or mountains. Landslides can happen for different reasons. Rivers can eat away at the base of hills and mountains, causing the earth above to fall. Heavy rains can also cause landslides when wet soil turns to mud. The slippery mud will then move downhill quickly.

## Slipping and sliding

8    Landslides can be as small as a few large rocks rolling down a hill. They can also be as large as the whole side of a mountain sliding away. The biggest landslides can move a lot of ground very quickly. They change the shape and size of landforms. They fill valleys with soil and rocks. Landslides can happen underwater, too.

Earthquakes can shake rocks and soil loose and cause a landslide.

The Kilauea Volcano in Hawaii has been erupting since 1983.

# Volcanoes

9    A volcano is an opening in Earth's crust where hot, melted rock and ash from inside Earth erupts, or shoots out. Some eruptions happen once every few years and last only a couple of hours. Other volcanoes continue erupting for weeks, months, or even years.

## Melting rocks

10    Volcanoes reshape Earth's surface. When the lava shoots out of the volcano, it flows down the sides and over the land below. The lava is so hot that it can melt rock. Boulders and hills can melt away. When the lava cools, it hardens into new rock. This new rock is full of minerals. After a few years, the new rock breaks down and turns into rich farmland.

**CLOSE READ**

## Synthesize Information

Highlight two sentences in the text that you can use to explain why volcanoes might affect where farmers grow their crops.

# Volcanic Islands

**Analyze Text Structure**

Underline the effects of underwater eruptions that help you recognize and explain the text structure on this page.

11   Volcanoes can create new islands. When a volcano erupts, lava flows out of it. Some volcanoes erupt underwater. As they erupt over and over, the lava cools and builds up a cone-shaped mountain around the opening. When the mountain gets big enough it breaks through the surface of the water, creating an island.

## Making islands

12   The Hawaiian Islands are volcanic islands found in the Pacific Ocean. The islands are the peaks of large mountains formed under the ocean by volcanic eruptions. Some Hawaiian Island volcanoes are no longer erupting. Others are still active and creating new land.

The Stromboli Volcano has been erupting for at least 2,000 years.

A tsunami can be as high as 115 feet (35 m). That is as tall as a ten-story building!

# Tsunamis

13   A tsunami is a giant wave. Tsunamis are caused by changes in the ocean floor. Underwater earthquakes, landslides, and volcanic eruptions can all cause tsunamis. The force from these natural disasters can make the water rise. This will start a wave that speeds through the water until it reaches land.

## Wall of water

14   A tsunami is one of the most damaging forces on Earth. It can race toward land as fast as a jet plane. It can wipe out villages, and even islands. It can move soil and rocks as much as 620 miles (1,000 km).

**CLOSE READ**

## Vocabulary in Context

The word *race* can be a noun meaning "a competition of speed" or a verb meaning "move quickly."

<u>Underline</u> context clues within and beyond the sentence that help you determine the meaning of *race* in paragraph 14.

**damaging** harming or dangerous

## Analyze Text Structure

<u>Underline</u> text evidence in paragraphs 15 and 16 that helps you recognize and explain the text structure on this page.

**produces** makes or forms

# Building Up and Tearing Down

15    Earth's processes can build up and tear down landforms. Landslides change the shape of hills and mountains. Tsunamis eat away at the land along the coast. Volcanoes build up Earth's surface and earthquakes tear it down.

### Our changing Earth

16    These changes can threaten the lives of people, plants, and animals. But, they are also a chance for new life to grow. New landforms become homes for plants and animals. New mineral-rich soil produces food to feed people around the world.

The island of Iceland is growing larger each year. It has many active volcanoes. The lava from these volcanoes creates new land.

Discovering new information about natural disasters can help save people's lives.

## On the Job

17    Scientists have a lot to learn about Earth's processes. Seismologists are people who study earthquakes. They want to learn when and where earthquakes will happen. Volcanologists are people who study volcanoes. They are looking for signs of a coming eruption. They study the buildup of pressure under the ground.

**CLOSE READ**

### Synthesize Information

Highlight two details in paragraph 17 that you could synthesize to create new understanding of how seismologists and volcanologists might affect people's safety.

# Develop Vocabulary

In informational text, authors often use subject-specific vocabulary words to explain a topic. When you read about the environment, you will learn scientific words to describe events that affect Earth.

**My TURN** Choose the two vocabulary words from the word bank that match the definitions in each box. Then use both words in a sentence that shows how they are connected.

**Word Bank**

surface     landforms     processes     damaging

| | Vocabulary Words | Sentence |
|---|---|---|
| **Describes Earth** | landforms<br>natural features of Earth's surface<br><br>surface<br>the outside or outermost part | The surface of the Earth is covered with landforms. |
| **Describes Actions** | harming or dangerous<br><br>series of actions that happen over time | |

# Check for Understanding

**My TURN** Look back at the text to answer the questions.

**1.** How can the reader identify this text as informational?

**2.** What is the most likely reason that the author included a diagram of the layers of the Earth?

**3.** What would happen if a landslide began on a high hill during heavy rains? Base your explanation on what you read in the text.

**4.** What evidence from the text would you use to support the claim that earthquakes, volcanoes, and landslides can change the Earth?

# Analyze Text Structure

Readers can best understand informational text by looking at how the author organizes ideas. The organization of ideas in a text is called **text structure**. For example, a scientific text may be organized by cause and effect. The cause is what happened. The effect is the result of what happened.

1. **My TURN** Go to the Close Read notes in *Earthquakes, Eruptions, and Other Events that Change Earth* and underline details that help you analyze text structure.

2. **Text Evidence** Use some of the parts you underlined to complete the chart. List one or more effects.

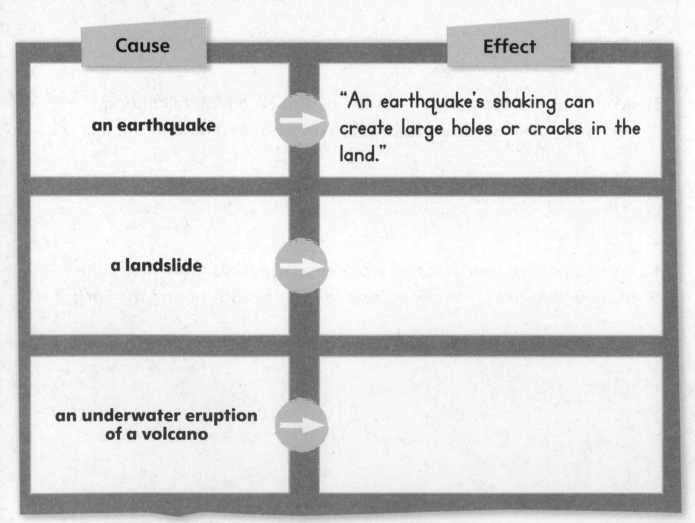

| Cause | | Effect |
|---|---|---|
| an earthquake | → | "An earthquake's shaking can create large holes or cracks in the land." |
| a landslide | → | |
| an underwater eruption of a volcano | → | |

# Synthesize Information

**Synthesize**, or combine, pieces of information you gather from a text to create new understandings about what you read.

1. **My TURN** Go back to the Close Read notes and highlight information in the text that you can synthesize to create new understandings.

2. **Text Evidence** Use some of your highlighted text evidence to support your new understanding of the ideas in the text.

| 1. Information in the Text | 2. Information in the Text Feature | Synthesize 1 and 2: What I Learned |
|---|---|---|
| Paragraph 3: Earth has "four layers." The inner core is a "solid ball of metal." The outer core is "liquid metal." The mantle is made of "solid rock and minerals." The "top layer is the crust." | The diagram shows Earth and its four layers. | The top layer of Earth with land and water is where we live. Compared to other layers of Earth, the crust is very thin. |
| Paragraph 10: | | |

# Reflect and Share

**Write to Sources** In this unit so far, you have read about extreme natural environments and natural events that change the environment. Choose an extreme environment and a natural event to compare and contrast. How are the challenges of living in the extreme environment and experiencing the natural event similar and different? Use evidence from the texts to write and support a response.

**Ask and Answer Questions** Before you write a response to a text, ask yourself questions about what you have read. Your answers to these questions will help shape your writing.

- How does the text describe the extreme environment or natural event?

- Which facts and details in the text can help me compare and contrast the extreme environment and the natural event?

Answer your questions by taking notes or underlining details in the texts. Use this evidence to write your response on a separate sheet of paper.

## Weekly Question

**How do changes on Earth affect its environment?**

# Academic Vocabulary

**Synonyms and Antonyms** Words that have the same or similar meanings, such as *cold* and *frigid*, are **synonyms**. Words that have opposite meanings, such as *hot* and *cold*, are **antonyms**.

**My TURN** For each word below,

1. **Read** the definition of the word.

2. **Write** a synonym and two antonyms for the word.

3. **Use** a print or digital dictionary to identify, use, and explain the meanings of the synonyms and antonyms you chose.

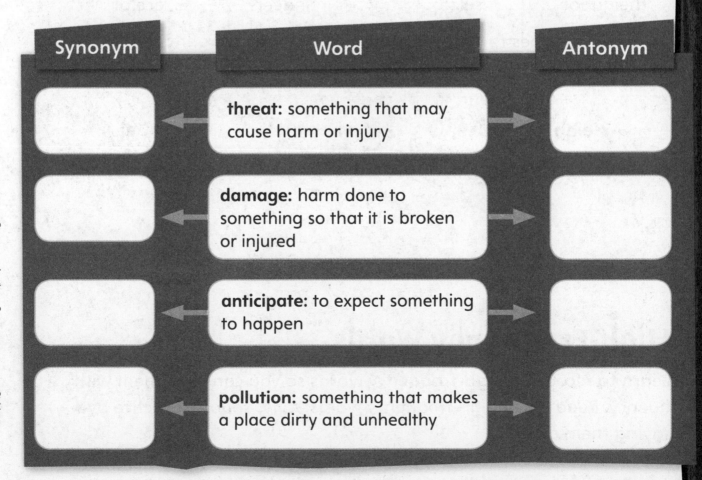

| Synonym | Word | Antonym |
|---|---|---|
| | **threat:** something that may cause harm or injury | |
| | **damage:** harm done to something so that it is broken or injured | |
| | **anticipate:** to expect something to happen | |
| | **pollution:** something that makes a place dirty and unhealthy | |

# Vowel Patterns

**Vowel Patterns *ei, eigh*** are letter combinations that have a single sound. The vowel pattern *eigh* can spell the long *a* sound, as in *eight*, or the long *i* sound, as in *heighten*. The vowel pattern *ei* can can spell the long *a* sound, the long *e* sound, or the long *i* sound.

The word *seismologists* in paragraph 17 of *Earthquakes, Eruptions, and Other Events that Change Earth* has the vowel pattern *ei*. The *ei* makes the long *i* sound. Say the word aloud and listen for the long *i* sound.

**My TURN** Read each word in the box. Then write each word in the correct column.

| neighbor<br>veiled | seize<br>sleigh | reindeer<br>vein | receipt<br>protein |
|---|---|---|---|

| **eigh**<br>long *a* sound | **ei**<br>long *a* sound | **ei**<br>long *e* sound |
|---|---|---|
| | | |
| | | |

# High-Frequency Words

Learn to recognize **high-frequency words** so you can read them with fluency. Read these high-frequency words: *built*, *square*. Practice by saying them aloud.

# Read Like a Writer

Authors use graphic features, such as photographs, to achieve the specific purpose of helping readers understand ideas in the text.

**Model !**  Read the sentence from *Earthquakes, Eruptions, and Other Events that Change Earth.*

> During a landslide, rocks and soil suddenly break loose and slide down hills or mountains.

*information also shown in the photograph*

**1. Identify** Natalie Hyde includes a photograph of a landslide near this text.

**2. Question** How does it help me understand the text?

**3. Conclude** It helps me see rocks and soil that have slid down a hill, causing damage.

Read the sentence.

> When the mountain gets big enough it breaks through the surface of the water, creating an island.

**MyTURN** Follow the steps to analyze the passage. Explain how the author uses a photograph to achieve the purpose of helping readers understand the text.

**1. Identify** Natalie Hyde includes a photograph near the text that shows

_____ .

**2. Question** How does it help me understand the text?

**3. Conclude** It helps me see _____

_____ .

# Write for a Reader

Writers use graphic features, such as photographs, to give extra details. Graphic features support the text by emphasizing a point or adding new information.

A photograph is worth a thousand words!

**My TURN** Think about how the photographs in *Earthquakes, Eruptions, and Other Events that Change Earth* help you understand the text.

**1.** Think about a natural event in your area that causes changes, such as a heavy rainstorm, a snowstorm, or many days without rain. Name the event and tell what it changes.

**Event:** _____

_____

**What It Changes:** _____

_____

**2.** Briefly describe the event and what it changes.

_____

_____

_____

**3.** Describe a photograph you could add. Explain how it would allow you to achieve the purpose of helping readers understand the text.

_____

_____

_____

# Spell Words with Vowel Patterns

**Vowel Patterns *ei*, *eigh*** spell the long *a* sound, as in *sleigh*; the long *e* sound, as in *seize*; and the long *i* sound, as in *heighten*. You will have to memorize how to spell words that have multiple sound-spelling patterns such as *ei* or *eigh*.

**My TURN** Read the words. Sort them by the spelling of the vowel pattern. Then identify the vowel sound.

| SPELLING WORDS | | |
| --- | --- | --- |
| ceiling | height | weigh |
| eighteen | neighbor | weight |
| eighty | receive | weightless |
| freight | | |

**eigh**                                 **ei**

_____     _____     _____

_____     _____     _____

_____     _____

# High-Frequency Words

Memorize high-frequency words to recognize them instantly in texts. Write these high-frequency words on the lines:

built _____

square _____

# Comparing with Adverbs

**Adverbs** tell more about the actions named by verbs. Some adverbs compare actions. **Comparative adverbs** compare two actions. To form most comparative adverbs, add -*er* to the end of the adverb. **Superlative adverbs** compare three or more actions. To form most superlative adverbs, add -*est*.

An adverb of **time** answers the question *when* or *how often*. An adverb of **manner** answers the question *how*. When an adverb ends in e, drop the final e before adding -*er* or -*est*. When an adverb ends in y, change the final y to an i before adding -*er* or -*est*.

| Adverb | Comparative Adverb | Superlative Adverb |
|---|---|---|
| fast (how?)<br>Shon runs **fast**. | fast**er**<br>Steph runs **faster** than Shon. | fast**est**<br>Derrick runs the **fastest** of them all. |
| early (when?)<br>I left **early**. | earl**ier**<br>I left **earlier** than Sue. | earl**iest**<br>Gia left **earliest** of all. |

**My TURN** Edit this draft for the correct use of adverbs.

Kim jumps high than Sydney. However, Sydney runs fast than Kim. The day of their basketball game, Kim arrives earliest than Sydney. Kim plays harder of all.

# Composing Like a Poet

When poets write, they have plenty of tools to use. **Poetic language** allows poets to turn ordinary words into something special. It allows readers to see the world in new and different ways.

**Learning Goal**

I can use knowledge of the sound and shape of poetry to write a poem.

Poetic language includes
- Vivid imagery
- Musical qualities
- Unusual comparisons

Read the poem about a tree. Notice how the poet uses poetic language to describe this ordinary object.

**My Friend**
Mighty oak tree, unafraid,
You give me peace, you give me shade.
Your limbs stretch upward to the sky,
You make me gaze and wonder why.
Bright green branches slowly sway,
We wave goodbye to this great day.

The words *mighty, unafraid,* and *bright green* are descriptive words that help me imagine the tree.

The words *stretch, sway,* and *wave* describe movements a person could make. These verbs make the tree seem like a person.

The rhyming words *unafraid/shade, sky/why,* and *sway/day* add a rhythm, or musical quality, to the description.

**My TURN** In your writing notebook, compose a poem about an ordinary object.

# Compose with Imagery

**Imagery** is the use of words that help the reader experience sensory details. Poets use imagery to create a picture in a reader's mind.

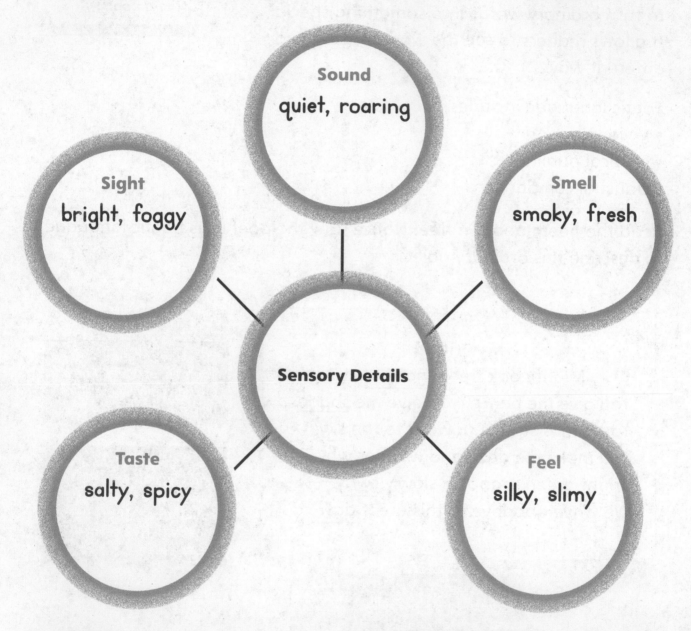

**Sound**
quiet, roaring

**Sight**
bright, foggy

**Smell**
smoky, fresh

**Sensory Details**

**Taste**
salty, spicy

**Feel**
silky, slimy

**My TURN** Read a poem from your classroom library. Look for words that the poet uses to create imagery and add them in the circles.

**My TURN** In your writing notebook, compose a short poem about a favorite place. Include sensory details.

# Compose with Rhythm and Rhyme

Poetry has characteristics that make it different from other forms of writing. Poets use elements of craft, such as rhythm and rhyme, when they compose poems. **Rhythm** is the pattern of sounds in speech or writing. Just like a song has a beat, a poem can have a beat, or rhythm.

**Rhyme** is two or more words that have the same ending sound. Many poems use rhyme at the ends of lines.

**Examples:** bag/rag    frog/dog

**My TURN** Read the poem several times. When you hear the rhythm, read the poem aloud and clap your hands to the rhythm.

**The Farmer's Market**

Bright orange pumpkins,
Lined up in a row,
Crunchy green vegetables,
The sun makes them grow!

Bright red tomatoes,
Some fresh homemade bread,
My mouth starts to water,
Let's buy jelly spread!

**My TURN** Write the pairs of words that rhyme in the poem.

**My TURN** Compose or revise a rhyming poem, making sure ending words rhyme. Read your poem softly and tap the rhythm.

# Compose with Alliteration

Poets use **alliteration** to express sounds and words. Alliteration is the repetition of a consonant sound or letter at the beginnings of words. Tongue twisters have alliteration.

Peter Piper picked a peck of pickled peppers.

Poets also use alliteration to create a mood. For example, words that begin with the letter *l* or *m* may create a peaceful mood.

Long days, lazy nights
Lullabies about love

**Onomatopoeia** refers to words that sound like what they mean. Onomatopoeia is a sound-device tool that poets use to help readers experience a poem.

**Examples:** hiss, sizzle, clickity-clack

**My TURN** Read the poem. Highlight the words that show alliteration. Underline the words that show onomatopoeia.

> **The Bee**
> Busy bee, you buzz all day,
> Pollinating plants on the prairie path.
> Humming, buzzing, zipping by,
> Hiding honey in your hive.

**My TURN** In your writing notebook, compose a short poem about your your favorite animal. Include alliteration or onomatopoeia.

# Compose with Figurative Language

**Figurative language** gives words a meaning beyond their dictionary definitions.

| Definition | Example | Meaning |
|---|---|---|
| A **simile** compares two unlike things that are alike in at least one way using the comparison words *like* or *as*. | The children ran *like* the wind. | The simile compares the speed of children running to the wind. |
| A **metaphor** is a comparison between two unlike things that are alike in at least one way without using any words of comparison. | Happiness *is* iced tea on a summer day. | The metaphor compares the quality of happiness to the joy of sipping iced tea. |

**My TURN** Read the poem. Highlight similes and underline metaphor.

My dog is hunting
        Like a panther in the forest.
She lowers her body,
        One paw placed slowly in front of the other.
She sneaks around the corner
        Like a thief in the night.
Her eyes are yellow moons
                Lighting her path.
Without notice, she sprints toward the tree,
        Fast as lightning.

**My TURN** Revise one of your poems by adding a simile or metaphor. Share your revised poem with your Writing Club.

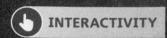
INTERACTIVITY

# EMERGENCY!

Earthquakes. Fires. Storms. Floods. Emergencies call for immediate action. Several organizations help people prepare for emergencies.

## NOAA (NATIONAL OCEANIC AND ATMOSPHERIC ADMINISTRATION)

One of NOAA's jobs is to keep track of the weather. NOAA alerts people when dangerous weather, such as a hurricane, tornado, or blizzard, is on the way. Warnings are posted to NOAA's Web site and broadcast on the radio.

*Listen for alerts.*

*Choose a place to meet in case of fire.*

## USFA (U.S. FIRE ADMINISTRATION)

Every year, about half a million buildings catch fire in the United States, and about 3,000 people lose their lives. The USFA suggests that families plan an escape route and choose a place to meet in case of a fire emergency at home.

## FEMA (FEDERAL EMERGENCY MANAGEMENT AGENCY)

FEMA deals with all kinds of emergencies. If there is a bad flood, a big storm, or a deadly explosion, FEMA is there to help. FEMA also provides information on how to prepare for emergencies. One of FEMA's suggestions is to put together an emergency kit with necessary supplies.

*Make an emergency supply kit.*

## Weekly Question

**What are some ways to prepare for an emergency?**

**Quick Write** Think about and take notes on how agencies such as NOAA, the USFA, and FEMA can help before, during, or after an emergency. Discuss your ideas with a partner, and listen actively to your partner's ideas.

**Learning Goal**

I can learn more about informational texts and analyze the text structure in a procedural text.

**Spotlight on Genre**

# Procedural Text

A **procedural text** is an informational text that explains how to perform a task.

Authors of procedural text use a **chronological,** or time-order, text structure. This text structure

- Shows the **sequence,** or order, of steps to complete a task
- Might use **numbers** and **bullet points** to organize instructions and information
- Includes **transitional words,** such as *next* or *then*, to help readers follow instructions

**Establish Purpose** The **purpose,** or reason, for reading a procedural text is often to learn how to do or make something. The structure of a procedural text helps readers understand the steps or order of the process.

Following steps is as easy as 1, 2, 3!

My **PURPOSE** _____

_____

_____

**TURN and TALK** With a partner, discuss different purposes for reading *A Safety Plan*. For example, you may want to learn how to stay safe in an emergency. Set your purpose for reading this text.

# PROCEDURAL TEXT
## ANCHOR CHART

Purpose: To explain how to complete a task

## CHARACTERISTICS OF PROCEDURAL TEXTS

- **TITLE**: identifies the process being described

- **SIGNAL WORDS**: SHOW STEPS IN A PROCESS; EXAMPLES INCLUDE first, next, and finally

- **MATERIALS LIST**: shows items needed for the process

- **NUMBERED LIST**: shows steps in order

- **CONCLUSION**: summarizes or encourages self-check

**Marcie Rendon**
is a Native American writer who lives in Minnesota. She writes books, short stories, plays, and poems. She especially likes to write about Native American life. Marcie is a mother and grandmother, and she enjoys teaching her grandchildren's dog to do tricks, such as playing the piano!

# A Safety Plan: In Case of Emergency

## Preview Vocabulary

As you read *A Safety Plan*, pay attention to these vocabulary words. Notice how they provide clues to the structure of the procedural text.

| | | |
|---|---|---|
| prepared | | emergency |
| memorize | responsible | instructions |

## Read

Before you begin, preview the text. Look at the headings, numbered and bulleted lists, and other text features. Follow these strategies when you read this **procedural text** the first time.

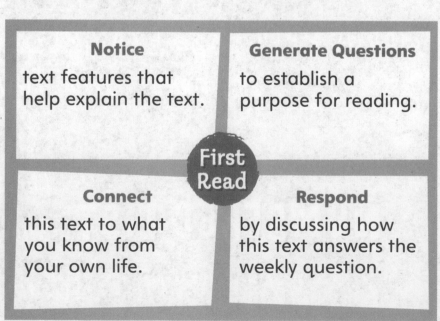

**Notice**
text features that help explain the text.

**Generate Questions**
to establish a purpose for reading.

**First Read**

**Connect**
this text to what you know from your own life.

**Respond**
by discussing how this text answers the weekly question.

# A SAFETY PLAN
## *In* Case *of* Emergency

 AUDIO

ANNOTATE

BY **Marcie Rendon**

## Analyze Text Structure

Underline details that help you recognize the text structure on this page and explain how this structure contributes to the author's purpose for writing the text.

**prepared** ready or have made ready for use at a later time

**emergency** a serious or dangerous situation

1  Life works out better when you're prepared. If you study for your test, you're likely to get a good grade. If your family makes a grocery list, you'll remember to get everything you need.

2  It makes sense to prepare for an emergency too. A disaster is an emergency that causes harm to people or places. You may never experience a flood, a tornado, or another kind of disaster. However, it's smart to prepare so you'll be ready to keep yourself safe.

3  Preparing for emergencies isn't hard. In fact, it can be fun! It will help you to feel safe and secure too.

4  Work with your family to make a plan. Put together a safety kit. Then you'll be ready for anything—just in case.

# Step One: Learn About Natural Disasters

5   The first step of making a safety plan is to learn about different types of natural disasters. In particular, learn about disasters that might occur in your area. The more you know, the better you'll be able to prepare.

6   The National Weather Service is an excellent source of information about natural disasters. Natural disasters are events in nature that harm a certain area. You can learn where they are most likely to happen and how to prepare for them. The National Weather Service Web site provides facts about weather events and safety.

7   You should know about the following types of natural disasters. None of these events happens often. In fact, a natural disaster may never happen where you live. However, being prepared will help you feel confident. If an emergency arises, you'll be able to think clearly and to help others.

## CLOSE READ

### Monitor Comprehension

Highlight two details you can use to ask a question to monitor your comprehension of this section of the text.

## Types of Natural Disasters

| | |
|---|---|
| **Earthquake** | a sudden and violent shaking of the ground as a result of movements within the earth |
| **Flood** | an overflow of a large amount of water, especially over what is normally dry land |
| **Hurricane or cyclone** | a storm with violent winds and heavy rain |
| **Landslide** | a sliding down of a mass of earth or rock from a mountain, hill, or cliff |
| **Thunderstorm** | a storm with thunder and lightning, often with heavy rain or hail |
| **Tornado** | a storm with violent rotating winds |
| **Tsunami** | a large ocean wave that reaches land, often caused by an undersea earthquake, a volcanic eruption, or a landslide |
| **Volcanic eruption** | an explosion of lava, rock fragments, hot air, and gas through a crater or vent in the earth's surface |
| **Wildfire** | a large, destructive fire that spreads quickly through forests, plains, or other natural areas |
| **Winter storm** | a storm dropping large amounts of snow, sleet, and/or freezing rain |

# Step Two: Make a Safety Plan

8    The second step of preparing for emergencies is to make a safety plan with your family. The plan will help you to locate one another. It will also help you to find a safe place to meet during an emergency.

9    You and your family should decide

- which family members will call each other in an emergency.

- which neighbors you will contact.

- which out-of-town or out-of-state relative or friend you will contact.

- where family members will meet.

**Analyze Text Structure**

Underline details that help you recognize and explain the author's purpose for using bullets in paragraph 9.

## Vocabulary in Context

In paragraph 12, the author uses the phrase "in your head" when explaining a calling plan.

Use context clues within and before the sentence to determine the meaning of the phrase "in your head."

<u>Underline</u> the context clues that support your definition.

**memorize** learn exactly and without the chance of forgetting

### The Calling Plan

10  Your family should create a calling plan. Make sure all family members have a paper copy. Keep the plan in a safe place. (You might want to keep yours in your school backpack.) Family members with cellular phones should save the phone numbers they will need in their contact lists.

11  It's important to have a contact person who is out of town or out of state. This person may be easier to reach during an emergency because the event may not be happening in his or her location.

12  Try to memorize your parents' or caregivers' phone numbers. If you don't have a phone and need to borrow someone else's, you'll have the most important phone numbers in your head.

**Tip:** Family members who have cellular phones should send a text message rather than call during an emergency. It's best to leave phone lines free. That way, if police, firefighters, or other emergency workers need to call, they'll be able to reach you.

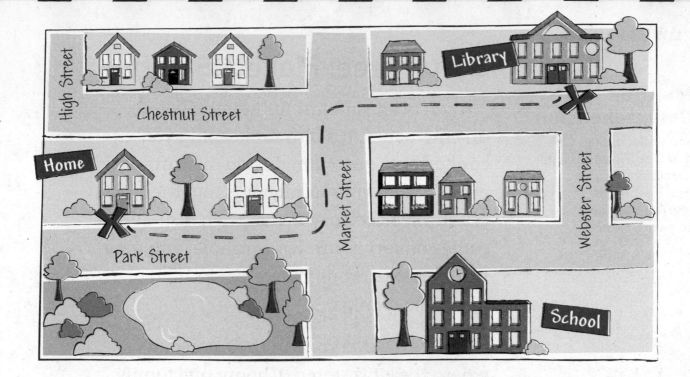

## The Meeting Plan

13   Decide with your family where you will meet in case of an emergency. In some situations, it will make sense to meet at your home. In other emergencies, you might not be able to get to your home or neighborhood. Choose a meeting spot outside your neighborhood. Make sure all family members know how to get there.

## Draw a Map

14   With your family, draw a simple map of your neighborhood. Mark the location of your home. Label it. Show the location of your school. Label it. Finally, mark the meeting spot outside your neighborhood. Label it and add street names. Draw a line showing the best route from one location to another.

**CLOSE READ**

### Analyze Text Structure

Underline text details that support the information given in the section headings. Explain the author's purpose for structuring the text this way.

### Monitor Comprehension

Look back at Step One and Step Two. Highlight details on this page that help you understand how the steps are related.

**responsible** in charge or in control of a job or duty

# Step Three: Make a Safety Kit

15  A safety kit isn't just for helping you in an emergency. It's also for keeping you comfortable and calm during and after the event. When your family puts together a kit, put in the necessary items. Then also add some comfort items. For example, you may want an extra comfy piece of clothing or a favorite blanket.

16  Make sure everyone in the family knows where the kit is stored. Choose one family member to be responsible for checking the kit twice a year. That person should check that everything in the kit is fresh and up to date. Look for expiration dates on medicine labels and other items. Your family should replace items that have expired.

17  Schedule kit checks on the days when your family changes the clocks for Daylight Saving Time. That way you won't forget to keep the kit updated.

514

## What Goes in a Safety Kit?

18    Here are important items to include in a safety kit.

### Analyze Text Structure

Underline details that help you explain the author's purpose for using numbers and bullets to structure this section of the text.

19    **1** **Food, water, and related supplies**

* One gallon of water per person per day, for three days

* A three-day supply of nonperishable food for each person (Nonperishable food is food that won't go bad. Include only foods you don't need to refrigerate or heat. Make sure it's food your family likes to eat!)

* A non-electric can opener

* Unbreakable plates, cups, and utensils

* Paper towels and plastic bags

20    **2** **Personal items**

* Clothes for each person for three days; include warm clothing, socks, and comfortable, sturdy shoes

* Toothbrushes, toothpaste, soap, and toilet paper

* A pillow and a sleeping bag or blanket for each person

* Diapers and other baby supplies, if needed

## Analyze Text Structure

<u>Underline</u> words that help you recognize the author's purpose for using bullets on this page. Explain how the purpose is different from her purpose for using bullets in paragraph 9.

21 **3 First-aid kit**

- Bandages, aspirin, and other supplies (The American Red Cross Web site has a complete list of what to include.)

- Prescription medicines, if needed

- Names and phone numbers of health-care providers

22 **4 Electronics and safety supplies**

- A battery-powered radio

- A cell phone and a solar charger

- A whistle (to signal for help if needed)

- Matches in a waterproof container (Let the adults handle these.)

- Flashlights, one per person

- Extra batteries

23 **5 Documents**

- Identification information for each family member

- Insurance and bank information

24 **6 Extras**

- Toys, games, and books

- Paper and pens or pencils

## Don't Forget the Pets!

If your family owns pets, you'll want to create a supply kit for them too. It should include the following items:

- A three-day supply of food and water for each pet

- A supply of medicines, if needed

- Copies of your pets' veterinary records

- Cat litter and litter box (if you have a cat!)

- Food dishes

## Monitor Comprehension

Highlight sentences that you can reread to monitor your comprehension of why instructions and weather updates are important.

**instructions** directions or orders

# During and After an Emergency

25   In any emergency, it's important to stay calm. Remember, if you've followed the steps on the previous pages, you and your family are well prepared! All you need to do now is to listen for instructions. Pay close attention to emergency workers, such as police, firefighters, or government officials. They will provide important information, such as whether to stay home or to move to another location.

26   In case of weather emergencies, use your portable radio to find the NOAA (National Oceanic and Atmospheric Administration) radio station. You can also get weather updates on a cellular phone. Information will be available on severe weather conditions and how long they're expected to last.

27  It's important to follow adults' instructions before, during, and after an emergency. Dangerous conditions such as fallen power lines or gas leaks can require extra caution. Emergency workers will give you the "all clear!" when it's safe to go outside.

28  Finally, you and your family may want to help your community recover from an emergency situation. Check with your local Red Cross or other agencies to find the best ways to help your neighbors or your town recover.

29  Don't forget to give your family a big hug too! You showed you can get through challenging times together, thanks to some careful planning. Good work!

**CLOSE READ**

## Analyze Text Structure

Underline details that help you understand how the text structure contributes to the author's purpose of describing how to stay safe after an emergency. Explain your answer.

# Develop Vocabulary

In procedural texts, authors choose precise words to explain how to make or do something. These words help the reader understand and follow the directions in the text.

**My TURN** Add the vocabulary word from the word bank to complete the chart. Then use each newly acquired vocabulary word in a sentence about making a safety plan.

### Word Bank

**prepared**  **emergency**  **responsible**  **memorize**

| Synonym | Vocabulary Word | Antonym | Sentence |
|---------|-----------------|---------|----------|
| remember | memorize | forget | Memorize your parents' phone numbers. |
| crisis | | peace | |
| ready | | unready | |
| in charge | | excused | |

# Check for Understanding

**My TURN** Look back at the text to answer the questions.

1. What characteristics help you identify this as a procedural text?

2. What do you think is the author's purpose for including the chart on natural disasters?

3. What text evidence supports the idea that families should create a safety plan together?

4. How can preparing for an emergency help keep people safe? Synthesize information from different sections of the text in your response.

# Analyze Text Structure

Authors of informational texts organize ideas in an overall **text structure**, such as cause and effect, problem and solution, and sequence. Analyze text structure to help explain the author's purpose for writing.

1. **My TURN** Go to the Close Read notes in *A Safety Plan*. Underline parts that help you analyze text structure.

2. **Text Evidence** Use some of the parts you underlined to complete the chart.

| Text Evidence | Text Structure | How Structure Contributes to Author's Purpose |
|---|---|---|
| Paragraph 1: "If you study for your test, you're likely to get a good grade. If your family makes a grocery list, you'll remember to get everything you need." Paragraphs 18–20: | cause and effect | The author connects positive effects of planning in everyday life as reasons to create a safety plan. |

# Monitor Comprehension

**Monitor comprehension**, or check your understanding, as you read. If your understanding breaks down, make adjustments. For example, you can reread, use background knowledge, ask questions, or annotate (mark up) the text.

1. **My TURN** Go back to the Close Read notes and annotate the text by highlighting evidence that helps you monitor your comprehension.

2. **Text Evidence** Use some of your highlighted text to complete the chart.

| Text Evidence | How I Can Check My Understanding | How This Adjustment Helped Me |
|---|---|---|
| "Step One: Learn About Natural Disasters"; "The first step of making a safety plan is to learn about different types of natural disasters." | I can ask a question and answer it by rereading. | I asked myself, "Why is this information included?" When I reread paragraphs 5 and 6, I realized that natural disasters can cause harm, so it is important to learn about them. |
| | | |

# Reflect and Share

**Write to Sources** Consider the informational texts you have read in this unit. Think about the types of emergencies described in the texts. What situations are easy to plan for? For what situations would planning be more difficult? Use these questions to help you write an opinion paragraph about the types of emergencies for which planning would be the easiest.

- - - - - - - - - - - - - - - - - - - - - - - - - - - - - - - - - - -

**Use Text Evidence** When writing an opinion, it is important to use text evidence to support your ideas.

- ◎ Look for details that connect safety planning with specific types of emergencies.
- ◎ Look for key words and phrases that support your opinion.
- ◎ Look for quotations that support your opinion.

Write your opinion paragraph on a separate sheet of paper. Use evidence from the texts to support your opinion.

- - - - - - - - - - - - - - - - - - - - - - - - - - - - - - - - - - -

## Weekly Question

**What are some ways to prepare for an emergency?**

# Academic Vocabulary

**Context Clues** are words and phrases that help you determine the meaning of unfamiliar words. Context clues can be found in the same sentence or in surrounding sentences.

**My TURN** For each sentence below,

1. **Underline** the academic vocabulary word.

2. **Highlight** the context clue or clues.

3. **Write** a brief definition based on the clues.

**Academic Vocabulary:** analysis, threat, anticipate, pollution

Dr. Brown thoroughly studied my test results. Then she shared the analysis of what she found with me.

**Definition:** _____

The family heard the warning that there was a threat of a tornado. They were ready for it because they had a safety plan.

**Definition:** _____

Before I pack clothes for a vacation, I think ahead and plan. I try to anticipate the weather conditions.

**Definition:** _____

Sara was upset when she saw ducks swimming with discarded cans, trash, and other pollution on the beach.

**Definition:** _____

# Words with Suffix -en

**Suffix -en** When the suffix -en is added to a word, the original word is usually read in the same way. An example would be adding -en to the word *hard*. The word part *hard* is read the same in the word *harden*.

| Rule | Word | New Word |
|------|------|----------|
| When the last two letters are consonants, add -en. | hard, quick | harden, quicken |
| When the word ends with e, drop the e and add -en. | take, ripe | taken, ripen |
| When the word ends with a vowel-consonant combination, double the final consonant and add -en. | flat, sad | flatten, sadden |

**My TURN** Read the following words with the suffix -en: *golden, widen, waken, sicken*. Then write two sentences using a word with the suffix -en.

1. _____

2. _____

# High-Frequency Words

**High-frequency words** are words that you may see often as you read. Read these high-frequency words: *syllables, direction*.

# Read Like a Writer

When the author's purpose is to explain a procedure, he or she may use a text structure that presents the steps in a process. Authors also use time-order words and text features such as images and labels.

**Model !** Read the passage from *A Safety Plan: In Case of Emergency*.

> ### Step One: Learn About Natural Disasters
>
> The first step of making a safety plan is to learn about different types of natural disasters.

*Headings and time-order words suggest text structure.*

1. **Identify** Marcie Rendon uses a heading and time-order word to show a process text structure.

2. **Question** How does this text structure help explain the text?

3. **Conclude** The text structure helps me understand how to start the process of making a safety plan.

Read the passage.

> ### Step Two: Make a Safety Plan
>
> The second step of preparing for emergencies is to make a safety plan with your family.

**My TURN** Follow the steps to analyze the passage. Explain how the author's use of text structure contributes to her purpose for writing.

1. **Identify** Marcie Rendon uses _____ to show a process text structure.

2. **Question** How does this text structure help explain the text?

3. **Conclude** It helps me understand _____.

# Write for a Reader

Writers might use a **text structure** that includes steps in a process to explain how to perform a task.

**My TURN** Think about how the author of *A Safety Plan: In Case of Emergency* uses the text structure of steps in a process. This structure helps the author achieve her purpose of telling readers how to prepare for emergencies. Now think about how you can use the text structure of steps in a process to write about how to do something.

1. Write something you would like to teach readers how to do.

_____

_____

2. Think about your purpose of explaining how to do something. Use the text structure of steps in a process to teach your idea.

_____

_____

_____

3. Explain how including steps in a process contributes to your purpose for writing.

_____

_____

_____

# Spell Words with Suffix -en

**Words with Suffix -en** sometimes have a spelling change before adding the suffix. Knowing the rules for adding the suffix -en can help you figure out how to spell these words.

**My TURN** Read the words. Sort the words by the spelling change that occurs when -en is added.

**SPELLING WORDS**

| | | |
|---|---|---|
| awaken | sharpen | brighten |
| given | lengthen | loosen |
| widen | gladden | lighten |
| soften | | |

| Add -en | Drop the final e and add -en | Double the final consonant and add -en |
|---|---|---|
| | | |
| | | |
| | | |
| | | |
| | | |

# High-Frequency Words

High-frequency words can be difficult to sound out. Write these high-frequency words on the lines.

syllables _____

direction _____

# Complex Sentences

A **complex sentence** is made up of two clauses, or groups of words with a subject and a verb. In a complex sentence, one clause cannot stand alone—a **dependent clause**. The other clause can stand alone—an **independent clause**. The dependent clause begins with a subordinating conjunction such as *before, after, when,* or *until*. If the dependent clause starts the sentence, a comma follows it.

| Dependent Clause | Independent Clause | Complex Sentence |
|---|---|---|
| **Before** adding the sugar | Mix the butter with a mixer. | Before adding the sugar, mix the butter with a mixer. |
| **After** my sister got sick | We all went to the doctor. | We all went to the doctor after my sister got sick. |
| **When** it is cold outside | We wear warm coats. | When it is cold outside, we wear warm coats. |
| **Until** my parents get home | I am in charge. | I am in charge until my parents get home. |

**My TURN** Edit this draft by combining dependent and independent clauses to create complex sentences. Use a subordinating conjunction to join clauses.

Daryl and I made lemonade. We got a pitcher. We poured in the lemon juice. We added the sugar. We poured in cold water. It reached the top. We added crushed ice. We served the lemonade. We had another cup. We still wanted more!

# Use Line Breaks and Stanzas

Poets choose a structure to organize their poems. The structure shows readers how the poems should be read. Poets use **line breaks** and **stanzas**, and sometimes even empty space, to create short lines or group lines into stanzas.

**Learning Goal**

I can use knowledge of the sound and shape of poetry to write a poem.

**My TURN** Read the poem. Then answer the questions.

---

**Who Has Seen the Wind?**

Who has seen the wind?
Neither I nor you:
But when the leaves hang trembling,
The wind is passing through.

Who has seen the wind?
Neither you nor I:
But when the trees bow down their heads,
The wind is passing by.

*Christina Rossetti*

---

**1.** How do the line breaks help create natural pauses?

**2.** How are the stanzas alike?

**My TURN** Compose your own poem. Put in line breaks, stanzas, and empty space to create the effect you want.

# Select a Genre

A **genre** is a category of writing. Poetry is one genre of writing. Examples of some other genres include personal narratives, opinion essays, and historical fiction. Some writers find it helpful to explore a single topic in two separate genres. Writing in one genre may bring out different ideas and details that can be used in the other genre.

**My TURN** Brainstorm topics, and decide on one for your poem. Then select another genre for that same topic. In your writing notebook, write about your topic in that genre. Finally, answer the questions.

1. What is your topic?

_____

2. What genre did you select? Why?

_____

_____

3. How would you describe the experience of writing about your topic in that genre?

_____

_____

_____

4. How can you use this writing to improve your poem?

_____

_____

_____

# Revise for Word Choice: Verbs

Here are some reasons to revise poetry for word choice:

- Choose specific verbs.
- Surprise an audience with an unexpected word.
- Improve a poem's sound or rhythm.
- Use a word that better fits the topic or mood.
- Combine ideas or rearrange words for clarity.

Because poetry uses fewer words than prose, or ordinary language, every word should say as much as possible. Use strong verbs to help readers experience action or emotion.

**My TURN** Read the poem. Revise it by writing two strong verbs that could replace each highlighted verb.

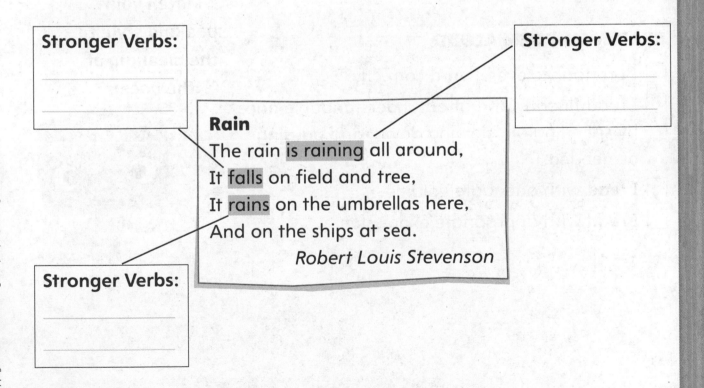

**Stronger Verbs:**
_____
_____

**Stronger Verbs:**
_____
_____

**Rain**
The rain is raining all around,
It falls on field and tree,
It rains on the umbrellas here,
And on the ships at sea.
*Robert Louis Stevenson*

**Stronger Verbs:**
_____
_____

**My TURN** As you revise your poem, choose verbs that help you create the effect you want to have on the reader

# Create an Audio Recording

Poets make **audio recordings** of their poems for different reasons.

- Poetry often has a musical quality that is better enjoyed when reading or hearing it aloud.
- A poet's expression, rate of speaking, and volume can give an audience extra information about a poem's mood, emotion, and meaning.
- An audio recording might reach audiences who are not able to read a poem.

**My TURN** Work with a partner. Take turns reading your poems aloud. Use the checklist to help you practice. Then create an audio recording of your poem.

## READING A POEM ALOUD

☐ I pronounce every word correctly.

☐ I read fluently and at an understandable pace by speeding up, slowing down, and pausing as needed.

☐ I read with adequate volume.

☐ I read with appropriate expression.

Match your speaking style to the meaning of the poem.

# Create a Visual Display

Writers might include **visual displays** to emphasize or enhance certain details in their poems. The sound of poetry adds to its meaning, and so does the look of poetry. This look includes the placement of words and lines on the page. However, it can also include other visual elements, such as colors, pictures, special lettering, and lines that form a shape. Poets can publish their poems online with visual displays and audio recordings of their poems.

**My TURN** Use the chart to brainstorm ideas for the visual display of your poem. Next, create the visual display. Finally, publish your visual display along with an audio recording of your poem.

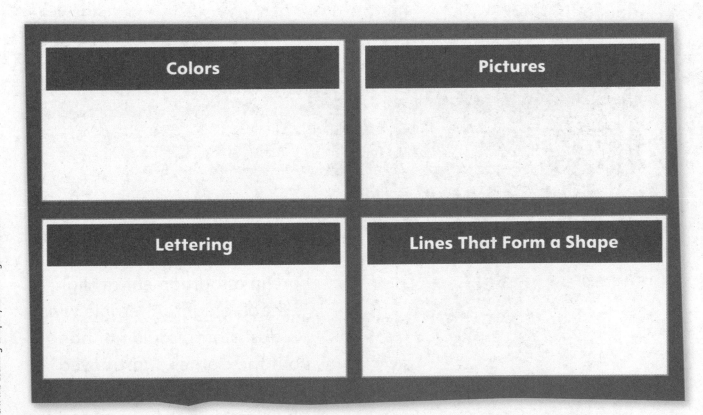

| Colors | Pictures |
| --- | --- |
| | |

| Lettering | Lines That Form a Shape |
| --- | --- |
| | |

**My TURN** Identify a topic, purpose, and audience. Then select any genre, and plan a draft by mapping your ideas.

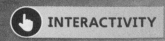 INTERACTIVITY

# THE DUST BOWL

In the 1930s, lack of rain and overused farmland created disaster for the Plains States. The Dust Bowl drought of the 1930s affected 19 states and lasted from 1931 to 1939. Dust storms brought high, strong winds that blew dust everywhere. Skies were dark for days during the storms. Homes were either destroyed or filled with dust. Food was scarce. People headed west to find work and a new life.

Read some eyewitness accounts in these diary entries of Mabel Holmes, who lived in Topeka, Kansas, to find out what life was like during the Dust Bowl.

Kansas

**MARCH 15 1935** Elma's boys are in a tournament at High School tonight. A terrible wind & dust storm, could not hang out the clothes. Max moved to 1134 Polk & at Gt Bend Ks & Scottsbluff Nebr. the wind & dust is so bad motorists have had to stop.

**MARCH 16 1935** Temp. went from 82 to 24 today. The dust wave blew allnight, at times could not see, everything covered with dirt. Dried the clothes in the bath room, got them ironed, Another war scare in Europe. Max was here all P.M. Several deaths & accidents from the Dust storms, trains were late.

**MARCH 20 1935** A severe dust storm raged over the city all day, could not see Dibbles plaza, nor to get around in the house without a light.

**MARCH 21 1935** The houses are in a terrible condition from the storm. Was over an hr. getting dust off of porches & walks, more dust flying, but do not need lights.

## Weekly Question

**How should people respond during a disaster?**

**Turn and Talk** With a partner, discuss how this firsthand account of the Dust Bowl helps you better understand how people cope with a disaster. Listen actively to your partner, and take notes on your discussion.

I can learn more about themes concerning *solutions* by analyzing point of view in historical fiction.

# Historical Fiction

**Historical fiction** is realistic fiction that takes place in a certain time period in the past. It combines imagination and fact. Historical fiction includes

- **Characters**, **settings**, and **events** that could be real, made-up, or a mix of the two
- A **first-person point of view** (the narrator is a character in the story) or a **third-person point of view** (the narrator is outside the story and telling the events)

**TURN and TALK** Discuss with a partner how you identified the point of view in a historical fiction text you have read.

**Be a Fluent Reader** Fluent readers read with expression. Practice reading dialogue in historical fiction until it sounds like natural speech.

When you read dialogue aloud,

- ◔ Raise or lower the pitch of your voice to express how the character feels.
- ◔ Read with excitement when you see an exclamation mark.

# HISTORICAL FICTION
## ANCHOR CHART

- - - - - - - - - - - - - - - - - - - - -

**Setting**
- The time period is real.
- The place is real.

**Characters**
- Characters may be real, made up, or both.

**Plot**
- Events can be real or made up.

**Point of view**
- The story is told in first-person or third-person point of view.

**Theme**
- The story often contains a theme, or message about life.

**Natalie Kinsey-Warnock** has always lived in Vermont, where her Scottish ancestors first settled in America. Her dozens of books for young people include *As Long As There Are Mountains*, which is a book based on her childhood on a dairy farm in a region of Vermont called the Northeast Kingdom.

# Nora's Ark

## Preview Vocabulary

As you read *Nora's Ark*, pay attention to these vocabulary words. Notice how they describe the challenges the family and their friends face.

| | | |
|---|---|---|
| **survived** | **astonished** | |
| **dangerous** | **piteously** | **relief** |

## Read

Preview the illustrations to establish a purpose for reading. Follow these strategies when you read this **historical fiction** text the first time.

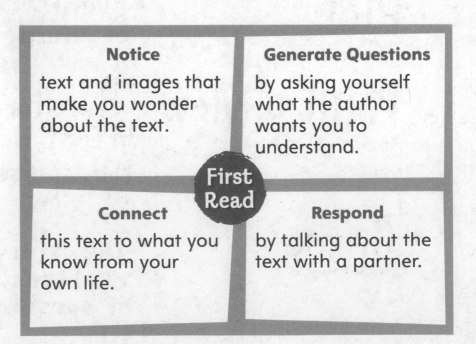

**Notice** text and images that make you wonder about the text.

**Generate Questions** by asking yourself what the author wants you to understand.

**First Read**

**Connect** this text to what you know from your own life.

**Respond** by talking about the text with a partner.

# NORA'S ARK

*by* Natalie Kinsey-Warnock

*illustrated by* Emily Arnold McCully

AUDIO

ANNOTATE

1    When I was born, Grandma said I was so small I looked like a little bird. That's why I was named Wren. Grandma may look small, too, but she's made of granite, and she says I'm tough, just like she is. Good thing, or we never would have survived the 1927 Flood.

2    Grandma and Grandpa lived on a little farm by a river in Vermont. They didn't have much money, but there was always plenty to eat— milk from Grandpa's cows, vegetables from Grandma's garden, apples and plums from the orchard, fish from the river, and maple syrup that Grandpa and Grandma made each spring.

**CLOSE READ**

## Analyze Point of View

Underline sentences that help you identify the point of view from which the story is told. Notice the pronouns used.

**survived** lived through or stayed alive

**Make Connections**

Highlight Wren's description that helps you compare and contrast houses in your community with Grandma's new house.

3   Grandpa was building Grandma a new house. It sat on a hill and, when finished, it would have electricity, a wringer washing machine, and best of all, an indoor bathroom.

4   "I don't need a new house, Horace," Grandma said. "We've lived here forty years, raised eight children, and been as happy as a family could be. That new house is just gravy."

5   "What do you mean?" I asked her.

6   Grandma thought how she could explain it to me.

7   "You like potatoes, don't you, Wren?"

8   "Yes, ma'am," I told her. Grandma made the best mashed potatoes in the world, with lots of milk, butter, and pepper in them. You could make a meal out of just her potatoes.

9   "You like gravy on them?"

10   "I reckon." Grandma did make good gravy. "But your potatoes taste good without gravy, too," I told her.

11    "Exactly," Grandma said. "Gravy tastes good, but you don't need it, and I don't need that new house. I like living here."

12    But Grandpa kept right on building.

## Vocabulary in Context

Use context clues within and beyond the sentence to determine the meaning of the word *torrents* in paragraph 14.

Underline the context clues that support your definition.

13   When it began to rain on November 2, 1927, no one along the river had any idea nine inches of rain would fall in two days. Life in Vermont was about to change forever.

14   The rain came down in torrents. It drummed so loudly on the roof we couldn't talk. Grandma spent the morning baking bread. By noon, she'd made twenty-seven loaves.

15   "Grandma, why'd you make so much bread?" I shouted.

16   Grandma watched the water stream down the windows.

17   "We might need it," she said, but I couldn't imagine how we'd eat twenty-seven loaves of bread.

18   When Grandpa came in for lunch, he poured a quart of water out of each boot.

19   "I've never seen the river rise so fast," he said. "I think we'd best get up to the new house."

20   For once, Grandma didn't argue. By the time she'd packed quilts, candles, her photo albums, and a sack of potatoes, the water was up to the porch.

21   Grandpa let all the cows and horses out of the barn.

22   "What will happen to them?" I asked.

23   "They'll get to higher ground and be all right," he said. "Don't worry, Wren." But I could tell he was the one who was worried.

24   I loaded all those loaves of bread into my old baby carriage, covered it with an oilcloth, and pushed it through the mud and rain to the new house.

25   "Guess I built this place just in time," Grandpa said.

26   "If I didn't know better, I'd think you caused this flood just so I'd have to move into the new house," Grandma said, but she seemed glad to be on higher ground, too.

27   We'd scarcely set foot inside when we heard pounding on the door.

**CLOSE READ**

## Analyze Point of View

Underline Wren's descriptions that help you understand her grandparents' feelings.

28   The three Guthrie boys stood on the porch, burlap bags in each hand. The bags squirmed and squawked.

29   "Our barn's flooded. Can we keep the chickens here?"

30   They emptied the chickens onto the kitchen floor.

31   "Some of our heifers are stranded in the fields," one of the boys said. "We're gonna see if we can push them to higher ground."

32   "I'll go with you," Grandpa said.

33   "May I go, too?" I asked.

34   "No!" Grandpa and Grandma both said at once.

35   "Be careful," Grandma told him, and he and the boys disappeared through the rain.

36   Even with all those chickens, the house seemed empty with Grandpa gone.

37   Grandma saw me shiver and wrapped a quilt around me.

38   "It's getting colder," she said. "I wish I had my cookstove here." She held me close as we stood watching the rain.

39   "I wish Grandpa would come back," I said.

40   "Me, too," said Grandma.

## Analyze Point of View

Underline details that reveal what Wren and Grandma think about having a horse in the house. How does the narrator's point of view help you understand her relationship with Grandma?

**astonished** very surprised or amazed

41  We both shrieked when a huge head appeared in the window. It was Major, one of the Fergusons' horses.

42  I was even more astonished when Grandma opened the door and led him in.

43  "You're bringing Major into the house?"

44  "We don't have a stove," Grandma said. "He's big. He'll add heat to the place."

45  Major took up half the kitchen. The other half was taken up by loaves of bread and chickens.

46  We had chickens in the cupboards, chickens on the shelves and in the baby carriage, even chickens roosting on Major's back.

47 Our next visitors were Mrs. Lafleur and her daughter, Madeleine. Mrs. Lafleur didn't speak much English.

48 "Our house wash away," Mrs. Lafleur said. "We row boat here."

49 Madeleine looked around the kitchen, and her eyes opened wide.

50 "Des poulets dans le chariot de bébé?" she said. I guess she'd never seen chickens in a baby carriage before.

**CLOSE READ**

## Analyze Point of View

Underline details that you can use to explain how Wren's point of view helps the reader understand Madeleine's reaction. Consider how your own point of view differs from that of the narrator or other characters.

## Make Connections

Highlight evidence that the safety of farm animals is important to people in a farming society.

51    By nightfall, the house was full to bursting. Besides Mrs. Lafleur and Madeleine, Mr. and Mrs. Guthrie, the Fergusons, and the Craig family had moved in, twenty-three people in all. There were also three horses, a cow, five pigs, a duck, four cats, and one hundred chickens.

52　The river rose until the house became an island, and we watched our neighbors' houses wash down the river.

**CLOSE READ**

## Vocabulary in Context

The word *wash* can mean "to make clean." It can also mean "to carry in a direction."

Underline context clues within the sentence that help you determine the meaning of *wash* as it is used in the text.

53   Mr. and Mrs. Guthrie had brought a side of salt pork with them, though we had no way to cook it. The Fergusons had saved their radio, a skillet, a bag of dried apples, and a three-legged cat. They were delighted to find Major alive and well and in our kitchen.

54   The Craigs had lost everything but the clothes on their backs.

55   "We're just glad we all got out alive," Mrs. Craig said, which only reminded Grandma and me that Grandpa had still not returned.

56   We had bread and dried apples for supper, and rainwater Madeleine and I scooped out of the Lafleurs' rowboat. The water had a few fish scales in it, but no one complained.

57  With no stove or beds, we all huddled together for warmth, sharing Grandma's quilts as best we could. We sang Scottish songs and "Row, Row, Row Your Boat" in a round, and Mrs. Lafleur taught us "À la Claire Fontaine," a tune that brought tears to our eyes even though we couldn't understand the words. Mrs. Guthrie told how her grandfather had fought at Gettysburg, and Mr. Craig kept us laughing with stories of his boyhood days in a logging camp in Maine. If it hadn't been for the thought of Grandpa out there somewhere, it would have almost seemed like a party.

## Vocabulary in Context

Use context clues within the sentence to determine the meaning of the word *forbid* in paragraph 59.

<u>Underline</u> the context clues that support your definition.

**dangerous** unsafe or likely to cause harm

58    I knew Grandma was worried about Grandpa. I was worried, too. He should have been home by now.

59    I wanted to ask Peter Ferguson if he would come with me to look for Grandpa, but I knew if Grandma overheard she'd forbid me to go, so when the sky was getting light, I sneaked out and sprinted for the rowboat.

60    Grandma was just getting into it.

61    "What are you doing here?" she wanted to know.

62    "Same as you, I reckon. Going to look for Grandpa."

63    "It's too dangerous," Grandma said. "Go back to the house," but I shook my head.

64    Grandma looked at me hard.

65    "All right," she said. "We'll look for him together."

66    I pushed us off into water that was full of furniture and trees and dead animals. Grandma had to be careful where she rowed. It was raining so hard I had to keep bailing water out of the boat.

67   Nothing looked the same. Fields had become lakes. Just the roofs of houses stuck up above the water.

68   On one of those roofs we saw a dog.

69   "Why, I believe that's Sam Burroughs' collie," Grandma said, and she rowed toward the house. The collie barked when she saw us coming.

70   I held on to the roof to steady the boat.

71   "Come on, girl," I said, and the dog jumped into the boat beside me. She whined and licked my face.

72   The strangest sight was yet to come. We rounded a bend in the river and I squinted, sure that my eyes were fooling me. Then I heard Grandma's voice behind me.

73   "Wren, are these old eyes failing me, or is that a cow in a tree?" Grandma asked.

## CLOSE READ

## Make Connections

Highlight details that describe what the narrator sees. Compare and contrast these descriptions to what people in a modern society might see during a flood.

## Make Connections

Highlight details that Wren sees and hears that help you explain the dangers living things might face during a flood.

**piteously** in a sad and suffering way

**relief** a feeling of happiness that follows worry

74  It was indeed. A red and white Ayrshire was wedged into the crook formed by two branches, and she was bawling piteously. Higher up in the branches was a man. He was hollering almost as loudly as the cow.

75  "I believe we've found your grandpa," Grandma said, relief flooding her face.

76  "I was on my way home when I got swept away by the water," Grandpa said. "I thought I was a goner, too, but when this cow floated by, I grabbed her tail and stayed afloat until she got hung up in this tree."

77 We pushed and pulled on that cow, but she was stuck fast and we finally had to leave her. Grandpa promised he'd come back and try to cut her free, but he was crying as we rowed away.

78 "Goodness," Grandma said. "All that fuss over a cow." But Grandpa wasn't crying over just one cow.

79 "All our cows drowned, Nora," he said. "The house, the barn, the horses, they're all gone."

80  Grandma wiped the tears from his cheeks.

81  "You're safe, and that's all that matters," she said.

82  "We'll have to start over," Grandpa said, and Grandma smiled.

83  "We can do that," she said.

84  Grandpa smiled back at her, and I knew then that, no matter what, everything would be all right.

85  The Craigs, Fergusons, Guthries, and Lafleurs were glad to see us. Madeleine even hugged me.

86  "She was afraid you'd drowned," Peter said. He blushed. "I was, too," he added.

87  When Grandpa saw all the animals in the kitchen, he burst out laughing.

88  "Nora, I thought I was building you a house, but I see it was really an ark."

## CLOSE READ

**Analyze Point of View**

<u>Underline</u> a sentence that reveals a change in the narrator's feelings.

**CLOSE READ**

**Make Connections**

Highlight the narrator's statement that helps you explain how a flood affects people and societies.

89   It took three days for the water to go down enough so our neighbors could go see what was left of their farms.

90   Grandpa put his arm around Grandma.

91   "I'll finish this house the way you want it, Nora," he said. But he shook his head when the Fergusons led Major out.

92   "I don't know as I'll ever be able to get those hoofprints out of this floor," he said.

93   I've now lived in my grandparents' house for more than forty years, and those hoofprints are still in the floor. I never sanded them out because they remind me of what's important: family and friends and neighbors helping neighbors.

94   Like Grandma said, everything else is just gravy.

**CLOSE READ**

## Analyze Point of View

Underline details that help you explain how the author uses Wren's point of view to share the central message of the story.

**Fluency** Practice reading accurately and with expression by reading paragraphs 89–94 aloud with a partner. As you read, pay attention to dialogue between characters.

# Develop Vocabulary

Authors use strong, precise words to add specific details. These words help the reader share in the experiences of characters in historical fiction.

**My TURN** Write the vocabulary word from the word bank for each definition. Then use the word in a sentence about *Nora's Ark*.

## Word Bank

survived    astonished    dangerous    piteously    relief

| Definition | Word | Sentence |
|---|---|---|
| unsafe or likely to cause harm | dangerous | The river was dangerous during the flood. |
| lived through or stayed alive | | |
| a feeling of happiness that follows worry | | |
| in a sad and suffering way | | |
| very surprised or amazed | | |

# Check for Understanding

**My TURN** Look back at the text to answer the questions.

1. How can the reader tell that *Nora's Ark* is historical fiction?

2. Why do you think the author has Wren describe herself and her grandmother as "tough" in paragraph 1?

3. What conclusions can you draw about Grandpa's feelings toward farm animals? Cite text evidence to support your response.

4. Connect the theme of this story to real life. What is the author's message, and how does it apply to society today?

# Analyze Point of View

A fictional story can be told from the **point of view** of a **narrator**, or storyteller. A character telling events gives a **first-person point of view**. A narrator outside of the story gives a **third-person point of view**. A narrator's or character's point of view is different from your point of view. Your point of view includes your own thoughts and opinions about the story.

1. **My TURN** Go to the Close Read notes in *Nora's Ark* and underline parts that help you analyze point of view.

2. **Text Evidence** Use some of the parts you underlined to complete the chart. Then explain how the narrator's point of view is different from your own point of view.

| What the Text Says | Narrator's Point of View | How Narrator's Point of View Helps Me Understand the Story |
|---|---|---|
| "That's why I was named Wren. . . . she says I'm tough, just like she is. . . . we never would have survived the 1927 Flood." | | |

How is the narrator's point of view different from your own point of view?

_____

# Make Connections

Historical fiction tells about life during an earlier time in history. As you read, think about what life was like during Wren's time. Then **make connections** between life in Wren's time in history and life in modern society.

1. **My TURN** Go back to the Close Read notes in *Nora's Ark* and highlight parts that help you make connections between life in 1927 and life today.

2. **Text Evidence** Use some of the parts you highlighted to complete the chart.

| What the Text Says | Life in Wren's Community in 1927 | Life in Today's Society |
|---|---|---|
| ". . . it would have electricity, a wringer washing machine, and best of all, an indoor bathroom." | Many farmhouses in 1927 did not have electricity or indoor bathrooms. | Many people today have electricity, indoor bathrooms, and electric washing machines. |
|  |  |  |

# Reflect and Share

**Write to Sources** Consider what you have learned about responding to a disaster in *Nora's Ark* and other texts you have read in this unit. What did you learn that could help your community prepare for a disaster? Use examples from *Nora's Ark* and at least one other text to write and support your response.

- - - - - - - - - - - - - - - - - - - - - - - - - - - - - - - - - - - -

**Interact with Sources** Writers interact with sources by taking notes or annotating text to help them answer questions. Before you write a response, discuss these questions with a partner, and use the questions to help you take notes on the text.

- ◐ Which details from the texts could help your community in an emergency?

- ◐ What are some examples from the texts of how people can help each other in an emergency?

Take notes or underline ideas and examples in the texts. Use this text evidence to write your response on a separate sheet of paper.

- - - - - - - - - - - - - - - - - - - - - - - - - - - - - - - - - - - -

### Weekly Question

How should people respond during a disaster?

# Academic Vocabulary

**Learning Goal**

I can develop knowledge about language to make connections between reading and writing.

**Figurative Language** gives words a meaning beyond their dictionary definitions. One type of figurative language is a simile, which compares two things using the word *like* or *as*.

**My TURN** For each sentence below,

**1. Read** each sentence and underline the simile.

**2. Match** the word in the word bank with the simile that best relates to the definition of the word.

**3. Choose** two similes. Use each simile and its related academic vocabulary word in a sentence.

| WORD BANK | | | |
|---|---|---|---|
| analysis | threat | damage | anticipate |

1. The pencil snapped in half like a twig. _____

2. She studied the scene as carefully as a detective. _____

3. Waiting for the starting signal, the runner is as still as a statue.

_____

4. The possible punishment loomed over us like storm clouds. _____

_____

_____

# Schwa

**A Schwa Vowel Sound** occurs in the unstressed syllable of a multisyllabic word. In the unstressed syllable, the vowel sound is pronounced, or read, like *uh*. Any vowel can spell the schwa sound.

The word *along* in paragraph 13 of *Nora's Ark* contains a schwa sound. The second syllable, *long*, is stressed. The unstressed syllable, *a*, spells the schwa vowel sound.

**My TURN** Read each multisyllabic word. Then write the word and divide it into syllables. Underline the syllable that has the schwa sound.

1. above _____          6. reckon _____

2. children _____       7. taken _____

3. albums _____         8. torrents _____

4. happen _____         9. seven _____

5. afraid _____         10. kitchen _____

# High-Frequency Words

**High-frequency words** appear often in text, so they are important to memorize. Read these high-frequency words: *ready, anything*. Practice to recognize them in your independent reading.

# Read Like a Writer

A first-person narrative is told from the narrator's point of view. The author chooses specific language to build the narrator's voice. Analyze the author's use of language to better understand a narrator.

**Model !** Read the sentence from *Nora's Ark.*

> Grandma may look small, too, but she's made of granite, and she says I'm tough, just like she is.

*details in the narrator's voice that convey feelings*

1. **Identify** Natalie Kinsey-Warnock uses specific language to build Wren's voice.

2. **Question** How do these words reveal Wren's feelings?

3. **Conclude** The author's use of language lets readers know that Wren respects Grandma as a tough woman.

Read the passage.

> Grandma saw me shiver and wrapped a quilt around me. "It's getting colder," she said. "I wish I had my cookstove here." She held me close as we stood watching the rain.

**My TURN** Follow the steps to analyze the passage. Describe how the author's use of language reveals the narrator's voice.

1. **Identify** Natalie Kinsey-Warnock uses specific language to build _____ voice.

2. **Question** How do these words reveal the narrator's feelings?

3. **Conclude** The author's use of language lets readers know that _____ .

# Write for a Reader

Writers choose specific language to reveal a
narrator's voice and to give readers details about
characters' thoughts and feelings.

Choose specific
words to convey
voice.

**My TURN** In *Nora's Ark*, Natalie Kinsey-Warnock chooses
specific language for Wren's voice. That language gives
details about Wren's feelings. Now you will choose specific
language to give details about characters.

1. Think of a story you would like to write about two characters. Plan
   your writing by brainstorming details about your characters and how
   they feel about each other.

   _____

   _____

   _____

2. Write from the main character's point of view using the details you
   brainstormed. Use specific language to reveal the narrator's voice and
   to show how he or she feels about the other character.

   _____

   _____

   _____

   _____

3. How did your use of language contribute to the narrator's
   voice and show how he or she felt about the other character?

   _____

   _____

# Spell Words with the Schwa Sound

**Words with the Schwa Sound** are usually multisyllabic. In multisyllabic words, one syllable is pronounced with more stress. The unstressed syllable is often the schwa vowel sound, pronounced as *uh*. The schwa sound can be spelled with any vowel, so memorizing how to spell words with the schwa sound is important.

**My TURN** Read the words. Sort the words by writing the word in the correct circle based on which letter spells the schwa sound. One word will fit in two categories.

| SPELLING WORDS | | |
| --- | --- | --- |
| citizen | gallon | nickel |
| decimal | global | notify |
| delicious | item | travel |
| economy | | |

Schwa with a

_____

_____

Schwa with e

_____

_____

Schwa with i

_____

_____

Schwa with o

_____

_____

Schwa with iou

_____

_____

# High-Frequency Words

Learn to recognize high-frequency words instantly so you can read them with fluency. Write the following high-frequency words on the lines.

ready _____

anything _____

# Pronoun-Antecedent Agreement

A **pronoun** is a word that takes the place of a noun or group of nouns. The **antecedent** is the noun or nouns to which the pronoun refers. The pronoun must agree with its antecedent in number (singular or plural) and person.

| Person | Singular Pronouns | Plural Pronouns |
|---|---|---|
| First Person | I, me, mine, my | we, us, ours, our |
| Second Person | you, your, yours | you, your, yours |
| Third Person | he, him, his, she, her, hers, it, its | they, them, theirs, their |

**Example sentences:**

The <u>boy</u> runs to the mailbox. <u>He</u> checks for the mail.

<u>My brother and I</u> went to the store. <u>We</u> bought some fruit.

**My TURN** Edit this draft by replacing four incorrectly used pronouns with pronouns that agree with their antecedents.

The storm was approaching fast. They was going to be a big one. My parents and I boarded up the windows. We set up boards as quickly as we could. My dad used her power drill to make the work go quicker. The neighbors ran out of boards. He came over to borrow some boards from us. We helped carry the boards to their house. It were heavy.

# Revise for Structure

The structure of a poem refers to how it is organized. Poetry might be arranged in **lines** and **stanzas**.

Read the poem. Notice the organization of lines and the stanzas.

## A Chill

What can lambkins do
All the keen night through?
Nestle by their woolly mother,
The careful ewe.

What can nestlings do
In the nightly dew?
Sleep beneath their mother's wing
Till day breaks anew.

If in field or tree
There might only be
Such a warm soft sleeping-place
Found for me!

*Christina Rossetti*

How a poet structures the **lines** in a poem may depend on the words that rhyme. The length of the lines may create the rhythm.

A group of lines is called a **stanza**. A stanza in poetry is similar to a paragraph in a story. In poetry, the lines in the stanza may center around one image.

**My TURN** Revise one of your own poems, making sure each line makes sense. Consider rearranging the lines according to words that rhyme. Make sure there is space between stanzas.

# Rearranging Ideas for Coherence and Clarity

To make their poems clearer, writers may rearrange ideas and poetic language to make an image more vivid or to change the rhythm or rhyme. Rearranged ideas might be single words, phrases, or lines. Here is how a writer added details and rearranged ideas.

A snake slithered down the tree.
He didn't see me, but stopped to hiss.
He slid away without a scene,
And he had smooth green scales.

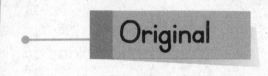

A slimy snake slithered down the tree.
He stopped to hiss, but not at me.
His scales were smooth and glossy green.
He slid away without a scene.

**My TURN** Rearrange the lines, ideas, or language of this stanza to make it clearer.

A leopard frog hopped down the lane,

He sings with his friends, all through the night.

Dark spots on his back, bright yellow and white.

He stopped to croak and not complain!

**My TURN** On one of your own drafts, rearrange the lines, ideas, or language to improve the clarity of your poem.

# Edit for Nouns

A **noun** names a person, place, or thing. An **abstract noun** describes an idea or concept. It describes something we cannot see, hear, taste, touch, or smell. Examples include *joy*, *friendship*, and *courage*.

A **singular noun** names *one* person, place, or thing. A **plural noun** names *more than one* person, place, or thing.

| Forming Plural Nouns | Singular | Plural |
|---|---|---|
| For most nouns, add -*s*. | boat | boats |
| If a singular noun ends in *ch*, *sh*, *x*, *s*, or *ss*, add -*es*. | beach<br>fox | beaches<br>foxes |
| If a singular noun ends in a consonant and *y*, change the *y* to *i* and add -*es*. | baby<br>party | babies<br>parties |
| **Irregular** plural nouns are not formed in any of the usual ways. | child<br>mouse | children<br>mice |

A **common noun** names any person, place, or thing. A **proper noun** names a specific person, place, or thing. They begin with a capital letter. Examples: Mr. Cho (title), Dallas (city), Labor Day (holiday).

**My TURN** Edit this paragraph for errors with nouns. Then highlight two abstract nouns.

Four horse are in their stables for the night. I cover them with blanket to keep them cozy and warm. My favorite horse is named spicy. Her strength and beauty amaze me.

**My TURN** Edit one of your own drafts for correct use of nouns.

# Edit for Comparative and Superlative Adjectives

An **adjective** describes a noun or pronoun. Most adjectives answer one of these questions: *What kind? How many? Which one?*
**Examples:** *fuzzy* dog, *five* turtles, *first* snow

Most adjectives have three degrees of comparison: positive, comparative, and superlative.
A **positive adjective** describes one noun.
A **comparative adjective** compares two nouns.
A **superlative adjective** compares three or more nouns.

| Positive (one) | Comparative (two) | Superlative (three or more) |
|---|---|---|
| deep | deep**er** | deep**est** |
| pretty | pretti**er** | pretti**est** |

**My TURN** Edit the paragraph by adding an appropriate adjective from the word bank to each sentence frame.

**Word Bank**

busy    yellow    larger    smallest    brighter

_____ daffodils grow in my garden. I wonder if daffodils are _____ than daisies. The tulips have _____ colors than the lilies. I watch the _____ bee as it buzzes all around. Will it find the tiny flowers? The _____ flowers in my garden are hidden from the sun.

**My TURN** Edit one of your poems for descriptive details by adding comparative and superlative adjectives.

# Edit for Punctuation Marks

**Punctuation marks** signal readers to pause, stop, or use expression.

- Declarative and imperative sentences end with a **period.**
- An interrogative sentence ends with a **question mark.**
- An exclamatory sentence ends with an **exclamation mark.**

The **comma** (,) tells readers to briefly pause. A comma separates clauses, phrases, and words to help the reader understand the author's meaning. It is also used in **compound sentences, items in a series,** and **addresses.**

**Examples:** Joe decorated the dining room, and Martha baked a cake.

I like tomatoes, carrots, and olives on my salad.

19 Rivertown St.

Tulsa, OK 74137

An **apostrophe** (') shows **possession** or replaces letters in a **contraction.**

**Examples:** Maria's hat       the boys' lockers       you will = you'll

**My TURN** Edit the paragraph by correcting punctuation errors.

Big Bend has tall mountains and there are many trails to hike. Some of the animals in the park include wolves, roadrunners and deer. Youll like this great park? Write to the park to learn more:

P. O. Box 129

Big Bend National Park TX 79834

**My TURN** Edit one of your poems for correct punctuation. Discuss your choices with your Writing Club.

 INTERACTIVITY

# Lesson From
# THE FOREST

The bases were loaded,
The fans were a blur.
I heard the folks chanting;
My name could be heard.

But the timing was off—
"STRIKE ONE!" came the shout.
The ump called two more.
The batter was out!

That batter was me,
And I wanted to hide.
Then I saw my grandpa
Walk up to my side.

He smiled down so gently,
And asked, "Want to go?"
I nodded—we left,
So my tears didn't show.

The next day, Gramps said,
"Let's go for a ride."
"Where are we headed?"
"The old burn," he replied.

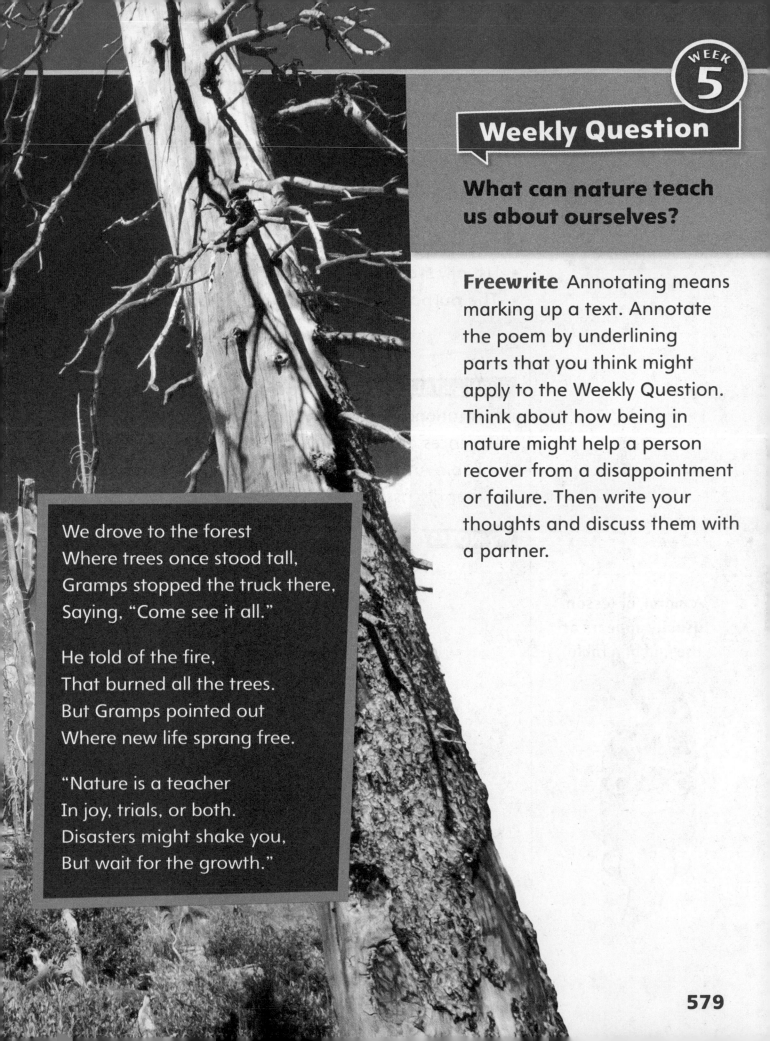

## Weekly Question

**What can nature teach us about ourselves?**

**Freewrite** Annotating means marking up a text. Annotate the poem by underlining parts that you think might apply to the Weekly Question. Think about how being in nature might help a person recover from a disappointment or failure. Then write your thoughts and discuss them with a partner.

We drove to the forest
Where trees once stood tall,
Gramps stopped the truck there,
Saying, "Come see it all."

He told of the fire,
That burned all the trees.
But Gramps pointed out
Where new life sprang free.

"Nature is a teacher
In joy, trials, or both.
Disasters might shake you,
But wait for the growth."

**Learning Goal**

I can learn more about themes concerning *solutions* by reading a text that helps me infer theme in traditional tales.

# Traditional Tales

A **fable** is a type of traditional tale. It is a brief story that gives a **moral,** or lesson. In a fable, the moral is

- The **theme,** or central message, of the story
- Usually **stated** in the text at the end of the story
- The **purpose,** or reason, for the story

**TURN**and**TALK**   How is a fable different from an informational text? With a partner, discuss key differences and examples of each genre. Use the Fable Anchor Chart to help you. Take notes on your discussion.

**My NOTES** _____

_____

_____

_____

_____

_____

_____

A moral, or lesson, usually appears at the end of a fable.

# Fable Anchor Chart

## Purpose

To teach a lesson

## Elements

- The characters are often animals that act and think like humans.

- The conflict is resolved by the end.

- Traits of characters are often compared.

- The theme is the moral, or lesson.

**Aki Sogabe** was born in Japan and made her first paper-cutting picture when she was in middle school. Now she is a master of the ancient art of Japanese paper cutting. She is an author, as well as the illustrator of several award-winning children's books that feature her detailed cut-paper artwork.

*from*
# Aesop's Fox

## Preview Vocabulary

As you read *Aesop's Fox*, pay attention to these vocabulary words. Notice how they help you understand the story events in the fable.

| | | |
|---|---|---|
| **elegant** | **remarkable** | |
| **flattery** | **spectacle** | **imitation** |

## Read

Preview the text and set a purpose for reading. Follow these strategies when you read this **traditional tale** the first time.

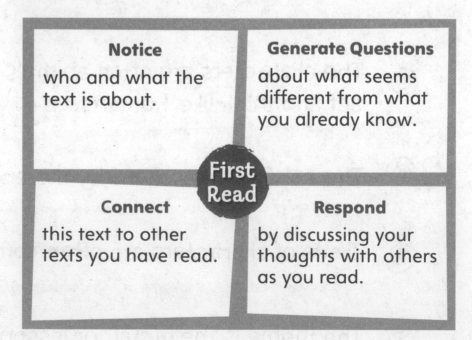

**Notice** who and what the text is about.

**Generate Questions** about what seems different from what you already know.

**First Read**

**Connect** this text to other texts you have read.

**Respond** by discussing your thoughts with others as you read.

*from*

# AESOP'S FOX

**retold and illustrated by**
**AKI SOGABE**

 AUDIO

 ANNOTATE

## Evaluate Details

Highlight details that help you determine Fox's problem and how he plans to solve his problem.

**elegant** graceful in style and beauty

1 One summer morning Fox woke up and started out on his search for breakfast. He couldn't find anything to eat in the forest, so he trotted over to the nearby farmyard and saw Rooster perched on the fence post.

2 "Good morning, Mr. Rooster," Fox said in his most friendly manner. "I didn't hear your beautiful voice this morning. Is anything wrong? My day doesn't start without your singing."

3 Rooster proudly shook his crest.

4 "I used to listen to your uncle's song," Fox continued. "Oh, he was a great singer. And so beautiful! I miss his voice very much."

5 Rooster waved his elegant crest from left to right and back again.

6 What a vain fellow! Fox thought.

7 "Can you sing as well as your uncle?" Fox asked.

8 "Of course I can. I sing much better," Rooster finally answered proudly. He opened his beak and took a deep breath.

9 "Wait!" said Fox. "When your dear uncle sang, he shut his eyes very tight and stretched his neck very straight. Then he sang his heart out."

10 "I can certainly do that," said Rooster. He shut his eyes very tight and stretched his neck very straight. *"Cock-a-doodle-doo! Cock-a-doodle-doo!"*

11 Fox leaped at him, seized him by the throat, and ran toward the forest.

12    The farmer saw Fox and began to chase
him. "Stop! Thief!" he cried, and came closer
and closer.

13    "My dear Fox," Rooster said as Fox held him
tightly in his jaws. "Why don't you just tell him
that I belong to you?"

14  What a good idea, Fox thought. He opened his mouth and called to the farmer, "This is my rooster! My breakfast!"

15  At that instant Rooster flew up to a tree branch.

16  The hungry fox said to himself, trotting away, "Think before you speak."

**CLOSE READ**

## Infer Theme

<u>Underline</u> details that help you infer the theme, or central message, before it is stated. How is the theme different from the topic, or what the fable is about?

17  As Fox walked along he heard some strange rasping sounds, and in a few moments he saw a large boar sharpening his tusks on the trunk of a tree.

18  *Zuuuk, zuuuk, zuuuk.*

19  "I beg your pardon," said Fox. "Why are you doing that?"

20  "I'm sharpening my tusks," Boar replied. "These are the only weapons I have to fight my enemies. Unlike you, I have no sharp claws or fast feet."

21  Fox looked about. Except for the noise Boar made, the forest was silent and peaceful. Surely this boar was a fool to spend his time this way when there was no need.

22  "But there's no danger here that I can see," Fox said.

23  "Not at this moment," replied Boar. "But when the hunters come after me with their dogs, then it will be too late to sharpen my tusks." He went back to the tree. *Zuuuk, zuuuk, zuuuk.*

24  Fox walked away and thought, He's right. If you are prepared to defend yourself, you have nothing to fear.

## Infer Theme

25   Fox was very hungry now. He soon came upon a large vineyard at the edge of the forest. Bunches of juicy grapes hung from a trellis. They looked ripe and ready to eat. They smelled delicious.

26   "What beautiful grapes!" Fox licked his lips and jumped up to get a bite of the purple bunches. But he couldn't reach them. He jumped again and again—and again—but the grapes remained beyond his reach. He could get nothing.

27   Finally he turned away and said angrily, "I didn't want those grapes anyway. Look at them! They are probably sour."

28   He walked back into the forest. Boar, who had been watching, said, "We often pretend to dislike what we can't have."

29   It was lunchtime now, and Fox was still without food.

## Infer Theme

Underline details that
help you infer the theme
before it is stated.
Distinguish the
theme from the
topic of the fable.

**remarkable**
extraordinary
or amazing

30    Then Fox saw Crow sitting on a branch with a piece of cheese in her beak.

31    Surely this is my chance to have something to eat! he thought. And so he addressed Crow.

32    "What a handsome bird you are," Fox said. "Your glossy feathers are remarkable. Why, I believe not even the peacock's splendor can equal yours."

33    Crow seemed interested but still held the cheese tightly in her beak.

34    "Your noble face and bright eyes are like Eagle's—No! Not even Eagle's. If you can sing like the nightingale," Fox continued, "I will tell all the beasts that you are Queen of the Birds."

35    Crow had listened closely and liked what she heard. This fox told the truth. She *was* handsome and her voice *was* beautiful. She opened her beak and sang, *"Caw! Caw!"*

36    "The piece of cheese fell into Fox's mouth. Fox gobbled it up and said to Crow, "Never believe flattery."

**flattery** praise
that is dishonest
or exaggerated

Use context clues before and beyond the sentence to determine the meaning of *alarmed*. Underline the context clues that support your definition.

37   After taking a nap Fox trotted down the path and saw Rabbit huddled in the underbrush, trembling. A few seconds later Deer ran past him with terror in her eyes. Fox became alarmed. Obviously some terrible danger lurked in the forest.

38   Peering over a hedge, he was surprised to see Old Lion snarling and pawing the ground. But when Fox looked more closely, he saw it wasn't Lion at all—it was Donkey. He was draped in a lion's skin and was enjoying the spectacle of the forest animals who ran in fear at the sight of him.

39   Fox leaped over the hedge and stood in front of Donkey.

40   "So you aren't afraid of the King of Beasts," Donkey said to Fox in a growly voice. "We'll see about that!" He bared his teeth and gave his best imitation of Lion's roar.

41   *"Hee-haw! Hee-haw!"*

42   Fox burst out laughing. "You can't frighten me," he said. "I see your gray ears under the lion's skin and I hear your bray." He trotted through the forest thinking, No matter how hard you try, you can't hide your true self.

**Evaluate Details**

Highlight details that help you determine a key idea about imitation.

**spectacle** entertaining sight or display

**imitation** a copy of something else

**CLOSE READ**

## Infer Theme

Underline details that help you infer the theme before it is stated. How is this theme different from the fable's topic?

43 It was late and Fox was getting hungry again. He sniffed the air for something good to eat, and this time his nose took him to a small hollow in a big oak tree. Inside he saw some fragrant bread and fruit that had been left by a woodcutter a short time earlier. Fox crept inside the hollow and ate every last morsel.

44 "That was delicious," said Fox. "I am finally satisfied. Time to go." But when he tried to crawl out of the hollow, he found he was stuck. He had eaten so much that his stomach was too big to squeeze through the narrow space. To make matters worse, his meal had made him very thirsty. "I can't even get a drink of water," cried Fox. "What shall I do?"

45 Raccoon passed by and heard Fox's lament. "You'll have to stay there until your stomach shrinks again," he said wisely. "Next time don't be so greedy."

46 Fox had to admit Raccoon was right. He settled back into the hollow.

47 "Ah, well," he said. "Time fixes everything."

48 Fox fell fast asleep. And by the time the moon rose, Farmer, Rooster, Boar, Crow, Rabbit, Deer, Donkey, and Raccoon had done the same.

# Develop Vocabulary

In traditional tales and other forms of fiction, authors use descriptive words to tell about characters and events. These words often help teach the moral, or lesson, of the fable.

**My TURN** Add the vocabulary word from the word bank to the chart to complete each sentence. Then identify the character the word describes and use the word in a sentence.

| Word Bank | | | |
|---|---|---|---|
| elegant | spectacle | flattery | imitation |

| Word | Tells About | Sentence |
|---|---|---|
| Imitation<br>means "copy or act like something or someone else." | Donkey | Donkey's imitation of Lion did not frighten Fox. |
| _____<br>means "praise that is dishonest or exaggerated." | | |
| _____<br>means "entertaining sight or display." | | |
| _____<br>means "graceful in style and beauty." | | |

# Check for Understanding

**My TURN** Look back at the text to answer the questions.

1. What story elements help you identify this text as a fable?

2. Explain the author's use of dialogue in paragraphs 9 and 10. How does it help you predict what will happen next?

3. What conclusion can be drawn about imitation from the interaction between Fox and Donkey?

4. Synthesize information to make a connection between the characters of Rooster and Crow.

# Infer Theme

The **theme** of a story is its central message, or what the author wants the reader to understand about life. To infer the theme and distinguish it from the story's **topic**, or subject, think about the problems the characters face and the lessons the characters learn.

1. **My TURN** Go to the Close Read notes in the fable and underline the parts that help you infer the different themes, or morals.

2. **Text Evidence** Use some of the parts you underlined to complete the chart.

| Fox's Interactions | Topic | Details | Theme |
|---|---|---|---|
| Fox and Rooster | how a hungry fox tries to catch a rooster | "He opened his mouth and called to the farmer..." "... Rooster flew up ..." | "'Think before you speak.'" |
| Fox and the grapes | | | |
| Fox and Crow | | | |

# Evaluate Details

Readers **evaluate details** as they read to determine key ideas. Readers use their evaluation of details to understand more about setting, characters, plot, and theme.

1. **My TURN** Go back to the Close Read notes and highlight details in the fable that help you determine key ideas.

2. **Text Evidence** Use some of the parts you highlighted to complete the chart. Evaluate the details you chose to determine the key ideas.

| Fox's Interactions | Details to Evaluate | Key Ideas About Theme |
|---|---|---|
| Fox and Rooster | "'Why don't you just tell him that I belong to you?'" | Rooster wants to trick Fox to escape. |
| Fox and Boar | | |
| Fox and Donkey | | |

# Reflect and Share

**Talk About It** Think about the characters you have read about this week. What traits do these characters have? How do these traits help or hurt the characters? Use these questions to help you discuss traits that lead to positive and negative results for the characters.

**Ask Relevant Questions** During a discussion, it is important to include others. You can do that by asking them questions that are relevant, or related, to the topic.

- Ask questions about what someone has said.
- Ask questions about what others think about an idea.

Use these sentence starters to ask relevant questions:

> What did you mean when you said . . . ?

> What do you think about the idea that . . . ?

After the discussion, think about how your classmates' comments affected your own opinions. Explain how your thinking has changed.

## Weekly Question

**What can nature teach us about ourselves?**

# Academic Vocabulary

**Learning Goal**

I can develop knowledge about language to make connections between reading and writing.

**Parts of Speech** are categories of words, such as nouns, verbs, adjectives, and adverbs. Some words may be used as more than one part of speech.

We **train** dogs at the park district. (verb)

Dad rides the **train** to work. (noun)

**My TURN** For each sentence below,

1. **Read** each sentence and underline the academic vocabulary word.

2. **Identify** the part of speech of the underlined word.

3. **Write** a sentence using the word as a different part of speech. You may change the form of the word, such as changing *pollution* to *pollute*. Identify the new part of speech.

| Sentence | Part of Speech | My Sentence |
|---|---|---|
| After analysis, Jamie realized her error. | | |
| Once the threat of the storm passed, we went back outside. | | |
| Getting too much sun can cause skin damage. | | |
| Air pollution is a problem. | | |

# Final Stable Syllables

**Final Stable Syllables *-le*, *-ture*, *-ive*, *-ize*** are letters at the end of the syllables that do not change. The letter combinations spell unique sounds. In the word *table*, the letters *ble* spell the sound you hear in the word *bull*. In the word *picture*, the letters *ture* spell the sound *chur*. When a word ends with the letters *ive*, the *i* could spell either a short or long *i* sound. When a word ends with the letters *ize*, the *i* spells a long *i* sound.

**My TURN** Read each sentence. Underline the words with final stable syllables.

1. You cannot survive for very long without water.

2. I need to apologize to my friend.

3. My mom prefers little dogs.

4. We should be sensitive to each person's culture.

# High-Frequency Words

**High-frequency words** do not follow regular word study patterns. Read these high-frequency words: *love*, *developed*.

# Read Like a Writer

Authors use imagery to achieve specific purposes. For instance, precise verbs help readers better picture the action in a text. The precise verbs *sprint*, *race*, and *dart* more clearly describe the general verb *run*.

**Model** Read the sentence from *Aesop's Fox*.

> He couldn't find anything to eat in the forest, so he trotted over to the nearby farmyard and saw Rooster perched on the fence post.

precise verb

1. **Identify** The author uses the precise verb *trotted*.

2. **Question** What is the author's purpose for using this verb?

3. **Conclude** The author's purpose is to give readers a more detailed description of how the fox walked.

Read the passage.

> He was draped in a lion's skin . . .

**My TURN** Follow the steps to analyze the passage. Describe how the author uses precise verbs.

1. **Identify** The author uses the precise verb _____.

2. **Question** What is the author's purpose for using this verb?

3. **Conclude** The author's purpose is to give readers a more detailed description of _____.

# Write for a Reader

Use precise verbs to help readers better picture the action in a text.

**My TURN** Think about how the use of precise verbs in *Aesop's Fox* helps readers picture the action. Then think about how you can use precise verbs to help readers picture actions in your own fable.

1. Write a precise verb on the line next to each general verb. You may want to use a dictionary or a thesaurus.

    jump: _____

    walk: _____

    carry: _____

    cry: _____

    laugh: _____

2. Start a draft of a fable on your own paper. Include as many of the precise verbs you wrote as you can. Then describe how your use of imagery helps readers picture the action.

    _____

    _____

    _____

    _____

    _____

# Spell Final Stable Syllables

**Final Stable Syllables *-le, -ture, -ive, -ize*** are always the same series of letters at the end of the final syllable of a multisyllabic word. Their spellings stay the same although their sounds may change.

**My TURN** Read and sort the words by their final stable syllable.

**SPELLING WORDS**

| | | |
|---|---|---|
| title | capture | posture |
| vegetable | organize | creature |
| humble | positive | finalize |
| active | | |

| Final Stable Syllable | Words |
|---|---|
| consonant + *-le* | |
| *-ture* | |
| consonant + *-ive* | |
| consonant + *-ize* | |

# High-Frequency Words

Write each high-frequency word on the lines.

love _____

developed _____

# Edit for Commas

A **comma** is a punctuation mark that has many uses. In writing, commas are used in dates, items in a series, and compound sentences, and to set off the exact words of a speaker.

| Comma Uses | Example |
|---|---|
| In the **date**, use a comma between the day and the year. | June 5, 2018 |
| Three or more items in a row form a **series**. Put a comma after each item in a series except for the last one. | Sam, Ben, and Jason went to the ballgame. |
| Put a comma before a coordinating conjunction such as *and*, *but*, or *or* to form a **compound sentence**. | I like painting, and I enjoy the classes on Saturdays. |
| When you write a **dialogue**, use a comma to separate the speaker's words from the speech tag. A speech tag, such as *said Mike*, identifies who is speaking. If the speech tag appears after the speaker's words, place the comma inside the quotation marks. If the speech tag appears before the speaker's words, place the comma outside the quotation marks. | "Your backpack is cool," said Renaldo. Luis said, "Thanks. I got it last summer." |

**My TURN** Edit this draft for correct use of commas.

On March 3 2018, Mike, Jamal and Lin bought a gift for their friend Justin, who lived in New York. Mike said "Let's ship it to him today!" They packed the gift in a box and they shipped it from the post office.

# Revise for Coherence and Clarity

A poem has **coherence** when everything in it is connected and makes sense. A poem has **clarity** when ideas are clear and easily understood. Poets revise for coherence and clarity by adding clear and relevant ideas and deleting unnecessary or confusing ideas. They also combine or group related ideas and rearrange ideas for sense and flow.

**My TURN** Revise this poem by: (1) adding a title, (2) deleting a line that does not belong, (3) combining ideas with a conjunction, and (4) rearranging the poem so that it is in a better order.

The sun settles

And so do I.

I tell it good night

With a yawn, a sigh.

The morning sun rises

And so do I.

I smile at the sun

The sun is a star

As it heats up the sky.

**My TURN** Revise a draft of one of your poems for coherence and clarity. Add, delete, combine, and rearrange ideas as needed.

# Edit for Adjectives and Adverbs

Use a **comparative adjective** to compare two people, places, or things. Use a **superlative adjective** to compare three or more nouns.

| Comparative Adjective | Superlative Adjective |
|---|---|
| Rod is **taller** than Cho. | Rod is the **tallest** boy in the class. |

**Adverbs** of time tell when or how often. Adverbs of manner tell how. Adverbs can have comparative and superlative forms, too.

| Comparative Adverb | Superlative Adverb |
|---|---|
| Ava ran **faster** than Mia. | Among everyone, Ava ran **fastest**. |

**My TURN** Edit the poem, choosing the correct comparative or superlative adjectives to replace the bold words.

The wind is strong than the door—

It flings it open wide.

The thunder is loud than the rain—

My friends, they run and hide.

But I am brave of us all—

I face the storm outside!

**My TURN** Edit a poem of your own for comparative and superlative adjectives and for adverbs that convey time and manner.

# Publish and Celebrate

Writers publish their poetry for many reasons. They may want

- to share their thoughts and feelings.
- to connect emotionally with an audience.
- an audience to feel something more deeply.

**My TURN** Publish your poem. Then answer these questions about your experience. Write complete words, thoughts, and answers legibly in cursive. Leave enough space between words.

How does your poetry sound?

_____

_____

_____

How does your poetry look?

_____

_____

_____

What feelings or mood does your poetry have?

_____

_____

_____

What kind of poetry will you write in the future?

_____

_____

_____

# Prepare for Assessment

**My TURN** Follow this plan to help you write a poem in response to a prompt.

1. **Study the prompt.**
   Read the prompt carefully. <u>Underline</u> the kind of writing you will do. Highlight the topic or idea you will write about.

   **Prompt:** Write a poem about something in nature that reminds you of your life.

2. **Brainstorm.**
   List three ideas for a poem based on the prompt. Highlight your favorite idea.

3. **Organize and plan your poem.**
   What will your poem say? How will your poem look and sound?

4. **Write your draft.**
   Use rhythm, rhyme, and imagery to help your poem come alive.

5. **Revise and edit your poem.**
   Use the skills you have learned to make changes and corrections as needed.

It might be easier to work on rhyme after you have written your draft.

# Assessment

**My TURN** Before you write a poem for your assessment, rate how well you understand the skills you have learned in this unit. Go back and review any skills you mark "No."

| | | Yes | No |
|---|---|---|---|
| **Ideas and Organization** | ◐ I can select a genre for writing.<br>◐ I can see something like a poet sees it.<br>◐ I can brainstorm ideas.<br>◐ I can plan my poetry.<br>◐ I can revise for structure.<br>◐ I can rearrange ideas for coherence and clarity. | ☐<br>☐<br>☐<br>☐<br>☐<br>☐ | ☐<br>☐<br>☐<br>☐<br>☐<br>☐ |
| **Craft** | ◐ I can identify what poetry sounds and looks like.<br>◐ I can use imagery and figurative language.<br>◐ I can use rhythm, rhyme, and alliteration.<br>◐ I can use line breaks and stanzas.<br>◐ I can make an audio recording and a visual display of my poetry. | ☐<br>☐<br>☐<br>☐<br>☐ | ☐<br>☐<br>☐<br>☐<br>☐ |
| **Conventions** | ◐ I can use nouns correctly.<br>◐ I can use adjectives and adverbs correctly including their comparative and superlative forms.<br>◐ I can use punctuation marks.<br>◐ I can revise my writing for choice of verbs. | ☐<br>☐<br>☐<br>☐ | ☐<br>☐<br>☐<br>☐ |

# COMPARE ACROSS TEXTS

## UNIT THEME

# Solutions

**TURN**and**TALK**   In a Word

With a partner, look back at each Unit 5 text to choose and record a word that best shows the unit theme of *Solutions*. Then, use those words as you answer the Essential Question.

WEEK
**3**

### A Safety Plan: In Case of Emergency

**Theme word:**

_____

**BOOK CLUB**

WEEK
**2**

### Earthquakes, Eruptions, and Other Events that Change Earth

**Theme word:**

_____

**BOOK CLUB**

WEEK
**1**

### Deep Down and Other Extreme Places to Live

**Theme word:**

_____

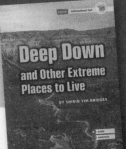

**Nora's Ark**

Theme word:

_____

WEEK
4

BOOK CLUB

WEEK
5

_from_ **Aesop's Fox**

Theme word:

_____

BOOK CLUB

## Essential Question

**My TURN**

In your notebook, answer the Essential Question: **How does the world challenge us?**

_Project_

WEEK
6

Now it is time to apply what you learned about solutions in your **WEEK 6 PROJECT:** Take a Trip!

# Take A TRIP!

## Activity

When a natural disaster happens, communities must find solutions to many problems. Recovering from a natural disaster can be difficult and take many years. Create a travel brochure that persuades readers to visit, or not visit, a place that is likely to be affected by a natural disaster.

## Research Articles

With your partner, read "Living on a Fault Line" to generate questions you have about the inquiry topic. With an adult's help, make a research plan for creating your travel brochure.

1. **Living on a Fault Line**

2. **The City I Love**

3. **A Mighty Flood**

## Generate Questions

**COLLABORATE** After reading "Living on a Fault Line," generate three questions you have about the article. Share your questions with the class.

1. _____

2. _____

3. _____

# Use Academic Words

**COLLABORATE** In this unit, you learned many words related to the theme of *Solutions*. Work with your partner to add more academic vocabulary words to each category. If appropriate, use this vocabulary in your travel brochure.

| Academic Vocabulary | Word Forms | Synonyms | Antonyms |
|---|---|---|---|
| analysis | analyses | examination investigation inspection | indifference ignorance |
| threat | threats threaten threatening | risk hazard danger | certainty safety protection |
| damage | damages damaged damaging | destruction breakage wreckage | recovery repair improvement |
| anticipate | anticipates anticipated anticipation | expect guess predict | doubt surprise shock |
| pollution | pollute polluted pollutant | dirtying contamination | cleanliness |

# Inform with Purpose

Use persuasive words, such as *should* and *need*, to convince readers to agree with you.

Authors write **argumentative text** to convince, or persuade, someone to think or do something. When reading argumentative text, identify

- the author's claim, or opinion;
- reasons that support the claim;
- facts and details that support the reasons; and
- the audience or reader the author wants to persuade.

**RESEARCH**

**COLLABORATE** Read "The City I Love" with your partner. Then, answer the questions about the text.

1. Whom does the author want to persuade? How do you know?

_____

_____

2. What is the author's claim?

_____

_____

3. Do the facts and opinions persuade you to agree with the author? Use a fact and an opinion from the text to explain why or why not.

_____

_____

_____

# Plan Your Research

**COLLABORATE** Before you begin researching places that are likely to be affected by natural disasters, you will need to plan your research. With help from an adult, use this activity to make a plan for how you will conduct research for your brochure.

| Definition and Example | Research Goal and Findings |
|---|---|
| The **topic** is the subject of the text.<br><br>**Example:** The topic of Maria's brochure is the Belden Youth Service Club. | To identify my topic, I will conduct research to find out<br><br>_____.<br><br>My topic:<br><br>_____ |
| A **claim** is a statement that tells the author's opinion about a topic.<br><br>**Example:** Maria thinks the Belden Youth Service Club is a valuable group and other students need to join. | To form my opinion, I will conduct research to find out<br><br>_____.<br><br>My claim:<br><br>_____ |
| Authors use **reasons** to support their claim and persuade readers to agree with their opinion.<br><br>**Example:** Students should join the Belden Youth Service Club because they can help people, learn valuable skills, and make new friends. | To develop my reasons, I will conduct research to find out<br><br>_____.<br><br>My reasons:<br><br>1. _____<br><br>2. _____<br><br>3. _____ |

Discuss your research plan with your partner. Add any suggestions to the chart.

# MARK the PAGE!

If you find a useful Web page while researching, you can bookmark it. **Bookmarking** allows you to return quickly to a Web page that has valuable information. With adult assistance, use bookmarking as you follow your research plan.

**EXAMPLE** Maria wants to find facts about the Belden Youth Service Club. She finds a Web page with valuable information. How can she bookmark the Web page so that she can return to it later?

http://beldenyouth_service.org

# Belden Youth Service Club

| Home | News | Opportunities | Resources | Contact Us |

**STEP 1** **Open Web page** Use your browser to go to the Web page you want to bookmark.

**STEP 2** **Press Ctrl+D or Command+D** Depending on the kind of computer you use, press the Ctrl (Control) and D keys on your computer keyboard at the same time. If you do not see the menu, press the Command and D keys on your keyboard. This will show you a bookmark menu.

**STEP 3** **Name the bookmark** Create a name for the bookmark or use the name that is shown.

**STEP 4** **Done or Add** Click the "Done" or "Add" box in the menu to bookmark the Web page.

**COLLABORATE** With your partner, review your research plan and go online to bookmark Web pages with the most valuable information for your brochure. Take notes as you conduct research. Be careful not to copy words or ideas, which is plagiarizing. To avoid plagiarism, retell ideas in your own words, which is paraphrasing. If you use exact words, be sure to use quotation marks and give credit to your sources.

Research Goal:

URL:

Relevant information:

How information supports my claim:


I will...

☐ retell or paraphrase while maintaining meaning and logical order.

☐ quote exact words in my brochure to make sure I do not plagiarize.


Research Goal:

URL:

Relevant information:

How information supports my claim:


I will...

☐ retell or paraphrase while maintaining meaning and logical order.

☐ quote exact words in my brochure to make sure I do not plagiarize.


Discuss your search results. Identify information that could improve your brochure.

# Persuade ME

Authors write an **argumentative text** to persuade their intended audience to support their opinion.

Before you begin making your brochure, answer the questions.

- What is the topic of your brochure?
- Who is my audience or reader?
- What is your claim, or opinion?
- What are your reasons? What is your supporting evidence?
- What images will you include?
- How will you organize the information in your brochure?

**COLLABORATE** Read the Student Model. Work with your partner to recognize the characteristics of an argumentative text.

## Now You Try It!

Discuss the checklist with your partner. Work together to follow the steps to create your brochure.

**Make sure your brochure includes**

☐ your claim, or opinion, about the topic.

☐ reasons that support your claim.

☐ facts and details that support the reasons.

☐ images that relate to the topic.

☐ organizing text features, such as a title and headings.

## Student Model

**Front**

BYSC

> **Underline** a sentence that defines the topic.

JOIN the
Belden Youth Service Club!

Do you like helping people?
Are you interested in saving
lives? Becoming a member of
the Belden Youth Service Club
means helping your community!

> **Highlight** the author's claim.

**Back**

Join to make new friends or
learn something new. Join to
teach someone else something
you know how to do. When
we share our time and talent,
everyone benefits.

To learn more about the Belden
Youth Service Club, come
to our next club meeting on
Tuesday after school in the
cafeteria!

**Inside**

Disaster
Relief

WHAT is the Belden
Youth Service Club?

The Belden Youth Service Club
is a group for kids who are
interested in helping their
community and people in need.
We decide on a project and work
together to make it happen.

> **Underline** a reason.

WHY Should You Join?

Being a member of the Belden
Youth Service Club has many
benefits. You will:

- Help people in our community
- Learn amazing lifesaving skills
- Make new friends
- Learn how to help
  in emergencies
- Be part of a team of more
  than 100 volunteers

> **Highlight** facts that support the reason.

# Cite Your Source!

A **works cited page** is a list of sources that an author actually used in the final draft. It is a separate page at the end of a research paper or project. When you cite a source, follow a specific format to give information.

This is how you cite a printed book.
Author, last name first (if more than one author, list in order they are listed on the book's title page). *Title of book*. Publisher, year of publication.

> Kinsey-Warnock, Natalie. *Nora's Ark*. HarperCollins, 2005.

This is how you cite a Web page.
Author, if known. "Title of Web Page." *Name of Web site*, date of site creation (if available). URL. Date you accessed, or visited, the site.

> "About Us—Belden Youth Service Group." *Belden Community Service*, 2017. www.url.here. Accessed 12 May 2017.

**RESEARCH**

**COLLABORATE** Read "A Mighty Flood." With your partner, examine the article and brainstorm sources of information that could help you learn more about the topic. Discuss the information you would need to cite these sources on a works cited page.

**COLLABORATE** Read the excerpt and examine one of the sources the author used. Use information from the source to create a works cited page with your partner. Use the examples on the Cite Your Source! page to help you.

# Recovering from Disaster

by Douglas Miller

May 10, 2017—After a tornado swept through Cedarburg yesterday, people are beginning to clean up. The town was hit hard by the tornado, which had winds of up to 127 miles per hour. Local officials estimate that nearly half of the town's homes were damaged or destroyed by the storm. However, hope is on the horizon. Volunteers arrived in vans and buses this morning with food, supplies, and support for the people of Cedarburg.

www.url.here. ◀ •••••••••••••••••••••••••••••••••• Web page URL

HOME    CALENDAR    EVENTS    **NEWS**

**Tornado Emergency Information** ◀ •••••••••••••• Title of Web page

**Tornado Facts:** The tornado that impacted Cedarburg touched down at 10:32 a.m. five miles west of town and dissipated at 10:43 a.m. near County Road 14. Local weather services recorded wind speeds as high as 127 miles per hour.

Town of Cedarburg   Updated May 9, 2017 4:14 p.m. ◀ •••••••••• Title of organization and Web page date

## Works Cited

# Present A SLIDE SHOW

A **slide show** is a presentation that uses a series of images. A presentation can include spoken words as well as visual information, such as slides. During a slide show, writers present information by speaking to the audience as they display images. Writers of argumentative texts can present a slide show to make and support a claim with images that persuade the audience.

Each year, thousands of people are affected by natural disasters. Relief workers provide help after disasters.

Volunteers help people in your community and communities around the world. They make a difference in people's lives.

Encourage people you know to become volunteer relief workers. Volunteers provide food, support, and shelter for victims of natural disasters.

**COLLABORATE** With your partner, discuss how you could use a slide show to present the information in your brochure. Follow agreed-upon rules as you collaborate. Begin by choosing key information from the brochure. Then discuss what kind of visual information would best get across the ideas from the brochure. Conduct research to find images for your slide show. Then, plan what you will say as you display each image.

Slide show ideas:

Image 1: Description:

Source:

What I will say when displaying this image:

Image 2: Description:

Source:

What I will say when displaying this image:

Image 3: Description:

Source:

What I will say when displaying this image:

# Revise

**Vocabulary** Reread your brochure with your partner. Have you included

- [ ] an informative description of the topic?
- [ ] a claim and reasons that support your claim?
- [ ] facts and details that persuade readers?
- [ ] text features, such as a title and headings, that organize information?

## Revise for Persuasive Language

In her first draft, the author of the Belden Youth Service Club brochure noticed that some of her text was not very engaging or persuasive. She revised the draft for coherence and clarity. She added, combined, and rearranged ideas to improve sentence structure and word choice.

Do you like helping people? Are you interested in saving lives? Becoming a member of the Belden Youth Service Club means helping your community!

∧ ~~Students should join the Belden Youth Service Club because it is fun. It also helps people in need.~~

# Edit

**Conventions** Read your brochure again.
Have you used correct conventions?

- ☐ spelling and punctuation
- ☐ correct grammar
- ☐ capitalization of specific places
- ☐ clear paraphrasing
- ☐ quotation marks for exact words

## Peer Review

**COLLABORATE** Exchange brochures with another pair. As you read, look for characteristics of argumentative text, including the writer's claim and supporting reasons. Discuss edits to correct errors in writing conventions and revisions that could make brochures more persuasive.

# Time to Celebrate!

**COLLABORATE** Imagine that you are a travel agent and your classmates are looking for a place to go. Present your persuasive brochure or slide show. Be sure to establish eye contact and speak with appropriate volume and rate. Enunciate, or pronounce, words clearly. Follow standard English conventions. After presenting, answer the questions.

Did your classmates agree with your claim? How could you tell? Write about your classmates' reactions.

_____

_____

_____

# Reflect on Your Project

**My TURN** Think about your travel brochure. Which parts are the strongest? What could you improve? Write your thoughts.

## Strengths

_____

_____

_____

## Areas of Improvement

_____

_____

_____

# Reflect on Your Goals

Look back at your unit goals. Use a different color to rate yourself again.

| SCALE | 1 | 2 | 3 | 4 | 5 |
|---|---|---|---|---|---|
| | NOT AT ALL WELL | NOT VERY WELL | SOMEWHAT WELL | VERY WELL | EXTREMELY WELL |

# Reflect on Your Reading

Based on the texts you read in this unit, synthesize, or put together, information about natural disasters. What information about natural disasters did you find most surprising?

_____

_____

_____

_____

_____

# Reflect on Your Writing

What connections did you make to personal experiences, ideas in other texts, and the world by writing poetry?

_____

_____

_____

_____

_____

# How to Use a Glossary

This glossary can help you understand the meaning, pronunciation, and syllabication of some of the words in this book. The entries in this glossary are in alphabetical order. The guide words at the top of each page show the first and last words on the page. If you cannot find a word, check a print or online dictionary. You would use a dictionary just as you would a glossary. To use a digital resource, type the word you are looking for in the search box at the top of the page.

**Example glossary entry:**

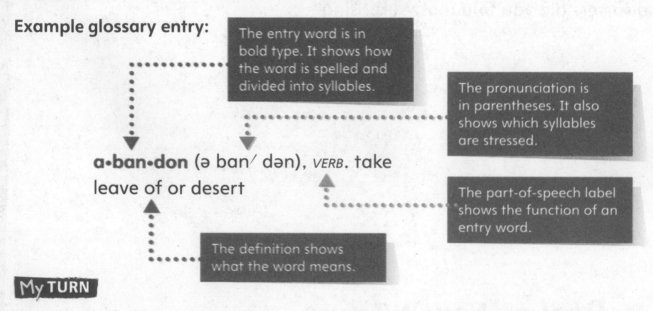

The entry word is in bold type. It shows how the word is spelled and divided into syllables.

The pronunciation is in parentheses. It also shows which syllables are stressed.

**a•ban•don** (ə ban⁄ dən), *VERB*. take leave of or desert

The part-of-speech label shows the function of an entry word.

The definition shows what the word means.

**My TURN**

Find and write the meaning of the word *generous*. Say the word aloud.

_____

Write the syllabication of the word. _____

Write the part of speech of the word. _____

How did the part of speech help you understand how the word is used?

_____

_____

Find the word *succeed* in the glossary. Note its meaning, syllabication, and pronunciation. Then use an online dictionary or other digital resource to check this information.

**TURN and TALK** Discuss how you can find the meaning of a word that is not in this glossary.

## Aa

**a•ban•don** (ə ban⁄ dən), *VERB.*
take leave of or desert

**ab•o•li•tion•ist**
(ab⁄ ə lish⁄ ə nist), *NOUN.* a person
or group that believes slavery
should be stopped

**a•chieve** (ə chēv⁄), *VERB.*
to succeed at something or
reach a goal

**ad•vice** (ad vīs⁄), *NOUN.* an opinion
or suggestion offered about a
situation

**a•nal•y•sis** (ə nal⁄ ə sis), *NOUN.* the
study of something in great detail

**an•tic•i•pate** (an tis⁄ ə pāt), *VERB.*
to expect something to happen

**ap•peared** (ə pird⁄), *VERB.* became
visible or able to be seen

**ar•riv•al** (ə rī⁄ vəl), *NOUN.* the act
of coming to a place

**as•ton•ished** (ə ston⁄ isht),
*ADJECTIVE.* very surprised or
amazed

## Pronunciation Guide

Use the pronunciation guide to help you pronounce the words correctly.

| | | |
|---|---|---|
| a in *hat* | ō in *open* | sh in *she* |
| ā in *age* | ȯ in *all* | th in *thin* |
| â in *care* | ô in *order* | ᴛʜ in *then* |
| ä in *far* | oi in *oil* | zh in *measure* |
| e in *let* | ou in *out* | ə = a in *about* |
| ē in *equal* | u in *cup* | ə = e in *taken* |
| ėr in *term* | u̇ in *put* | ə = i in *pencil* |
| i in *it* | ü in *rule* | ə = o in *lemon* |
| ī in *ice* | ch in *child* | ə = u in *circus* |
| o in *hot* | ng in *long* | |

**at·tracts** (ə trakts/), VERB. interests or brings toward

## Bb

**ben·e·fit** (ben/ ə fit), NOUN. something that helps a person or thing

## Cc

**cer·e·mo·nies** (ser/ ə mō/ nēs), NOUN. formal religious or public events

**chal·lenge** (chal/ ənj), NOUN. a difficult situation or contest

**com·mand** (kə mand/), VERB. to direct or give an order

**com·mu·ni·ty** (kə myü/ nə tē), NOUN. a group of people living in the same area

**com·pa·ny** (kum/ pə nē), NOUN. being together with another person or other people

**com·plain** (kəm plān/), VERB. express a feeling of unhappiness about something

**con·struct·ed** (kən struk/ ted), VERB. built or made

**con·sum·er** (kən süm/ mər), NOUN. a person who buys goods

**con·vince** (kən vins/), VERB. to persuade or cause someone to believe

**cur·i·ous** (kyu̇ r/ ē əs), ADJECTIVE. interested in knowing or seeing

## Dd

**dam·age** (dam/ ij), NOUN. harm done to something so that it is broken or injured

**dam·ag·ing** (dam/ ij ing), ADJECTIVE. harming or dangerous

**dan·ger·ous** (dān/ jər əs), ADJECTIVE. unsafe or likely to cause harm

**de·feat** (di fēt/), NOUN. a loss or setback of some kind

**de·stroyed** (di stroid/), VERB. completely ruined

**de·ter·mined** (di tėr′ mənd), _ADJECTIVE_. committed or firmly decided

**dis·tin·guish** (dis ting′ gwish), _VERB_. to tell the difference between two things

**dis·turbed** (dis tėrbd′), _VERB_. bothered or moved the position of

**do·nate** (dō′ nāt), _VERB_. to give as a way to help others

# Ee

**el·e·gant** (el′ ə gənt), _ADJECTIVE_. graceful in style and beauty

**e·mer·gen·cy** (i mėr′ jən sē), _NOUN_. a serious or dangerous situation

**en·cour·age** (en kėr′ ij), _VERB_. to give someone hope to keep trying

**e·nor·mous** (i nôr′ məs), _ADJECTIVE_. huge or very large

**e·qual·i·ty** (i kwäl′ ə tē), _NOUN_. the right for all people to be treated the same

**e·ven·tu·al·ly** (i ven′ chü ə lē), _ADVERB_. finally or after a long time

**ex·treme** (ek strēm′), _ADJECTIVE_. far from normal or average

# Ff

**fa·mil·iar** (fə mil′ yər), _ADJECTIVE_. common, well-known

**fig·ured** (fig′ yərd), _VERB_. believed or thought

**flat·ter·y** (flat′ ər ē), _NOUN_. praise that is usually dishonest or exaggerated

**fur·i·ous** (fyůr′ ē əs), _ADJECTIVE_. intense, raging, or violent

# Gg

**gen·e·ra·tion** (jen′ ə rā′ shən), _NOUN_. a group of individuals born and living at the same time

**gen·er·ous** (jen′ ər əs), _ADJECTIVE_. giving or showing kindness toward others

# Hh

**her•it•age** (her′ ə tij), *NOUN*. family or cultural history and traditions that are passed down through the years

**hor•ri•bly** (hôr′ ə blē), *ADVERB*. in a very bad way

# Ii

**i•mag•ined** (i maj′ ənd), *VERB*. believed or thought was possible

**im•i•ta•tion** (im′ ə tā′ shən), *NOUN*. a copy of something else

**im•mi•grants** (im′ ə grəntz), *NOUN*. people who come to live in another country

**im•pressed** (im prest′), *ADJECTIVE*. affected in a favorable way

**in•flu•en•tial** (in′ flü en′ shəl), *ADJECTIVE*. having a great effect on someone or something

**in•sist•ed** (in sist′ ed), *VERB*. stated firmly

**in•struc•tions** (in struk′ shənz), *NOUN*. directions or orders

**in•ter•fered** (in′ tər fird′), *VERB*. got involved in the matters of others

**in•ter•view** (in′ tər vyü), *NOUN*. a formal meeting where one or more persons questions another person

# Ll

**la•ment•ing** (lə ment′ ing), *VERB*. expressing feelings of sadness

**land•forms** (land′ fôrmz), *NOUN*. natural features of Earth's surface, such as mountains and valleys

# Mm

**med•i•cine** (med′ ə sən), *NOUN*. a substance used for treating an illness

**mem•o•rize** (mem′ ə rīz′), *VERB*. learn exactly and without the chance of forgetting

# Oo

**of•fer•ing** (ô′ fər ing), *VERB*. giving or presenting

**op•por•tu•ni•ty** (op′ ər tü′ nə tē), *NOUN*. a chance for a good experience or improvement

# Pp

**pa·tience** (pā/ shəns), NOUN. the ability to wait without getting upset

**per·mis·sion** (pėr mish/ ən), NOUN. formal or official approval to do something

**pit·e·ous·ly** (pit/ ē əs lē), ADVERB. in a sad and suffering way

**pol·lu·tion** (pə lü/ shən), NOUN. something that makes a place dirty, unsafe, or not suitable to use

**pre·pared** (pri pârd/), ADJECTIVE. ready or have made ready for use at a later time

**proc·ess·es** (pros/ es ēz), NOUN. series of actions that happen over time

**pro·duc·es** (prə düs/ ez), VERB. makes or forms

# Rr

**re·claimed** (ri klāmd/), VERB. took back

**re·gion** (rē/ jən), NOUN. area of land

**re·lief** (ri lēf/), NOUN. a feeling of happiness that follows worry

**re·mark·a·ble** (ri mär/ kə bəl), ADJECTIVE. extraordinary or amazing

**re·mem·bered** (ri mem/ bərd), VERB. thought of something that occurred in the past

**re·spon·si·ble** (ri spon/ sə bəl), ADJECTIVE. in charge or in control of a job or duty

# Ss

**slav·er·y** (slā/ vər ē), NOUN. a system in which people are owned by others

**spec·ta·cle** (spek/ tə kəl), NOUN. entertaining sight or display

**spec·tac·u·lar** (spek tak/ yə lər), ADJECTIVE. wonderful or very beautiful

**sta·tion·ar·y** (stā/ shə ner/ ē), ADJECTIVE. not moving

**suc·ceed** (sək sēd′), *VERB.* to do well or achieve a goal

**sur·face** (sėr′ fis), *NOUN.* the outside or outermost part

**sur·vived** (sər vīvd′), *VERB.* lived through or stayed alive

**sus·tain·a·bil·i·ty** (sə stā′ nə bil′ i tē), *NOUN.* a way of doing or making something that does not harm the environment and uses resources wisely

# Tt

**tem·per** (tem′ pər), *NOUN.* a person's state of mind or feelings of anger

**ter·ri·bly** (ter′ ə blē), *ADVERB.* in an awful or very bad way

**threat** (thret), *NOUN.* something that may cause harm or danger

**tra·di·tion** (trə dish′ ən), *NOUN.* custom or belief passed down among a group of people

**trans·formed** (tran sfôrmd′), *VERB.* changed or made very different

**trans·port** (trans′ pôrt), *VERB.* carry or move from one place to another

**tri·um·phant** (trī um′ fənt), *ADJECTIVE.* joy-filled or winning

**twin·kle** (twing′ kəl), *VERB.* sparkle or shine with a flickering light

# Vv

**vi·o·lence** (vī′ ə ləns), *NOUN.* acts that cause great harm, such as damage or injury

# CREDITS

## Text

**Candlewick Press**
GRANDDADDY'S TURN. Text copyright © 2015 by Michael S. Bandy and Eric Stein. Illustrations copyright © 2015 by James E. Ransome. Reproduced by permission of the publisher, Candlewick Press.

**Crabtree Publishing Company**
Earthquakes, Eruptions, and Other Events That Change Earth by Natalie Hyde. Used with permission from Crabtree Publishing Company.

**Curtis Brown Ltd.**
"Miss Stone" copyright © 2002 by Nikki Grimes. Originally published by Creative Classroom Publishing LLC. Currently published in AMAZING FACES (Lee & Low Books). Reprinted by permission of Curtis Brown, Ltd.

**Gina Maccoby Literary Agency**
Nora's Ark, text copyright 2005 by Natalie Kinsey-Warnock. Used by permission of the Gina Maccoby Literary Agency.

**HarperCollins Publishers**
Little House on the Prairie by Laura Ingalls Wilder, text copyright 1935, 1963 Little House Heritage Trust. Used by permission of HarperCollins Publishers. Please Note: "LITTLE HOUSE" (R) is A Registered Trademark of HarperCollins Publishers, Inc.
By the Shores of Silver Lake by Laura Ingalls Wilder, text copyright 1939, 1967 Little House Heritage Trust. Used by permission of HarperCollins Publishers. This selection may not be re-illustrated without written permission of HarperCollins Publishers, Inc.

**Henry Holt & Company**
The House That Jane Built: A Story About Jane Addams by Tanya Lee Stone, reprinted by Henry Holt Books for Young Readers. Caution: Users are warned that this work is protected under copyright laws and downloading is strictly prohibited. The right to reproduce or transfer the work via any medium must be secured with Macmillan Publishing Group, LLC d/b/a Henry Holt & Company.
Green City: How One Community Survived a Tornado and Rebuilt for a Sustainable Future by Allan Drummond, Caution: Users are warned that this work is protected under copyright laws and downloading is strictly prohibited. The right to reproduce or transfer the work via any medium must be secured with Macmillan Publishing Group, LLC d/b/a Henry Holt & Company.

**Houghton Mifflin Harcourt Publishing Company**
AESOP'S FOX, retold and illustrated by Aki Sogabe. Copynght © 1999 by Aki Sogabe. Reprinted by permission of Houghton Mifflin Harcourt Publishing Company. All rights reserved.

**Lee & Low Books**
In Daddy's Arms from IN DADDY'S ARMS, I AM TALL. Text Copyright ©1997 by Folami Abiade. Illustrations Copyright © 1997 Javaka Steptoe. Permission arranged with LEE & LOW BOOKS, Inc., New York, NY 10016. All rights not specifically granted herein are reserved.
Firefighter Face from AMAZING FACES. Illustration by Chris Soentpiet. Illustrations Copyright © 2010 Chris Soentpiet. Permission arranged with LEE & LOW BOOKS, Inc., New York, NY 10016. All rights not specifically granted herein are reserved.
The Race from IN LOVE TO MAMA: A TRIBUTE TO MOTHERS. Text Copyright ©2001 by Jennifer Trujillo. Illustrations Copyright © 2001 Paula S. Barragan. Permission arranged with LEE & LOW BOOKS, Inc., New York, NY 10016. All rights not specifically granted herein are reserved.

**Prospect Agency, LLC**
Firefighter Face by Mary E. Cronin. Used with permission from the author.

**Rocky Hill Group**
Granddaddy's Turn: A Journey to the Ballot Box by Michael S. Bandy and Eric Stein, used with permission from LSH/Rocky Hill Group, Inc.

**Scholastic Library Publishing**
Frederick Douglass by Josh Gregory. All rights reserved. Reprinted by permission of Children's Press an imprint of Scholastic Library Publishing, Inc.
Milton Hershey: Chocolate King, Town Builder by Charnan Simon. All rights reserved. Reprinted by permission of Children's Press an imprint of Scholastic Library Publishing, Inc.

**Simon & Schuster, Inc.**
Mama Miti: Wangari Maathai and the Trees of Kenya by Donna Jo Napoli. Copyright © 2010 by Donna Jo Napoli. Reprinted with the permission of Simon & Schuster, Inc. All Rights Reserved.

## Photographs

Photo locators denoted as follows Top (T), Center (C), Bottom (B), Left (L), Right (R), Background (Bkgd)

10 (T) Darleine Heitman/Shutterstock,(B) Michael Jung/Shutterstock; 11 Used with permission from Prospect Agency LLC. 16 (L, R, B) NASA, (Bkgd) Elena Polina/123RF; 20 Geoffrey Swaine/Rex Features/ AP Images; 60 Choreograph/123RF; 64 Used with permission from Michael Bandy.; 94 (T) Digital Image Library/Alamy Stock Photo, (B) Stocktrek Images, Inc./ Alamy Stock Photo, (Bkgd) Photolinc/Shutterstock; 95 (T) JT Vintage/Glasshouse Images/Alamy Stock Photo; 98 Fine Art Images/Heritage Image Partnership Ltd/ Alamy Stock Photo; 106 Fine Art Images/Heritage Image Partnership Ltd/Alamy Stock Photo.; 130 (T) Interim Archives/Contributor/Getty Images, (B) Steve Larson/Denver Post/Getty Images; 131 (T) RitchardD/ Shutterstock, (B) Matt Moyer/Millrock Productions, Inc./ Corbis/Getty Images; 134 Used with permission from Donna Jo Napoli.; 164 (T) Catwalker/Shutterstock, (B) Maria Evseyeva/Shutterstock; 165 Chris Dorney/ Shutterstock; 168 The Race Poem from the collection Love to Mama A Tribute to Mothers. Text copyright © 2001 by Jennifer Trujillo. Permission arranged with Lee & Low Books, New York, NY 10016.; 169 Hilary Morgan/ Alamy Stock Photo; 202 Florian Kopp/imageBROKER/ Alamy Stock Photo; 208 (T) KidStock/Blend Images/ Getty Images, (B) RosaIreneBetancourt 7/Alamy Stock Photo; 211 Image Source/DigitalVision/Getty Images; 130 Roberto Sorin/Shutterstock; 164 PhotoStock10/ Shutterstock; 170 Used with permission from Prospect Agency LLC. 198 Asiseeit/iStock/Getty Images; 204-205

# CREDITS

Terraxplorer/E+/Getty Images; **206-207** Romakoma/ Shutterstock; **214** (Bkgd) Maciej Bledowski/Alamy Stock Photo.; **215** Library of Congress Prints and Photographs Division Washington[LC-USZ62-13484]; **220** (BL) Paul Fearn/Alamy Stock Photo, (Bkgd) Rainer Lesniewski/ Alamy Stock Vector; **224** Used with permission from Macmillan Publishers Ltd; **257** Dennis MacDonald/ Age Fotostock/Alamy Stock Photo; **259** Library of Congress Washington[LC-USZ62-119343]; **262** Used with permission from Josh Gregory.; **265** Everett Collection Inc/Alamy Stock Photo; **266** North Wind Picture Archives/ Alamy Stock Photo; **267** Hulton Archive/Getty Images; **268** Library of Congress Prints and Photographs Division [LC-DIG-ppmsca-38382]; **269** (TL) JT Vintage/Glasshouse Images/Alamy Stock Photo, (CR) Library of Congress Prints and Photographs Division [LC-USZ62-119343], (BL) Library of Congress Prints and Photographs Division [LC-DIG-ppmsca-07773]; **270** (BL) Everett Collection Inc/Alamy Stock Photo, (BR) Photo Researchers/ Science History Images/Alamy Stock Photo; **272** (TL) NAWROCKI/ClassicStock/Alamy Stock Photo, (TR) North Wind Picture Archives/Alamy Stock Photo; **273** (TL) Bettmann/Getty Images, (TR) Library of Congress Prints and Photographs Division [LC-DIG-highsm-09902]; **274** Library of Congress Prints and Photographs Division [LC-DIG-highsm-09902]; **275** (B) Library of Congress Prints and Photographs Division [LC-USZ62-93268]; **292** (Bkgd) Alison Hancock/Shutterstock; **293** Oyls/ Shutterstock; **297** Bettmann/Getty Images; **299** H. Mark Weidman Photography/Alamy Stock Photo; **301** Andre Jenny/Alamy Stock Photo; **302** (CL) Courtesy of Hershey Community Archives, Hershey, PA, (B) Courtesy of Hershey Community Archives, Hershey, PA; **303** Courtesy of Hershey Community Archives, Hershey, PA; **305** (BC) Jozsef Szasz-Fabian/Shutterstock; **306** Courtesy of Hershey Community Archives, Hershey, PA; **307** Courtesy of Hershey Community Archives, Hershey, PA.; **308** (BR) Bygone Collection/Alamy Stock Photo; **312** (B) Superstock; **313** (B) Courtesy of Hershey Community Archives, Hershey, PA, (TC) Centli/Shutterstock; **330** Drserg/Shutterstock; **330-331** (Bkgd) Pluie_r/ Shutterstock; **334** Used with permission from Macmillan Publishers Ltd.; **370** (T) Karelnoppe/Shutterstock, (CL) Unge255_photostock/Shutterstock, (CR) Rawpixel.com/ Shutterstock, (B) Maria Ivanushkina/Shutterstock; **370** (Bkgd) VectorPot/Shutterstock, (B) Pixelheadphoto digitalskillet/Shutterstock; **408** Richie Chan/Shutterstock; **412** Ed Metz/Shutterstock; **414** Gabbro/Alamy Stock Photo; **415** (T) C. Steimer/Arco Images GmbH/Alamy Stock Photo, (C) Joel Sartore/National Geographic/Getty Images, (B) Jim and Lynne Weber/Shutterstock; **416** Zack Frank/Shutterstock; **418** Newman Mark/Prisma by Dukas Presseagentur GmbH/Alamy Stock Photo; **424** (Bkgd) Peky/Shutterstock.; **430** (T) Poprotskiy Alexey/ Shutterstock, (B) Monkey Business Images/Shutterstock, (Bkgd) Stephane Bidouze/Shutterstock; **431** (T) Helen Hotson/Shutterstock; **434** Shirin Yim Bridges; **435** Mark Lloyd/Alamy Stock Photo; **436** Donatas Dabravolskas/ Shutterstock; **437** (T) Işabella Pfenninger/Shutterstock, (B) Dr Morley Read/Shutterstock; **438** (T) US Marines Photo/Alamy Stock Photo,(B) Mark Lloyd/Alamy Stock Photo; **439** (T) Interfoto/Travel/Alamy Stock Photo, (B)

US Marines Photo/Alamy Stock Photo; **440** Jose More/ VWPics/Alamy Stock Photo; **441** Keith Kapple/SuperStock/ Alamy Stock Photo; **442** Dave stamboulis/Alamy Stock Photo; **442** (Bkgd) Tony Waltham/Robertharding/ Alamy Stock Photo; **443** (T) Aleksandra H. Kossowska/ Shutterstock;(B) Dave stamboulis/Alamy Stock Photo; **444** (T) GillesBarbier/imageBROKER/Alamy Stock Photo, (B) Ariadne Van Zandbergen/Alamy Stock Photo; **445** Ton koene/Alamy Stock Photo; **446** (L) Alison Wright/ National Geographic Creative/Alamy Stock Photo, (R) Tbkmedia.de/Alamy Stock Photo; **447** Tatiana Kholina/ Shutterstock; **448** Robert Matton AB/Alamy Stock Photo; **448** (Bkgd) Outdoor-Archiv/Klauer/Alamy Stock Photo; **449** (BR) Top-Pics TBK/Alamy Stock Photo; **450** V. Belov/Shutterstock; **451** (TL) Ragnar Th Sigurdsson/ ARCTIC IMAGES/Alamy Stock Photo, (TR) Anders Ryman/ Alamy Stock Photo, (B) tbkmedia.de/Alamy Stock Photo; **452** F1online digitale Bildagentur GmbH/Alamy Stock Photo; **453** (TR) Fotomicar/Shutterstock, (TL) MaxyM/ Shutterstock, (BR) Radu Bercan/Shutterstock; **474** Used with permission from Crabtree Publishing Company.; **476** (TL) Think4photop/Shutterstock; **477** (B) Webspark/ Shutterstock; **478** Somjin Klong-ugkara/Shutterstock; **479** (T) Designua/Shutterstock, (BR) Dorling Kindersley/ Getty Images; **480** La Prensa Grafica/AP Images; **481** Shutterstock; **482** (CL) Pierre Leclerc/Shutterstock, (B) luigi nifosi/Shutterstock; **483** Sadatsugu Tomizawa/ AFP/Jiji Press/Getty Images; **484** (B) Maria Luisa Lopez Estivill/123rf; **485** (T) Ragnar Th Sigurdsson/ ARCTIC IMAGES/Alamy Stock Photo; **502** Tom Reichner/ Shutterstock; **503** Welcomia/123RF, IrinaK/Shutterstock; **507** Iakov Filimonov/Shutterstock; **508** Jessica Lynn Culver/Moment/Getty Images; **510** (BL) Minerva Studio/ Shutterstock, (CL) Fesus Robert/Shutterstock, (TL) Brisbane/Shutterstock, (C) Gece33/iStock/Getty Images; **511** (R) ILI/Juice Images/Alamy Stock Photo, (L) Arek_ Malang/Shutterstock; **512** Redpixel.PL/Shutterstock; **515** Serg_V/123RF; **516** Lawrence Manning/Corbis/Getty Images; **517** Sergey Novikov/Shutterstock; **518** Kzenon/ Shutterstock; **519** Aldomurillo/E+/Getty Images; **536** Library of Congress Prints and Photographs Division Washington[LC-DIG-ppmsca-31916]; **537** (T) Library of Congress Prints and Photographs Division[LC-DIG-hec-38293], (B) Library of Congress Prints and Photographs Division Washington[LC-USF34-002505-E]; **540** Copyright © 2017 by Natalie Kinsey-Warnock. Used by permission of The Gina Maccoby Literary Agency.; **578** (Bkgd) Ryan DeBerardinis/Shutterstock; **582** Used with permission from Aki Sogabe.; **616** Tommy E Trenchard/ Alamy Stock Photo; **622** Martin Shields/Alamy Stock Photo; **625** Andrea Booher/FEMA; **626** (T) Tom Uhlman/ Alamy Stock Photo, (C) Jim West/Alamy Stock Photo, (B) Douglas R. Clifford/Tampa Bay Times/ZUMA Wire/Alamy Stock Photo; **629** Syda Productions/Shutterstock.

## Illustrations

**19, 167, 223, 433, 581** Ken Bowser; **63, 261, 295, 473** Olga & Aleksey Ivanov; **97, 333, 505** Ilana Exelby; **99–113** Amal; **133, 373, 539** Valeria Cis; **208, 620** Karen Minot; **375–389** Laura Osolini; **418** Rob Schuster; **502– 503** Scott Burroughs; **513** Jodi O'Rourke